Housing Issues, Laws and Program Series

IMPROVING CONSUMER MORTGAGE DISCLOSURES

Housing Issues, Laws and Program Series

Pluralism in Housing Provision in Developing Countries: Lessons from Brazil
Ramin Keivani, Alex Abiko and Edmundo Werna (Authors)
2004 ISBN: 1-59033-857-X

Housing the Poor: An Overview
Morton J. Schussheim (Editor)
2003 ISBN: 1-59033-724-7

Fannie Mae and Freddie Mac: Scandal in U.S. Housing
James R. Cristie (Editor)
2006 ISBN: 1-60021-356-1

HUD Housing Programs for Persons with disabilities
Ervin C. Felker (Editor)
2009 ISBN: 978-1-60741-113 0

Re-Use of Construction and Demolition Waste in Housing Developments
V.W.Y. Tam and C.M. Tam (Authors)
2008 ISBN: 978-1-60456-362-7

Department of Housing and Urban Development Appropriations
Maggie McCarty, Libby Perl, Bruce E. Foote, Eugene Boyd, Meredith Peterson, David Randall Peterman, and John Frittelli (Authors)
2008 ISBN: 978-1-60456-789-2

Housing: Socioeconomic, Availability, and Development Issues
Edward P. Hammond and Alex D. Noyes (Editors)
2009 ISBN: 978-1-60692-371-9

Green Affordable Housing
Gerald N. Burlinghouse (Editor)
ISBN: 978-1-60692-831-8

Improving Consumer Mortgage Disclosures
Jason C. Castleman (Editor)
2009 ISBN: 978-1-60692-923-0

Housing Issues, Laws and Program Series

IMPROVING CONSUMER MORTGAGE DISCLOSURES

JASON C. CASTLEMAN
EDITOR

Nova Science Publishers, Inc.
New York

LIBRARY OF CONGRESS CATALOGING-IN-PUBLICATION DATA

Available upon request

ISBN: 978-1-60692-923-0

Published by Nova Science Publishers, Inc. ✝ New York

CONTENTS

PREFACE

Recent developments in the subprime home loan market have triggered concern in Congress and the public at large as to whether borrowers were fully informed about the terms of their mortgage loans. Some observers have suggested that some borrowers in the subprime market may have been victims of predatory lending practices or other discriminatory activity. Bills introduced in the 110th Congress, such as S. 1299 (Senator Charles Schumer et al.) and S. 2452 (Senator Christopher Dodd et al.) would seek to remedy perceived abuses particularly with higher-priced mortgage lending. This book describes current issues and recent changes to the Home Mortgage Disclosure Act (HMDA) of 1975. Also included are brief explanations of how recent reporting revisions may affect the reporting of loans covered by the Home Ownership and Equity Protection Act of 1994 as well as those insured by the Federal Housing Administration

Despite a long history of mortgage cost disclosure requirements and many legislative and regulatory proposals, little empirical evidence exists to document the effect of the current disclosures on consumer understanding of mortgage costs, consumer mortgage shopping, or consumer mortgage choice. In this study, we conducted 36 in-depth interviews with recent mortgage customers, and quantitative consumer testing with over 800 mortgage customers, to examine how consumers search for mortgages, how well consumers understand current mortgage cost disclosures and the terms of their own recently obtained loans, and whether better disclosures could improve consumer understanding of mortgage costs, consumer shopping for mortgage loans, and consumers' ability to avoid deceptive lending practices. The potential for improving consumer understanding of mortgage costs through better disclosures was tested using prototype disclosures developed for the study. The prototype disclosures were developed for fixed-rate loans, including those with interest-only and balloon payments, but could be extended to incorporate the key features of adjustable-rate, hybrid, and payment option loans.

In: Improving Consumer Mortgage Disclosures
Editor: Jason C. Castleman

ISBN 978-1-60692-923-0

Chapter 1

REPORTING ISSUES UNDER THE HOME MORTGAGEDISCLOSURE ACT*

Darryl E. Getter

ABSTRACT

Recent developments in the subprime home loan market have triggered concern in Congress and the public at large as to whether borrowers were fully informed about the terms of their mortgage loans. Some observers have suggested that some borrowers in the subprime market may have been victims of predatory lending practices or other discriminatory activity. Bills introduced in the 1 10th Congress, such as S. 1299 (Senator Charles Schumer et al.) and S. 2452 (Senator Christopher Dodd et al.) would seek to remedy perceived abuses particularly with higher-priced mortgage lending.

This chapter describes current issues and recent changes to the Home Mortgage Disclosure Act (HMDA) of 1975. Also included are brief explanations of how recent reporting revisions may affect the reporting of loans covered by the Home Ownership and Equity Protection Act of 1994 as well as those insured by the Federal Housing Administration.

INTRODUCTION

Recent mortgage repayment problems and subsequent increases in foreclosures have generated concern in Congress as to whether borrowers are taking out high interest loans that they cannot afford.[1] There are at least four possible explanations why some borrowers receive higher-priced loans. First, borrowers with weak credit histories may face higher borrowing costs than borrowers with better credit histories if lenders require more compensation for taking on greater credit or default risks. Second, the actual costs of the mortgage may have been hidden or simply not transparent when borrowers entered into the lending transaction. Hidden costs can surprise a borrower and cause financial distress, which

* This is an edited, excerpted and augmented edition of a CRS Report RL34720, dated October 24, 2008.

may lead to foreclosure. Third, borrowers may have entered into high cost loans as a result of discrimination. According to the Federal Reserve Board, minorities are still more likely to pay rates above specified pricing thresholds (prior to controlling for some related borrower characteristics).[2] Fourth, recent mortgage repayment problems may reflect a rise in various forms of predatory lending. In short, borrowers may have obtained expensive mortgage loans for a variety of reasons, which may have resulted in recent repayment problems.

Various legislation has been enacted to oversee lending practices in the mortgage market. The Home Mortgage Disclosure Act (HMDA) of 1975 requires the disclosure of mortgage loan information so regulators can monitor mortgage lending activity.[3] In addition, the 1994 Home Ownership Equity Protection Act (HOEPA), enacted as an amendment to the Truth-In-Lending Act (TILA) of 1968, requires additional disclosures to consumers for high cost refinance and other non- purchase loans secured by their principal residences.[4] The Real Estate Settlement Procedures Act (RESPA) of 1974 is designed to protect mortgage borrowers from paying excessive fees related to real estate transactions. RESPA requires standardized disclosures about the settlement or closing costs of residential mortgages.

This chapter briefly describes the role of HMDA reporting for monitoring higher- priced lending activities, discusses policy issues, and summarizes recent regulatory decisions made by the Federal Reserve Board, the agency that implements these statutes.[5] This chapter also discusses how HOEPA and federally insured mortgage loans may be affected by recent regulatory changes.

Background on HMDA Reporting

HMDA was enacted in 1975 to assist government regulators and the private sector with the monitoring of anti-discriminatory practices.[6] HMDA is implemented by the Federal Reserve Board via Regulation C (12 CFR Part 203), and the public loan data set is available at the Federal Financial Institutions Examination Council's website.[7] HMDA data is used to assist with the supervision and enforcement of fair lending compliance.[8] The Office of the Comptroller of the Currency (OCC), for example, is a federal agency that uses the HMDA data to assist with its fair lending and Community Reinvestment Act (CRA) examinations of nationally chartered banks.[9]

Reporting Issues Prior to 2008

Redlining and Frequency of Rejection

When HMDA was enacted, there was concern that less affluent and minority neighborhoods did not enjoy the same access to financial services as do other neighborhoods. Financial institutions allegedly accepted deposits but did not make mortgage loans in certain neighborhoods, and these lending practices were viewed as contributing to further neighborhood deterioration. HMDA required institutions covered under the law to report home mortgage originations by geographic area, financial institution type, borrower race, sex, income, and whether the loans were for home purchase or refinance.[10] This information would show geographical patterns of mortgage originations and help regulators determine where further investigation of redlining, or geographical discrimination, was necessary.

In 1989, Congress expanded HMDA to include the race, sex, and borrower income of those applicants that were rejected as well as those who were approved.[11] This change allowed regulators to monitor the frequency that applicants from certain groups were denied mortgage loans relative to other groups.[12] The HMDA data could then be used to track any differences in denial rates by income, race, and gender.

Risk-Based Pricing

Beginning in the 1990s, credit became increasingly available for less creditworthy borrowers. Instead of turning down loan requests for borrowers of lower credit quality, lenders began charging these borrowers higher interest rates to compensate for the additional risk. As a result, regulators monitoring discrimination began to show greater concern about the mortgage loan rates charged to different groups of borrowers.

Congress expanded HMDA in 2002 to include rate-spread information. At the time, the rate-spread was defined as the difference between the annual percentage rate (APR), which is the annual total cost of a loan, and the rate on U.S. Treasury securities of comparable maturity. The flat mortgage interest rate was not chosen because, by definition, it contains only the cost of the principal loan amount expressed as a percentage. The APR, however, includes the cost of the principal loan amount, insurance, and other fees — all expressed as a percentage. The law requiring rate-spread information was implemented in 2004.[13]

Reporting Requirements and Coverage

All home-secured mortgage loans do not get reported under HMDA, for at least three reasons. First, covered institutions, or those subject to HMDA reporting requirements, include only those banks, savings and loans, credit unions, and mortgage and consumer finance companies that meet thresholds regarding asset size or percentage of business related to housing-lending activity. Lenders that do not have offices in metropolitan statistical areas are also not required to report HMDA data. Second, Regulation C requires lenders to report only loans that meet certain rate-spread thresholds. The reporting thresholds for first mortgage loans had been those with a spread of 3 percentage points; for the second mortgage loans, the reporting threshold was 5 percentage points. Loans not meeting these rate-spread thresholds would not be reported. Third, home equity loans taken out for purposes other than home improvements or other home related purposes are not reported under HMDA. Given that only loans meeting statutory requirements are reported, HMDA currently covers approximately 80% of the national mortgage market.[14]

Difficulties Identifying High-Priced Lending Abuses

The HMDA data, like all databases, has its caveats. When using the HMDA data to identify high-priced lending activity, understanding data limitations is important to correctly interpret the empirical findings. Key issues are presented below.

Lack of Credit History Information

The HMDA data has been criticized for not including more variables that could be used to either verify or rule out discrimination. An example of a relevant variable is borrower credit history information. Some borrowers pay more for their loans relative to others because they exhibit higher levels of credit risk. Having credit history information would be necessary to determine if observed pricing differentials reflect differences in financial risk or discrimination. Other useful variables include borrower characteristics, such as total assets and debts, and loan characteristics, such as the loan-to-value ratio. Given that HMDA data do not include all relevant information that bears on lender risk, the basis for individual lending decisions is portrayed incompletely.

Lenders are not required to report every variable used to evaluate applicants because the HMDA data is released to the public, which could compromise the privacy of individuals holding reported loans. It is possible that public users of HMDA data would be able to match collected information with local records and determine the identity of individuals. Because federal regulator agencies can obtain loan data from financial institutions they wish to examine more closely, the reporting of all borrower information to HMDA is not necessary for those agencies that enforce fair lending and fair housing laws.

Federal agencies also follow Interagency Fair Lending Examination Procedures, provided by the Federal Financial Institutions Examination Council (FFIEC), to evaluate unlawful discrimination in the prime market.[15] These procedures include review of (1) sample bank loan files; (2) loan prices relative to compensation of brokers; (3) whether the institutions use pricing models that are empirically based and statistically sound; and (4) whether the disparities are substantial.[16] Hence, even if more variables were collected, HMDA data are intended for use in targeting institutions for closer examination but not as the sole basis for enforcing antidiscrimination laws in individual cases.[17]

Reporting Problems with the APR

With greater usage of complex nontraditional mortgage loan products, the APR may become increasingly difficult indicator to interpret.[18] The APR tells nothing about balloon payments, prepayment options, or the length of term that an adjustable interest rate is locked.[19] In addition, closing costs vary by state, which means local differences will always persist. Hence, the APR measure may provide little information about relative pricing, because the underlying loan products and terms vary substantially.

Movements in Interest Rates

Changes in short-term relative to long-term rates, also known as yield curve rotations, may affect loan reporting to HMDA. Given that mortgage loans are often priced on rates that better reflect the expected life-span of the loan (as opposed to rates that match the entire mortgage term), the HMDA data can reflect a duration-matching problem rather than a problem of excessive higher-priced lending.[20] For example, borrowers often sell their homes or refinance into a new mortgage before their existing mortgage expires. Regulation C, however, had required the rate-spread calculation for 30-year (fixed or adjustable rate) mortgage loans to use the 30-year Treasury yield as the benchmark rate. Suppose Treasury market interest rates change so that shorter-term rates rise relative to longer-term rates. The rate-spreads calculations, which may have even been negative under a steeper yield curve, will increase and may become positive, potentially resulting in more loans meeting the HMDA thresholds. Consequently, such timing or duration mismatches captured by the rate-spread calculations, which increase when the differences in duration between APR and benchmark rates are large, could result in more 30-year fixed rate mortgages reported as HMDA rate- spread loans.

Interest rate changes may also affect the reporting of higher-priced lending in particular if the proportion of adjustable-rate mortgages (ARMs) relative to fixed-rate mortgages increases. A flattening of the yield curve is likely to cause the rate-spreads on both fixed rate mortgages and ARMs to be similar in size. As a result, ARMs would have higher rate spreads relative to those computed under steeper yield curves, and there would be an increase in the number of ARMS reported as high-priced loans.[21]

Recent Modifications to Regulation C

To address some concerns described above, the Federal Reserve has changed the benchmark rate used to calculate the rate-spread for reporting HMDA loans.[22] The Federal Reserve proposes use of the average mortgage rates found in the Primary Mortgage Market Survey (PMMS) conducted by Freddie Mac as the benchmark rates for rate-spread calculations.[23] The reporting thresholds for first mortgage loans will now be those with a spread equal to or greater than 1.5 percentage points; for the second mortgage loans, the reporting threshold will be equal to or greater than 3.5 percentage points. The use of an average prime mortgage rate, which the PMMS reports on a weekly basis, is likely to follow the rates of prime mortgage rates more closely than Treasury rates. Whenever the yield curve changes, a rate-spread computed as the difference between a mortgage rate and an average prime mortgage rate is likely to show less volatility than one computed as the difference between a mortgage rate and a Treasury rate. As a result of this regulatory change, it may become easier to attribute an observable increase in rate-spread reported loans to actual changes in lending practices, which ultimately is the objective for HMDA reporting.

IMPLICATIONS FOR HOEPA LOANS

The 1994 Home Ownership Equity Protection Act (HOEPA) is an amendment to the Truth-In-Lending Act (TILA) of 1968. TILA requires lenders to disclose the cost of credit and repayment terms of all consumer loans before borrowers enter into any transactions.[24] HOEPA imposes additional disclosure requirements for consumers obtaining high cost refinance and other non-purchase (closed-ended second) loans secured by their principal residences. A loan is considered to be a HOEPA loan if either the APR exceeds the rate of a comparable Treasury security by more than 8 percentage points on a first mortgage, 10 percentage points on a second mortgage, or if the consumer pays total points and fees exceeding the larger of $561 or 8% of the total loan amount.[25] Should a loan satisfy any of these criteria, the borrower must be provided with disclosures three days before the loan is closed in addition to the three-day right of rescission generally required by TILA, which means a total of six days to decide whether or not to enter into the transaction. In 2002, revisions to Regulation C required lenders to report HOEPA loans in HMDA, and they must also identify such loans as being subject to HOEPA requirements.26 HOEPA, however, is implemented via Regulation Z (12 CFR Part 226, sections 31, 32, and 34).

HOEPA has been extended to cover more loans.27 Since 2002, coverage has been extended by lowering the price trigger from 10 to the current 8 percentage points above a comparable Treasury security. The Federal Reserve Board has also amended Regulation Z to apply HOEPA rules to all mortgage lenders (and not just those supervised and examined by the Federal Reserve).28 The amended rule added four key protections. The first protection prohibits lenders from making loans based upon the home value without regard for the borrower's ability to repay the loan from income and assets. Second, verification of income and assets will be required for determining repayment ability. Third, higher-cost loans may not have prepayment penalties that last for more than two years, and prepayment penalties are not allowed for loans in which the monthly payment can change during the initial four years. Finally, escrow accounts for property taxes and homeowners' insurance must be established for all first lien mortgages. Additional protections covered in the rule are described in the Federal Reserve announcement.29

HOEPA loans may have been considered a subset of the larger set of HMDA loans when both rate spread calculations relied upon comparable U.S. Treasury securities for the benchmark rates. Now that the Federal Reserve has modified the benchmark rates used to compute HMDA rate spreads, HMDA and HOEPA rate spreads will be calculated under separate methods. The benchmark rate for computing HOEPA loans is defined by federal statute, and modification of the benchmark rate for HOEPA loans would be left for Congress to decide. Loans meeting the existing HOEPA thresholds may still simultaneously meet the newly adopted HMDA thresholds. HOEPA rate spreads, however, will now be more sensitive to Treasury yield curve movements than HMDA rate spreads.

IMPLICATIONS FOR FHA-INSURED LOANS

Mortgage insurance is usually required for borrowers lacking either a downpayment or home equity of at least 20% of the property value. Prime (or conventional) as well as subprime homebuyers may purchase private mortgage insurance. The Federal Housing Administration (FHA) is a federally operated mortgage insurance program that primarily serves first-time and less creditworthy borrowers.30 Should the borrower default on a FHA-insured mortgage loan obligation, the lender will be reimbursed for the loss. The FHA is a self-financing program under which premiums must be sufficient to cover its costs and expected losses. FHA fees are collected via an upfront premium charge when the loan is originated and an annual premium charge thereafter.

After passage of the Housing and Economic Act of 2008, FHA received the statutory authority to charge up to 3% in its upfront premium and 0.55% annually.31 Consequently, the bulk of the total mortgage insurance premium must be collected upfront, and FHA has little flexibility to collect a larger portion of the insurance fees via the annual premium mechanism. FHA-insured mortgage loans, therefore, run the risk of hitting the 1.5% threshold of reportable HMDA rate-spread loans. The FHA upfront premium charges would likely be calculated in the APR of the mortgage loan, which would cause the rate-spread to be higher.

The flexibility to shift how the FHA insurance fees are collected or, more specifically, to make greater use of the annual premium mechanism, arguably has at least three advantages. First, annual premium collections would reduce the risk of FHA loans being incorrectly identified as higher-priced loans under HMDA reporting requirements. Second, computing refunds or premium reductions via the annual premium may arguably be easier should FHA borrowers become eligible for rebates.32 Third, under certain circumstances, an annual premium mechanism may also reduce financial burdens on FHA borrowers. For example, borrowers planning to reside in their homes for a relatively short period of time would not incur additional interest costs due to financing large insurance premiums into their mortgage loans.

REFERENCES

[1] For more detailed information on subprime lending, see CRS Report RL3 3930 *Subp rime Mortgages: Primer on Current Lending and Foreclosure Issues*, by Edward Vincent Murphy.

[2] See Robert B. Avery, Kenneth P. Brevoort, and Glenn B. Canner, "Higher-Priced Home Lending and the 2006 HMDA Data," *Federal Reserve Bulletin*, September 2006.

[3] P.L. 94-200, 12 U.S.C. Sections 2801-2809.

[4] TILA is contained in Title I of the Consumer Credit Protection Act, P.L. 90-301, 81 Stat. 146, as amended by 15 U.S.C. Section 1601 et seq. TILA requires lenders to disclose the cost of credit and repayment terms of mortgage loans before borrowers enter into any transactions. The Federal Reserve Board implements TILA through Regulation Z.

[5] The Real Estate Settlement Procedures Act (RESPA), which was enacted in 1974 under P.L. 93-533, 88 Stat. 1724, 12 U.S.C. Sections 2601-2617, is another piece of legislation designed to protect mortgage borrowers from paying excessive fees related to real estate transactions. RESPA requires standardized disclosures about the settlement or closing costs of residential mortgages. See CRS Report RL34442, *HUD Proposes Administrative Modifications to the Real Estate Settlement and Procedures Act*, Darryl E. Getter.

[6] P.L. 94-200, 12 U.S.C. Sections 2801-2809.

[7] See [http://www.ffiec.gov/hmda/].

[8] Reference to fair lending laws and regulations typically encompasses enforcement of the Fair Housing Act, which is Title VIII, Section 800 of the Civil Rights Act of 1968 (P.L. 90- 284, 82 Stat. 73, 81-89). For more information on fair lending examination procedures as well as definitions of discrimination types, see [http://www.occ.treas.gov/handbook/ fairlep.pdf].

[9] See [http://www.occ.treas.gov/handbook/hmda.pdf]. The Community Reinvestment Act of 1977 is Title VII of P.L. 95-128, 12 U.S.C. 2901. Regulated financial institutions are required by law to demonstrate that their deposit facilities serve the convenience and needs of the communities where they are chartered to do business. See [http://www.bos.frb.org/ commdev/commaff/cra.pdf] and CRS Report RL34049, *Community Reinvestment Act: Regulation and Legislation*, by Walter W. Eubanks.

[10] See [http://www.fdic.gov/news/news/press/2005/pr3005a.html].

[11] P.L. 101-73, 103 Stat 183. Sections 1211(d) and 1212.

[12] See [http://www.federalreserve.gov/boarddocs /speeches/2005 /20050603 /default. htm].

[13] P.L. 107-155, 116 Stat 81.

[14] See [http://www.federalreserve.gov/BoardDocs/Speeches/2005/2005033 1/default.htm] and [http://www.frbatlanta.org/invoke.cfm?obj ectid=37B8 10A9-5056-9F12-12E8EB3 12 FB29 1A7&method=display_body].

[15] See [http://www.dallasfed.org/ca/pubs/fair.html] and [http://www.ffiec.gov/PDF/ fairlend.pdf].

[16] The Department of Justice, which investigates fair lending cases, establishes a *pattern and practice* of discrimination before it charges lenders with violating federal discrimination laws. See [http://www.usdoj .gov/crt/housing/housing_pattern .htm].

[17] See [http://www.federalreserve.gov/newsevents/press/bcreg/200704 12a.htm].

[18] For more information on non-traditional mortgage products, see CRS Report RL3 3775, *Alternative Mortgages: Risks to Consumers and Lenders in the Current Housing Cycle*, by Edward Vincent Murphy.

[19] Regulation Z requires lenders to assume the interest rate situation at the time of origination will continue for the term of the loan when calculating the APR for adjustable- rate loans.

[20] If investors (lenders) are promised returns associated with longer-term loans but receive returns associated with shorter-term loans, they may be unwilling to make future loans, especially if yields consistently fail to meet expectations. Hence, mortgage originators price mortgages using rates that closely match the expected duration or mortgage life. Lenders may account for prepayment or early termination risk by pricing mortgages using Treasury rates equal to or less than 10 years.

[21] For a formal analysis concerning the extent to which the increase in HMDA reportable rate-spread loans between 2004-2006 can be attributed to the flattening of the yield curve, see Chau Do and Irina Paley, "Explaining the Growth of Higher-Priced Loans in HMDA: A Decomposition Approach," Journal of Real Estate Research, Vol. 29, No. 4 (2007) pp. 441- 447.

[22] See [http://www.federalreserve.gov/newsevents/press/bcreg/2008 1020b.htm.pdf].

[23] See [http://www.freddiemac.com/].

[24] TILA is contained in Title I of the Consumer Credit Protection Act, P.L. 90-301, 81 Stat. 146, as amended by 15 U.S.C. Section 1601 et seq. The Federal Reserve Board implements TILA through Regulation Z.

[25] The $561 figure is for 2008. The Federal Reserve Board adjusts this number annually based upon changes to the Consumer Price Index. See [http://www.occ.treas. gov/ftp/bulletin/2007-32a.pdf] and [http://www.ftc.gov/bcp/edu/pubs/ consumer/homes/ rea19.shtm]. The figure for 2009 will be $589. See [http://www.federalreserve.gov/ newsevents/press/ bcreg/20080805a.htm].

[26] See [http://www.federalreserve.gov/boarddocs/press/bcreg/2002/2002062 1/default.htm] and [http://www.bankersonline.com/lending/jh_regc.html].

[27] See [http://www.federalreserve.gov/boarddocs/press/boardacts/200 1/200112142/ attachment.pdf].

[28] See [http://www.federalreserve.gov/newsevents/press/bcreg/200807 14a.htm].

[29] For more detailed information about HOEPA, see CRS Report RL34259, *A Predatory Lending Primer: The Home Ownership and Equity Protection Act (HOEPA)*, by David H. Carpenter.

[30] For an introduction to the FHA program, please see CRS Report RS20530, *FHA Loan Insurance Program: An Overview*, by Bruce E. Foote and Meredith Peterson.

[31] P.L. 110-289, 122 Stat. 2654. For the current FHA premium pricing structure, see [http://www.hud.gov/offices/adm/hudclips/letters/mortgagee/files/0822ml.doc].

[32] See letter that discusses FHA having to resume payment of distributed shares to customers when a surplus of reserves had accumulated in the Money Market Insurance Fund at [http://www.gao.gov/archive/2000/rc00280r.pdf].

In: Improving Consumer Mortgage Disclosures
Editor: Jason C. Castleman

ISBN 978-1-60692-923-0

Chapter 2

IMPROVING CONSUMER MORTGAGE DISCLOSURES. AN EMPIRICAL ASSESSMENT OF CURRENT AND PROTOTYPE DISCLOSURE FORMS[1]

James M. Lacko and Janis K. Pappalardo

---

[1] This is an edited, excerpted and augmented edition of a Federal Trade Commission publication, dated June 2007.

This is a chapter of the Bureau of Economics of the Federal Trade Commission. The views expressed in this chapter are those of the staff and do not necessarily represent the views of the Federal Trade Commission or any individual Commissioner.

EXECUTIVE SUMMARY

Despite a long history of mortgage cost disclosure requirements and many legislative and regulatory proposals, little empirical evidence exists to document the effect of the current disclosures on consumer understanding of mortgage costs, consumer mortgage shopping, or consumer mortgage choice. In this study, we conducted 36 in-depth interviews with recent mortgage customers, and quantitative consumer testing with over 800 mortgage customers, to examine how consumers search for mortgages, how well consumers understand current mortgage cost disclosures and the terms of their own recently obtained loans, and whether better disclosures could improve consumer understanding of mortgage costs, consumer shopping for mortgage loans, and consumers' ability to avoid deceptive lending practices. The potential for improving consumer understanding of mortgage costs through better disclosures was tested using prototype disclosures developed for the study. The prototype disclosures were developed for fixed-rate loans, including those with interest-only and balloon payments, but could be extended to incorporate the key features of adjustable-rate, hybrid, and payment option loans.

The key findings of the study are:

- Current mortgage cost disclosures failed to convey key mortgage costs to many consumers.
- Prototype disclosures developed for the study significantly improved consumer recognition of mortgage costs, demonstrating that better disclosures are feasible.
- Both prime and subprime borrowers failed to understand key loan terms when viewing the current disclosures, and both benefitted from improved disclosures.
- Improved disclosures provided the greatest benefit for more complex loans, where both prime and subprime borrowers had the most difficulty understanding loan terms.

The study also demonstrates the importance of consumer testing in the development and evaluation of consumer disclosures.

Study Method

We used two methods to examine consumer understanding of mortgage disclosures—in-depth consumer interviews and quantitative consumer testing.

In-Depth Consumer Interviews

Thirty-six in-depth interviews were conducted with consumers who had obtained a mortgage within the previous four months. The interviews, conducted in several waves between September 2004 and February 2005, examined how consumers shopped for their mortgages, how well they understood the terms of the loans they had recently obtained, how well they understood various loan terms and the currently required mortgage cost disclosures, and how they reacted to the initial version of the prototype cost disclosures developed for the quantitative testing phase of the study.

A wide variety of loan types had been obtained by interviewed consumers, including fixed-rate, adjustable-rate, interest-only, balloon, bi-weekly payment, payment option, and combination (piggy-back) loans. Approximately half of the consumers obtained their loans from a prime lender and the other half from a subprime lender. All lived in Montgomery County, Maryland, a suburb of Washington, D.C., but their demographic characteristics and experience with mortgage transactions varied widely.

During the telephone calls in which we recruited recent mortgage customers for the interviews, borrowers who agreed to participate in the study were asked a series of questions about the terms of their recently obtained mortgage. Participants were then asked to bring the loan documents they had received for this mortgage to the interview. The cost disclosures in these documents were then used to assess the accuracy of the borrowers' perceptions of their loan costs.

Quantitative Consumer Testing

Quantitative consumer testing within a controlled experiment was conducted with 819 recent mortgage customers in 12 locations across the country. The testing, conducted in October through December 2005, examined the extent to which consumers could understand and use current mortgage cost disclosures and prototype disclosures developed for the study. About half of the participants had obtained their loan from a subprime lender and the other half from a prime lender.

Respondents were given cost disclosure forms for two hypothetical mortgage loans and asked a series of questions about various costs and terms of the loans, including the loan amount, settlement costs, charges for optional products and services, total up-front costs, interest rate, APR, cash due at closing, monthly payment, payments for property taxes and homeowner's insurance, balloon payment, and prepayment penalties. The questions asked consumers to compare the two loans and identify which was higher or lower on particular loan costs, to examine one loan and identify the amount of various costs, and to identify whether particular costs or terms were present in a loan.

The tests were conducted with two different loan-cost scenarios, one with relatively simple loans and the other with more complex loans that included features such as optional credit insurance, interest-only monthly payments that did not include escrow for taxes and insurance, a large balloon payment, and prepayment penalties. The results of 25 questions (or combinations of questions) were analyzed to assess the ability of respondents to understand and use the disclosure forms. Twenty-one questions were used in the simple-loan scenario because some of the loan terms were not present in these loans.

Half of the respondents used the current mortgage cost disclosure forms during the tests and half used the prototype form developed for the study. The current disclosure forms consisted of the Truth-in-Lending Act ("TILA") statement that is required for closed-end, fixed-rate residential mortgages under the Truth in Lending Act, and the Good Faith Estimate of Settlement Costs ("GFE") required under the Real Estate Settlement Procedures Act ("RESPA"). The GFE used in the tests was an enhanced version that included information not required by the current regulations, including the amount of money borrowed, the interest rate, the total monthly payment amount, an itemization of the monthly payment, the cash due at closing, and the total settlement charges. Many lenders use some variation of an enhanced GFE that goes beyond the regulatory requirements. The form used in the tests followed this practice so that it would more closely reflect the information that many consumers actually receive. The use of an enhanced GFE implies, however, that the test results will understate any problems that consumers may have with a GFE that merely complies with the regulations.

Prototype Mortgage Cost Disclosures

A prototype mortgage cost disclosure form was developed to test whether better disclosures would enable consumers to more easily recognize loan costs, more easily comparison shop for the best deal, and more readily recognize and avoid deceptive lending practices.

The prototype disclosures were developed for fixed-rate loans, including those with interest-only and balloon payments. Adjustable-rate, hybrid, and payment option loans would require additional disclosures that described how the interest rate, monthly payment, or both, may change over the course of the loan. The study focused on fixed-rate loans in order to first test whether better disclosures could be designed for these relatively simpler loan products.

If the prototype disclosures are shown to be more effective than current disclosures for fixed-rate loans, additional disclosures for adjustable-rate, hybrid, and payment option products could be added. An additional page that described the adjustable-rate and option features, and their potential impact on the interest rate and payments of the loan, could be added, and a prominent disclosure could be added to the first page to direct consumers to the additional disclosures and perhaps provide the maximum monthly payment possible in the loan.

The principles followed in designing the prototype form were simple and straightforward. The key mortgage costs that consumers need to understand when obtaining a loan were included in the form. Information that is less important or confusing was excluded. Costs were conveyed in simple, easily-to-understand language. The form was organized and formatted so that the various costs could be easily recognized and identified.

The design of the prototype was not restricted to include all of the disclosures currently required in the TILA statement and GFE form. We attempted to start anew, as if the current disclosures did not exist, and ask what mortgage cost information was most important for consumers. We were guided by a general financial analysis of the key costs of a mortgage, the types of consumer problems encountered in the deceptive lending cases investigated by the FTC, our experience in designing and evaluating consumer disclosures, and the insights gained from the in-depth consumer interviews conducted in the first part of the study.

The content and format considerations resulted in a three-page disclosure form. The first page provides a summary of all key loan costs; the second and third pages provide additional detail. This allows consumers to easily review the overall cost of the loan and compare it to other loan offers, as well as fully understand the details and source of the costs. An example of the prototype form appears at the end of this Executive Summary. Additional examples for loans with other terms appear in Appendix H of the chapter.

The prototype form provides a number of cost disclosures not required in the current TILA and GFE forms, including:

- Disclosure of the total loan amount, rather than the "amount financed," and an itemization that divides the total into the categories of money borrowed to purchase or refinance a home, cash for debt consolidation or a home equity loan, financed settlement charges, and financed charges for optional products or services.
- Disclosure of the total charges for settlement services.

Stronger disclosure of charges for optional credit insurance, and expansion of the disclosure to include all types of optional products and services, with clearer notice that the optional items are not required for the loan, and that charges should not be included if the consumer does not want to purchase the items.

- Disclosure of total up-front charges, and an itemization that divides the total into two categories: settlement and optional charges.
- Disclosure of the amount of cash due at closing, and an itemization that divides the total into the categories of down payment, payments for settlement services, and payments for optional products or services.
- Disclosure of the interest rate.
- Highlighted disclosure of any balloon payment.
- Enhanced prepayment penalty disclosures, including a specific statement of whether a prepayment penalty is included in the loan (as opposed to the current statement that the borrower "may" be charged a penalty), and if so, the size of the penalty and the conditions under which it will apply.
- Disclosure, in purchase loans, of the house price, down payment, and amount of price financed.
- Disclosure of the total monthly payment, rather than only the principal and interest portion, and an itemization that divides the total into the categories of principal and interest, property taxes, homeowner's insurance, mortgage insurance, and any monthly billed, optional products or services.
- Disclosure of whether the monthly payment includes property taxes and homeowner's insurance, and if not, the additional monthly amounts that must be paid by the borrower.
- Consumer tips and warnings on the benefits of comparison shopping, not relying on oral promises, and verifying costs at closing.

Results

The study produced four major findings: (1) current mortgage cost disclosures failed to convey key mortgage costs to many consumers; (2) prototype disclosures developed for the study significantly improved consumer recognition of mortgage costs, demonstrating that better disclosures are feasible; (3) both prime and subprime borrowers failed to understand key loan terms, and both benefitted from the improved disclosures; and (4) improved disclosures provided the greatest benefit for more complex loans, where both prime and subprime borrowers had the most difficulty understanding loan terms. These findings were obtained from both the in-depth consumer interviews and the quantitative consumer testing, with the exception that the consumer interviews did not examine the impact of the improved disclosures on particular types of borrowers or for particular types of loans.

In-Depth Consumer Interviews

The in-depth consumer interviews found that many borrowers were confused by the current mortgage cost disclosures and did not understand key terms in the disclosure forms, such as the APR, amount financed, and discount fees. Many borrowers also did not understand important costs and terms of their own recently obtained mortgages. Many had loans that were significantly more costly than they believed, or contained significant restrictions, such as prepayment penalties, of which they were unaware. Many of these borrowers did not learn of these costs and terms until at or after the loan settlement, and some appeared to learn for the first time during the interview. Some of these borrowers reported that they had spent considerable time shopping and comparing loan offers, but still experienced problems or misunderstandings. Others relied primarily on their loan officer or mortgage broker to explain the loan terms, or on the reputation of the lender or the recommendation of a friend or relative, rather than examining and verifying the loan terms themselves. Both prime and subprime borrowers were confused by the current mortgage disclosures, and both experienced significant misunderstandings about the terms of their recently obtained loans. Borrowers were nearly unanimous in their strong positive reaction to the initial version of the prototype disclosure form developed for the study; most characterized it as a substantial improvement over the current forms in organization and readability.

Quantitative Consumer Testing

The quantitative consumer testing, conducted with 819 recent mortgage customers, confirmed and quantified the shortcomings of the current mortgage cost disclosures and the improvements provided by the prototype disclosure form. The testing also provided much greater detail on consumer understanding of various individual loan costs in the current and prototype forms. The following summarizes many of the detailed results that support the four major findings of the study.

1) Current mortgage cost disclosures failed to convey key mortgage costs to many consumers
- The failure to convey key mortgage costs was evident across a wide range of loan terms and among substantial proportions of study participants.
- About a fifth of the respondents viewing the current disclosure forms could not correctly identify the APR of the loan, the amount of cash due at closing, or the monthly payment (including whether it included escrow for taxes and insurance).
- Nearly a quarter could not identify the amount of settlement charges.
- About a third could not identify the interest rate or which of two loans was less expensive, and a third did not recognize that the loan included a large balloon payment or that the loan amount included money borrowed to pay for settlement charges.
- Half could not correctly identify the loan amount.
- Two-thirds did not recognize that they would be charged a prepayment penalty if in two years they refinanced with another lender (and a third did not even recognize that they "may" be charged such a penalty).
- Three-quarters did not recognize that substantial charges for optional credit insurance were included in the loan.
- Almost four-fifths did not know why the interest rate and APR of a loan sometimes differ.
- Nearly nine-tenths could not identify the total amount of up-front charges in the loan.
- Because the GFE used in the tests was an enhanced version that included information not required by the current regulations, the results understate the problems faced by consumers who receive a GFE that merely complies with the law. Many of the key costs examined in the tests would not be disclosed in a form that merely met the regulatory requirements.

2) Prototype disclosures developed for the study significantly improved consumer recognition of mortgage costs, demonstrating that better disclosures are feasible
- Respondents viewing the current disclosure forms answered an average of 61 percent of the test questions correctly. Respondents viewing the prototype form answered 80 percent of the questions correctly, a 19 percentage point improvement.
- 80 percent of the respondents viewing the prototype form were able to answer 70 percent or more of the questions correctly, compared to only 29 percent of the respondents viewing the current forms, an improvement of 51 percentage points.
- The prototype form performed better than the current forms in 17 of the 21 questions in the simple-loan scenario and 23 of the 25 questions in the complex-loan scenario. (Thirteen and 16 of the differences in the two scenarios, respectively, were statistically significant.)
- Many of the improvements provided by the prototype form were quite large. In the complex-loan scenario, for example, the prototype outperformed the current forms by more than 10 percentage points in 15 questions, more than 30 percentage points in eight questions and more than 50 percentage points in four questions.
- The prototype disclosures provided improvements across a wide range of loan terms and for substantial proportions of respondents. The improvements provided by the prototype form included:

- 66 percentage point increase in the proportion of respondents correctly identifying the total amount of up-front charges in the loan.
- 43 percentage point increase in the proportion of respondents recognizing that the loan contained charges for optional credit insurance.
- 37 percentage point increase in the proportion correctly identifying the amount borrowed.
- 24 percentage point increase in the proportion recognizing that a prepayment penalty would be assessed if the loan was refinanced in two years.
- 21 percentage point increase in the proportion correctly identifying why the APR and interest rate may differ in a loan.
- 16 percentage point increase in the proportion correctly identifying the APR amount.
- 15 percentage point increase in the proportion correctly identifying the amount of settlement charges.
- 13 percentage point increase in the proportion correctly identifying which of two loans was less expensive.
- 12 percentage point increase in the proportion correctly identifying the interest rate amount.
- 9 percentage point increase in the proportion recognizing that settlement charges were financed and included in the loan amount.
- The prototype form also conveyed the correct prepayment penalty amount to 59 percent of the respondents, and the correct amounts of property taxes and homeowner's insurance charges, for a loan in which the charges were not included in the monthly payment, to 79 percent of the respondents. This information is not included in the current forms.

- A comparison of the percentage of respondents using the current and prototype forms who could not correctly identify various loan costs is presented in the chart in Figure ES-1. The chart illustrates the improvements provided by the prototype form.
- Although the prototype form provided significant improvements in consumer understanding, some consumers still failed to recognize key costs, and, in some cases, represented substantial proportions of prototype- form respondents. Forty-one percent of prototype form respondents, for example, could not identify the amount of prepayment penalties (though this was a substantial improvement over the 95 percent who could not do so with the current forms), and 30 percent did not recognize that the loan included a large balloon payment, an identical percentage as in the current-forms group. Further development of the disclosures may provide additional improvements that better convey these costs.

3) Both prime and subprime borrowers failed to understand key loan terms when viewing the current disclosures, and both benefitted from improved disclosures

- Prime borrowers viewing the current disclosure forms answered an average of 62.0 percent of the questions correctly, compared to 59.6 percent for subprime borrowers, a difference of only 2.4 percentage points.
- Although prime borrowers performed better than subprime borrowers in most of the questions, the differences were almost always small and, with only two exceptions, not statistically significant.

- The prototype form provided similar benefits to both prime and subprime borrowers. In the complex-loan scenario, for example, the prototype form increased the average percentage of questions answered correctly by 21.6 percentage points for prime borrowers and 22.4 percentage points for subprime borrowers.
- In the 23 questions in which the prototype form performed better than the current forms, prime borrowers obtained a larger percentage point improvement in 11 questions and subprime borrowers obtained a larger improvement in 12 questions.

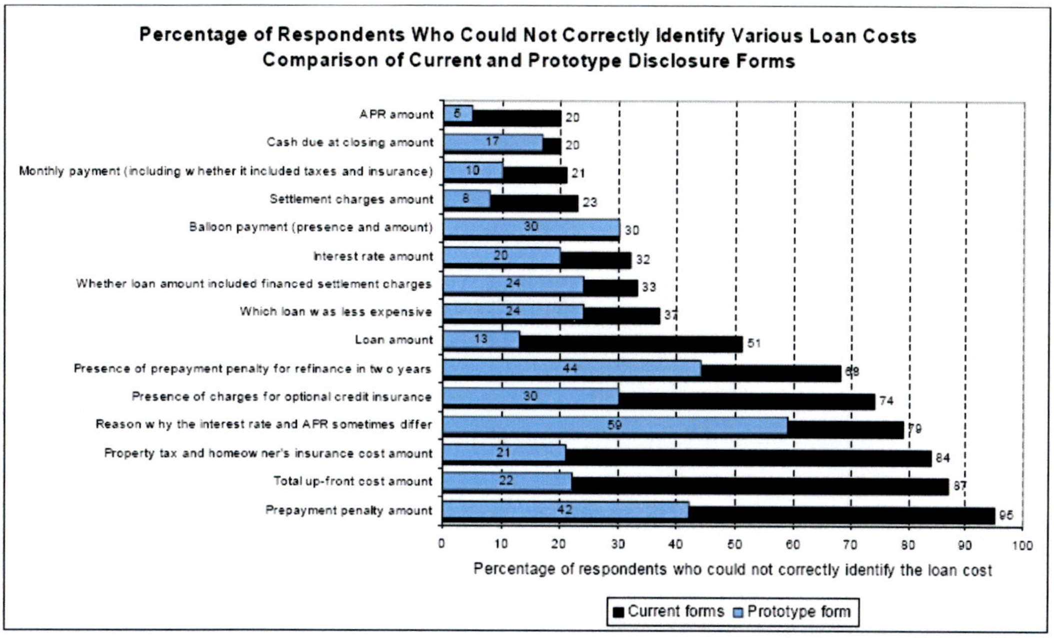

Figure ES-1. Percentage of Respondents Who Could Not Correctly Identify Various Loan Costs Comparison of Current and Prototype Disclosure Forms.

4) Improved disclosures provided the greatest benefit for more complex loans, where both prime and subprime borrowers had the most difficulty understanding loan terms.

- Respondents viewing current disclosure forms answered 66 percent of the questions correctly in the simple-loan scenario, compared to 56 percent in the complex-loan scenario, a difference of 10 percentage points. Similarly, respondents viewing the prototype form answered 82 percent of the questions correctly in the simple-loan scenario, compared to 78 percent in the complex-loan scenario, a difference of four percentage points.
- The prototype form increased the percentage of questions answered correctly by 22 percentage points in the complex-loan scenario, compared to 16 percentage points in the simple-loan scenario.

If loans in the subprime market tend to have more complex features than loans in the prime market, these results suggest that borrowers in the subprime market may have greater difficulty understanding their loan terms than borrowers in the prime market, and improved disclosures may provide a greater beneficial impact in the subprime market.

In summary, the consumer testing found that current mortgage cost disclosures failed to convey key mortgage costs to both prime and subprime borrowers, and that prototype disclosures developed for the study significantly improved consumer recognition of mortgage costs, demonstrating that better disclosures are feasible. Improved disclosures provided the greatest benefits for more complex loans, where both prime and subprime borrowers had the most difficulty understanding loan terms.

These findings may be even stronger in real-world transactions. Although in real-world transactions borrowers will have greater incentive to understand loan costs, because their homes and savings are at risk, they also may face a number of factors that make it more difficult to understand their loan costs. The consumer testing was conducted in a quiet, experimental setting. Respondents did not face the time pressure of a loan closing, a large stack of other closing paperwork, or deceptive tactics aimed at obscuring loan costs, all of which are likely to aggravate the difficulties consumers have understanding their loan terms. These difficulties may be especially acute for refinance loans, for which the TILA disclosures need not be provided until closing. Further difficulties are introduced because the settlement costs disclosed earlier in the GFE are subject to change at closing.

The differences between prime and subprime borrowers also may be larger in real-world transactions. The study results were obtained holding constant the complexity of the loans. In actual market transactions, subprime borrowers may be more likely to face loans with complex features, which the study found were more difficult to understand. Adjustable-rate, hybrid, and payment option loans, which were not tested, are likely to create even greater difficulties. Time pressure at closing, voluminous other paperwork, and any deceptive practices are likely to especially aggravate understanding difficulties for these more complex loans. Many subprime borrowers also face pressures not typically faced by prime borrowers, such as the need to obtain a loan quickly in order to address family financial difficulties, or the experience of being turned down by several lenders before being approved for a loan. All of these considerations suggest that subprime borrowers may face even greater difficulties understanding their loan terms than indicated by the study results, and may benefit the most from improved disclosures.

CONCLUSIONS

If consumers do not understand the costs and terms of their mortgages, they may pay more for their mortgages than necessary, obtain inappropriate loan terms, fall prey to deceptive lending practices, and experience unpleasant surprises and financial difficulties during the course of their loans. The results of the study show that current mortgage disclosures fail to convey key mortgage costs and terms to many consumers, leaving them susceptible to these problems.

This study also demonstrates that better cost disclosures can significantly improve consumer recognition of loan costs. Further development of the disclosures may provide additional improvements that better convey these costs to even more consumers. Better cost disclosures have the potential for providing greater consumer understanding of loan costs, more efficient comparison shopping, reduced vulnerability to deceptive lending practices, and enhanced competition in the marketplace. This study demonstrates that it is possible to achieve such improvements.

The study also illustrates the importance of consumer testing in the development and evaluation of consumer disclosure policy. Although some disclosures may be so simple and straightforward that testing is not necessary, for most disclosures, particularly those regarding something as complicated and difficult to understand as mortgage transactions, testing is essential to ensure that the disclosures effectively convey the desired information to consumers.

Mortgage Loan Offer
FS Mortgage Company
456 Main Street
Mortgagetown, Virginia 22189
(703) 555-2767

LOAN "T"

Page 1 of 3

Borrower: James and Clara Borrower — Offer Date: October 14, 2005
Property Location: 123 Your Street, Hometown, VA 22189

This page provides a summary of your loan, our charges for the loan, and your loan payments. See pages 2 and 3 for important details on each of these items.

YOUR LOAN

Loan Type Summary	10 year interest-only balloon	
Loan Amount	$ 189,313.43	
Loan Term	10 years (120 monthly payments)	

OUR LOAN CHARGES

Interest Rate	6.65%	Fixed rate
Up-Front Charges	$ 7,658.43	Total settlement charges
	$ 6,230.00	Charges for optional products and services
	$ 13,888.43	Total up-front charges
Monthly-Billed Charges	None	
Annual Percentage Rate (APR)	6.88%	The cost of credit, including both interest payments and other finance charges, expressed as an annual rate.

YOUR LOAN PAYMENTS

Cash Due at Closing	$ 0.00	
Monthly Payments	$ 1,254.95	Payments number 1–119 (Includes required payments for property taxes and hazard insurance.)
Balloon Payment	$ 190,568.38	Payment number 120 – You will have to pay this amount at the end of the 10 year loan term.

PENALTIES AND LATE FEES

Prepayment Penalty	None
Late Fee	A 5% late fee will be charged on payments more than 7 days late.

FS Mortgage Company	LOAN "T"	Page 2 of 3

This page and the next provide explanations and important details about your loan amount, our charges for the loan, and your loan payments. See page 1 for a summary of these items.

LOAN AMOUNT DETAILS

Loan Amount	$ 150,000.00	Refinance current mortgage loan
	$ 20,000.00	Cash paid to borrower
	$ 5,425.00	Consolidation of borrower's other debts
	$ 7,658.43	Financed settlement charges
	$ 6,230.00	Financed charges for optional products and services
	$ 189,313.43	Total Loan Amount

OPTIONAL CHARGES DETAILS

Optional Products and Services Charges	$ 3,900.00	Credit life insurance
	$ 2,330.00	Credit disability insurance
	$ 6,230.00	Total Optional Product and Services Charges

These products and services are NOT required for the loan. Tell your loan provider if you do not wish to purchase them and make sure that you obtain a revised offer sheet with these charges removed.

CASH DUE AT CLOSING DETAILS

Cash Due at Closing	$ 0.00

MONTHLY PAYMENT DETAILS

Monthly Payment

Itemization of initial monthly payment

$ 1,049.11	Principal and interest
$ 145.83	Property tax escrow
$ 60.00	Hazard (homeowners) insurance
$ 0.00	Private mortgage insurance (PMI)
$ 0.00	Monthly-billed optional products or services
$ 1,254.95	Total initial monthly payment

Taxes and Insurance — Property taxes and hazard insurance ARE included in your monthly loan payment.

FS Mortgage Company	LOAN "T"	Page 3 of 3

SETTLEMENT CHARGES DETAILS

This page lists the settlement services included in the settlement charges shown on page 1. ALL of the settlement services you need to close the loan are included.

Settlement Services Package	$5,230.00	This package includes the following services: Origination and lender services: Loan origination; Appraisal; Credit report; Lender's property survey; Lender's property inspection; Pest inspection Title services: Settlement agent; Title search and examination; Title document preparation; Lender's title insurance; Attorney services; Notary fee Government taxes and fees: County recording fee; State and local tax stamps
Interest Charge for Partial Month	$ 275.93	This charge is for the daily interest charges from the day of your settlement until the end of the month. For this loan this amount is $ 34.4914 per day for 8 days (if your closing date is 10/24/05).
Prepaid Items	$ 0.00 $ 720.00	Property taxes (0 months at $_____ per month) Hazard insurance (12 months at $ 60.00 per month)
Reserves Deposited with the Lender	$1,312.50 $ 120.00	Property taxes (9 months at $ 145.83 per month) Hazard insurance (2 months at $ 60.00 per month)
Total Settlement Charges	**$7,658.43**	**Total Settlement Charges**

HOW TO PROTECT YOURSELF

COMPARISON SHOP TO FIND THE BEST DEAL — The lender or broker providing this loan is not necessarily shopping on your behalf or providing you with the lowest cost loan.

DO NOT RELY ON ORAL PROMISES TO CHANGE THESE TERMS — Obtain all changes in writing.

SAVE THIS OFFER SHEET AND COMPARE TO DOCUMENTS AT CLOSING — Before you sign any papers at your loan closing (loan settlement), make sure that the costs have not been increased.

Federal law requires that this offer sheet be provided to the borrower within three (3) business days after the borrower has applied for a loan. If the loan terms change prior to acceptance by the borrower, a new offer sheet must be provided. Notify the Federal Trade Commission (FTC) if the lender does not abide by the terms set forth in this offer or does not provide this offer sheet within three days of application: Federal Trade Commission (FTC), 600 Pennsylvania Avenue, N.W., Washington D.C., 20580, telephone (877) FTC-HELP (382-4357), web site www.ftc.gov.

INTRODUCTION

Mortgages are the largest loans that most consumers ever obtain, and mortgage payments are the largest ongoing monthly expense that most consumers face. At the end of 2005, consumers held over $9 trillion in outstanding mortgage debt. Over the five years from 2001 to 2005, consumers borrowed an average of nearly $3 trillion a year through mortgage loans to finance the purchases of homes and refinance existing loans.[1]

Choosing the wrong mortgage can cost consumers thousands of dollars in unnecessary up-front costs and larger monthly payments, result in unpleasant surprises and financial difficulties during the course of the loan, and, in some cases, even threaten a consumers' homeownership and financial solvency. Some consumers may make these unfortunate choices on their own but others may fall prey to the misrepresentations and other deceptive lending practices used by unscrupulous lenders and brokers.

Consumers can better avoid these problems if they understand the costs and terms of their mortgages. By comparing loan offers from competing lenders, and by understanding the cost and terms of the loans, consumers can make accurate comparisons and identify the least expensive loan that fits their needs.

1.1. Current Mortgage Cost Disclosures

For decades federal law has required that various costs and terms of a mortgage be disclosed to borrowers in the Truth-in-Lending Statement ("TILA statement") and Good Faith Estimate of Settlement Costs ("GFE").[2] In his 1966 Special Message to the Congress on Consumer Interests, President Johnson advocated the passage of truth in lending legislation that would disclose the cost of credit to consumers:

> The right of the consumer to know the actual cost of his credit has been ignored for too long. Credit is a commodity. The consumer has just as much right to know the cost of borrowing money as to know the price of any other article he buys. . . . I therefore renew my recommendation for legislation requiring lenders to state the full cost of credit, simply and clearly, and to state it before any credit contract is signed. This legislation will help consumers: budget their incomes more intelligently, because they will know the price of credit in the same clear terms as the price of milk or gasoline; compare credit costs so they shop for the best combination of quality and price—including all of the charges involved; [and] avoid unscrupulous lenders who use excessive credit charges and other sharp practices. This legislation will also help the legitimate lender by offering protection against any competitor who seeks to gain business by misrepresenting credit costs. It will insure the fair and effective competition that legitimate lenders desire.[3]

When the Truth in Lending Act ("TILA") was eventually enacted in 1968, the first paragraphs of the statute presented the Congressional statement of findings and declaration of purpose:

> The informed use of credit results from an awareness of the cost thereof by consumers. It is the purpose of this [statute] to assure a meaningful disclosure of credit terms so that the

> consumer will be able to compare more readily the various credit terms available to him and avoid the uninformed use of credit . . . .[4]

Similarly, in 1974, Congress declared in the statement of findings and purpose of the Real Estate Settlement Procedures Act ("RESPA") that:

> . . . significant reforms in the real estate settlement process are needed to insure that consumers throughout the Nation are provided with greater and more timely information on the nature and costs of the settlement process . . . . It is the purpose of this chapter to effect certain changes in the settlement process for residential real estate that will result in more effective advance disclosure to home buyers and sellers of settlement costs . . . . [5]

The TILA and GFE disclosures are generally viewed as having improved the information available to consumers.[6] Consumer advocates view the TILA disclosures, in particular, as a "cornerstone of consumer credit legislation," and note that prior to the enactment of TILA, creditors did not use a uniform way of calculating interest rates, making it difficult for consumers to determine the cost of credit or to compare costs across different lenders.[7]

At the same time, however, questions have been raised concerning whether the disclosures have fully met their stated purpose and effectively informed consumers of the cost of credit, particularly in regard to mortgage transactions. In 1996, for example, Congress directed the Board of Governors of the Federal Reserve System ("FRB"), which is responsible for implementing the TILA disclosures, and HUD, which is responsible for implementing the GFE disclosures, to simplify and improve the disclosures, and create a single disclosure document that would meet the purposes of both acts.[8] In 1998, the two agencies submitted a joint report to Congress. The report concluded that "the current TILA and RESPA disclosure rules may fall short of meeting their intended goals," because consumers may receive the disclosures too late to find them helpful in comparison shopping, the cost estimates they receive under RESPA may differ significantly from the final figures, and consumers may find some of the cost information presented in the TILA disclosures not readily understandable.[9]

The agencies recommended that improvements be made to the TILA and GFE disclosures to make them more understandable and useful for consumers, that the timing of the disclosures be coordinated and provided to consumers as early as possible, and that disclosed closing costs be made more reliable by imposing stricter tolerances on cost estimates and allowing lenders to offer guaranteed packages of settlement services.[10]

A joint report by HUD and the Department of the Treasury ("Treasury"), issued in 2000, repeated the call for improved disclosures of the type envisioned in the FRB-HUD report, as part of its recommendations for addressing the problems of abusive lending.[11] Although the agencies concluded that lending abuses were due to a number of factors, and that better disclosures on their own would not curb abuses, they concluded that complicated disclosures of loan costs can confuse even the most knowledgeable borrowers, fail to inform borrowers of their loan costs, and fail to protect borrowers from abusive practices. The agencies concluded that improved disclosures could increase consumer awareness of loan costs and enable borrowers to better protect themselves.

In 2002, HUD announced a rulemaking to make changes to the GFE and other RESPA rules to accomplish a number of the recommendations put forth in the FRB-HUD report. In its proposal, HUD described shortcomings of the current GFE disclosures:

> . . . the process of financing or refinancing a home . . . remains too complicated, too costly, and too opaque for many borrowers. . . . Settlement cost disclosures need to be improved so that the information they provide is simpler, clearer, more reliable, and reasonably available to facilitate shopping, increase competition, and lower settlement costs.[12]
>
> The current GFE format contains a long list of individual charges that can be overwhelming, often confuses consumers, and seems to provide little useful information for consumer shopping . . . . the current disclosure fails to highlight the major costs and seems to lead only to a proliferation of charges [13]

The HUD proposal sought to improve the GFE by consolidating settlement costs into a few major categories, with a single total amount disclosed for each, and adding additional information about the loan, including the interest rate, APR, adjustable-rate terms, loan amount, monthly payment, any balloon payment, and an indication of whether the loan contained a prepayment penalty. HUD also proposed a mortgage broker compensation disclosure, which added payments received from the lender to the broker's disclosed origination fee. HUD's proposal also would have made settlement costs less subject to change (some costs could not be changed, and others could be changed only within a small tolerance), and removed regulatory barriers to allow guaranteed packages of mortgages and settlement services to be made available to borrowers.[14] HUD ultimately withdrew the proposed rule before it was finalized, but indicated that it would reexamine the proposal, revise as necessary, and repropose the rule at a later date.[15]

In December 2004, the FRB announced that it was undertaking a comprehensive review of the TILA disclosures and other provisions of Regulation Z. The review, which, the FRB noted, was the first since 1982, was to take place in stages, beginning with the rules for non-mortgage, open-end credit. The FRB noted that significant changes to the TILA mortgage disclosures would best be considered in connection with HUD's future rulemaking.[16]

In 2006, the GAO examined the disclosures made by various lenders to inform consumers of the risks of alternative mortgage products, such as interest-only and payment option loans. The GAO found that the disclosures lacked important information, and were poorly written because they used language too complex for many adults to understand, used small, hard-to-read typeface, and made ineffective use of white space and headings, all of which made it difficult to read the disclosures and to identify important information.[17] The FRB, along with other banking agencies, recently issued industry guidance on disclosures (and safety and soundness issues) for these types of loans that urged lenders to provide balanced information about the benefits and risks of the loans, particularly the risks of payment shock and negative amortization.[18] The FRB will also consider additional disclosures for these products during its comprehensive review of TILA disclosures.[19]

1.2. Previous Studies of Mortgage Disclosures

Despite the importance of consumer mortgage decisions, decades of experience with federal mortgage disclosures, a general perception that these disclosures are inadequate and confusing, and repeated calls for improvement, little empirical evidence exists to document the effect of the current disclosures on consumer understanding of mortgage costs, consumer mortgage shopping, or consumer mortgage choice. There does not appear to be any study that directly examines consumer understanding of mortgage disclosures.

Several studies have examined consumer knowledge of loan terms. For example, a recent study by the FRB compared the distribution of responses from a survey asking consumers about the terms of their mortgage loans to the distribution of loan terms in lender-reported data.[20] The authors found that the distributions were similar for basic loan terms, such as the type of mortgage (fixed, adjustable, or balloon), loan term (maturity), and amount of annual mortgage payments, suggesting that consumers correctly understand these terms. Consumers with adjustable-rate loans, however, appeared to substantially underestimate the per-period and lifetime caps on interest rate increases, and many were unaware of their index rate. The authors also found statistically significant differences in the distributions for current interest rates, which suggests that some consumers may underestimate their current rates.

Another study, also conducted at the FRB, tested consumers' general understanding of the APR by asking whether the interest rate of a mortgage loan would be higher, lower, or the same as the APR. Only 10 percent of the respondents correctly responded that the interest rate would be lower.[21]

Although both studies provide valuable insight into consumers' knowledge of mortgage terms, they provide less insight into consumer understanding of mortgage disclosures. Both studies measure consumer knowledge a substantial time after consumers viewed the disclosures. The second study includes consumers who had obtained their mortgage up to five years earlier, and the first study includes consumers with a mortgage, regardless of when the mortgage was obtained. In the intervening time, consumers may have forgotten loan terms that they knew when they obtained the mortgage, or learned terms that they did not know earlier. Also, there is no way of knowing how many of the consumers actually read the disclosures, or even received them, or how many obtained information from sources other than the disclosures.

The authors of the first study also note another limitation: the comparison of distributions is a weaker test of accuracy than a test that examines whether individual consumers report their mortgage terms accurately, because if consumers make offsetting errors, the distributions may match, even though individual consumers do not accurately report their terms. The authors note, however, that the results are not subject to this limitation if the distributions do not match.

Another recent study of mortgage disclosures was conducted at the FTC. The study was conducted in an experimental setting in which consumers were given mortgage disclosures and asked a series of questions that directly assessed their ability to understand and use the information.[22] The focus of the study, however, was on the impact of a proposed mortgage broker compensation disclosure. Consumer understanding of other loan terms was not examined, and the disclosure forms, while including other loan terms, did not correspond to the current TILA and GFE forms. Thus, while the results of the study provide an illustration of the difficulties in formulating consumer disclosures, and the importance of consumer testing, they do not provide insight into consumers' understanding of current mortgage disclosures.

A number of consumer surveys have been conducted over the years to assess the impact of the TILA disclosures.[23] These surveys have consistently found that most consumers disagree with a statement that "most people read their TILA statement carefully," and that most agree that "some information in the TILA statements is not very helpful" and that

"TILA statements are complicated." A number of surveys have asked consumers to identify the APRs on their current loans, and a number have asked the same about hypothetical loans. Both use prevailing market rates to assess the accuracy of the responses. The studies find that substantial proportions of consumers remained unaware of APRs even after the TILA disclosures were implemented. The studies differ, however, in their findings of whether awareness increased in the years following TILA implementation. The studies involving the consumers' own loans show substantial improvement over time, but the studies involving hypothetical loans show little improvement. All of these surveys provide useful insight into consumers' opinions of the TILA disclosures, their awareness of market rates, and their knowledge, at the time of the survey, of the APRs on their own loans, but, like the studies discussed above, provide less direct insight into consumer understanding of the disclosures.

1.3. A Study of Consumer Understanding of Mortgage Cost Disclosures

In this study, we attempt to fill that gap by examining how consumers search for mortgages, how well consumers understand mortgage cost disclosures and loan agreements, and whether better disclosures could improve consumer understanding of mortgage costs, consumer shopping for mortgage loans, and consumers' ability to avoid deceptive lending practices.

The FTC's interest in these issues derives from its responsibility as the primary federal consumer protection agency. The agency uses law enforcement and regulatory actions to help ensure that markets are competitive and free of deceptive and unfair marketing practices. FTC staff also conducts research to inform and support the agency's competition and consumer protection missions, increase its understanding of markets and consumer behavior, and promote the welfare of consumers.

The FTC's law enforcement jurisdiction includes nonbank lenders and brokers that account for a large part of the mortgage market. In recent years, the FTC has brought legal actions against a number of lenders and brokers for the deceptive marketing and advertising of mortgage loans.24 Several of these actions have resulted in large monetary judgments, with a total recovery of more than $320 million in redress for consumers. Although, in some of these cases, the creditors failed to provide, or provided incorrect, TILA disclosures to borrowers, the FTC's experience has shown that even if the required disclosures are provided, unscrupulous lenders can still mislead borrowers about the cost of a loan.[25]

FTC staff has a unique mix of experience and expertise relevant to the study of consumer mortgage disclosures, including experience investigating and prosecuting deceptive lending cases; experience interpreting the marketing messages made by sellers and assessing their impact on consumers; expertise in developing and assessing consumer disclosures and other consumer protection policies; expertise in designing, conducting, and analyzing consumer research, including the testing of consumer disclosures; and expertise in the economic analysis of consumer, firm, and market behavior.

In this study, we examine consumer use and understanding of mortgage cost disclosures: both the current TILA and GFE disclosures and a prototype of improved cost disclosures developed for the study. We used two methods to examine the disclosures: 36 in-depth, qualitative interviews that probed the experience and understanding of recent mortgage customers, and quantitative consumer testing that examined whether the disclosures accurately conveyed key loan costs to 819 recent mortgage customers. The interviews were conducted in several waves between September 2004 and February 2005, and the consumer testing was conducted in October through early December 2005. Approximately half of the participants in both phases of the study obtained their mortgages from a subprime lender.

The prototype of improved cost disclosures was developed to test whether better disclosures would enable consumers to more easily recognize loan costs, more easily comparison shop, and more readily recognize and avoid deceptive lending practices. The design of the prototype was not restricted to include all of the disclosures currently required in the TILA statement and GFE form. In developing the prototype, we attempted to start anew, as if the current disclosures did not exist, and ask what mortgage cost information was most important for consumers. We were guided by a general financial analysis of the key costs and features of a mortgage, the types of consumer problems encountered in the deceptive lending cases investigated by the FTC, our experience in designing and evaluating consumer disclosures, and the insights gained from the in-depth consumer interviews conducted in the first part of the study.

The two methods used in the study complement and reinforce each other, and the disadvantages of each are offset by the strengths of the other, making the combined study more informative than if either method had been used on its own. The qualitative interviews provide an in-depth view of the experience and understanding of recent mortgage customers, but are based on a relatively small sample. The quantitative testing uses a much larger sample, and examines the disclosures in a more precise and uniform manner, with results that can be statistically analyzed, but does so within the context of an experiment rather than actual consumer transactions. However, if the two methods obtain similar results, one can be more confident that the findings are not skewed by either the small sample of the qualitative interviews or the experimental context of the quantitative testing.

The results of both the consumer interviews and quantitative testing show that current mortgage disclosures fail to convey key mortgage costs to many consumers. The failure to convey key mortgage costs was evident across a wide range of loan terms and among substantial proportions of study participants. The failure of the current disclosures to convey key loan costs to many consumers may make it easier for some lenders to engage in deceptive practices that mislead consumers about the cost of a loan. Many of the practices seen in deceptive lending cases have involved loan terms that the current disclosure forms have particular difficulty conveying to consumers, such as optional credit insurance, balloon payments, prepayment penalties, and the financing of high fees and optional charges in the loan amount.

The results of the quantitative testing also show that better disclosures can significantly improve consumer recognition of mortgage costs. In the tests, the prototype disclosures performed significantly better than the current disclosures across a wide range of loan terms and for substantial proportions of respondents. Some of the improvements were quite large. These results were supported by the opinions expressed by recent mortgage customers in the qualitative interviews, who portrayed the prototype disclosures as a substantial improvement over the current disclosures they had recently received. Although the quantitative testing showed that there is room for further improvement of the prototype disclosures, the prototype provides a starting point for the development of better disclosures.

The findings of the study also show that both prime and subprime borrowers failed to understand key loan terms, and both benefitted from the improved disclosures. Improved disclosures provided the greatest benefit for more complex loans, where both prime and subprime borrowers had the most difficulty understanding loan terms. The study also demonstrates the importance of consumer testing in the development and evaluation of consumer disclosures.

CONSUMER INTERVIEW METHODOLOGY

In the first phase of the study, 36 in-depth, qualitative interviews were conducted with recent mortgage customers. Nearly half of the interviews were conducted with borrowers who had obtained their loans from a subprime lender. The interviews examined how the borrowers shopped for their mortgages, how well they understood the terms of their own recently obtained mortgages, how well they understood mortgage terms and current mortgage disclosures, and how they reacted to draft prototype disclosures developed for the study. A key component of the research plan was to recruit borrowers who would agree to bring to the interview the loan documents received in their recent mortgages, which allowed a review of the documents to be incorporated into most of the interviews.

The qualitative interviews complemented the quantitative consumer testing conducted later in this study. The qualitative nature of the interviews provided insights into consumers' experiences that could not be obtained through a more structured survey. The interviews allowed for the collection of rich detail about the real-life experiences of consumers who recently obtained a mortgage, and an in-depth examination of their understanding of both mortgage disclosures and the terms of their own recent mortgage. Although the interviews are based on a much smaller sample of consumers than the consumer testing, and cannot be statistically analyzed in the same manner as the results of the testing, they offer insights that cannot be obtained solely through the examination of consumer understanding in an experimental environment. The interviews also aided in the development of the prototype disclosure form, and allowed us to test consumer reaction to an initial version of the prototype to ensure that the development was proceeding in the right direction.

The research plan for the interviews consisted of identifying a sample of recent mortgage customers, both prime and subprime; recruiting respondents from the sample who were willing to participate and bring their mortgage documents to the interview; conducting individual, in- person, in-depth interviews with each respondent; and analyzing the transcripts of the interviews to identify patterns, differences, and similarities in the experiences and understandings of the respondents.

2.1. Preliminary Focus Groups

Two focus groups were held prior to the interviews. The topics discussed in the focus groups were similar to those discussed in the interviews: respondents' experiences obtaining their mortgages, their understanding of the terms of their recent mortgages, and their use and understanding of current mortgage disclosures. The focus groups were conducted to provide some preliminary information on these topics and to assess the feasibility of conducting in-depth interviews. Observations made during the focus groups indicated that in-depth interviews on these same topics would be feasible, and provided insights that assisted the development of the interview topics and the drafting of the interview script. Because the focus groups were intended to be a preliminary stage in the development of the interviews, the results of the focus groups are not presented here. The focus groups, however, did not yield any observations inconsistent with those of the in-depth interviews.

2.2. Identification of Recent Borrowers

Interview respondents were recruited from lists of consumers who had obtained a mortgage in the previous four months in Montgomery County, Maryland, a suburb of Washington D.C. The lists were compiled from public records maintained at the Montgomery County courthouse.[26]

Two methods were used to identify recent mortgage customers in the courthouse records. Records of mortgages recorded on random, recent dates were identified from the county database. This yielded mortgages primarily from prime lenders. To identify a sufficient number of mortgages from subprime lenders, recently recorded mortgages were searched for the names of lenders on HUD's subprime lender list.[27] Mortgage transactions involving only a home equity line of credit were excluded.[28]

The population of Montgomery County, Maryland has higher average levels of education and income than the overall population of the country.[29] Given these characteristics, one must consider the possibility that the interview respondents would be more astute shoppers, and better able to understand their mortgages, than average borrowers across the country. If the interviews had shown that the respondents generally understood their mortgages, and had few problems, one might question whether the findings were an artifact of the particular population sampled for the study. But the actual findings, described below, show the opposite—that most respondents had difficulty understanding mortgage terms and many did not understand important terms of their recently obtained mortgages. These findings may be strengthened by the relatively high average levels of education and income in the population from which the sample was drawn, because borrowers with less education and income may have exhibited even greater difficulties.

The population of Montgomery County also is more ethnically diverse than the overall U.S. population.[30] This diversity was considered desirable for the study, as it would hopefully make it easier to obtain a racially and ethnically diverse group of respondents.

2.3. Recruitment of Respondents

Recent mortgage customers identified from the courthouse records were contacted by telephone and recruited for the study.[31] Potential respondents were told that the research was being conducted ". . . for a government agency that is trying to learn how consumers shop for mortgages . . . ." If the potential respondent asked for the name of the agency, they were told that the research was for the Federal Trade Commission.

To be eligible for the study, respondents had to confirm that they had taken out a mortgage within the previous four months to purchase or refinance a home, and were either the sole or joint household decision maker on the mortgage. Respondents also had to agree to bring their mortgage documents to the interview to share with the interviewer.

Potential respondents also were asked a series of demographic questions, including their age, education, race, and ethnicity. Recruiters were instructed to recruit a sample of respondents that included a diverse mix of each of these attributes, as well as a mix of purchase and refinance loans, location within the county, and gender.

Qualified respondents were invited to participate in a one hour interview and informed that they would be paid $100 for their participation.[32] Respondents who were joint decision makers were invited to bring their partner to the interview, and were offered compensation of $150 if both attended.

Qualified respondents who agreed to participate in the study were then asked a series of questions about the features of their mortgage, which could later be compared to the actual terms specified in their loan documents, to assess how well respondents understood the terms of their loan.

2.4. Description of Respondents

The final sample consisted of 36 consumer interviews.[33] Thirty-two of the interviews were conducted with individuals and four with couples. Respondents in 20 of the interviews had obtained their loan from a prime lender, and respondents in 16 of the interviews had obtained their loan from a subprime lender. Thirty-five of the interviews involved mortgage transactions completed within four months of the interview, and one within five months.

The sample included respondents with a wide range of life circumstances and reasons for obtaining a mortgage, including individuals purchasing their first home, young married couples starting families, middle-aged couples facing college expenses, a single woman running her own business, married couples operating their own businesses, individuals refinancing in response to divorces, and retirees. Some of the borrowers were experiencing financial distress, others seemed to have strong financial positions. The occupations of the respondents also varied widely, and included several schoolteachers, a school principal, a nurse, military personnel, computer specialists, homemakers, a salesman, a director of corporate security, a couple of attorneys, several small business owners, several retirees, and a person on employment disability.

Respondents in both the prime and subprime groups were split almost equally between male and female. Each group included nine respondents age 35 to 54, and five respondents age 55 to 64. Four and two of the respondents in the prime and subprime groups, respectively, were 18 to 34 years old, and two in the prime group were 65 years or older.[34] The 20 prime respondents included two African-Americans, one Hispanic-American, and one person with a multi-racial background. The 16 subprime respondents included three African-Americans, two Asian-Americans, and one American Indian.

All of the prime respondents had educations that included at least some college, including 10 who were college graduates and five who had attended graduate or professional school. Thirteen of the subprime respondents also had educations that included at least some college, including six who were college graduates and four who had attended graduate or professional school. Two of the subprime respondents were high school graduates, and one had attended a technical or trade school.

The most recent transaction of most respondents in both groups was a refinance of an existing loan (15 and 14 of the prime and subprime respondents, respectively). Five of the prime respondents and two of the subprime respondents had obtained purchase loans.

2.5. Interview Procedure

The interviews were conducted in several waves between September 2004 and February 2005 by personnel of a consumer research firm at research facilities in Bethesda and Gaithersburg, Maryland. The lead moderator for each interview had substantial experience conducting qualitative research interviews on issues related to consumer financial services.

When respondents arrived at the interview facility they were asked if they had brought their mortgage documents, and if so, whether they would allow the researchers to photocopy them. Respondents who did not wish their documents to be copied were asked if they would allow the researchers to record key terms from the documents. All respondents who brought their documents were asked if the documents could be examined during the course of the interviews. Information copied or recorded from respondents' mortgage documents, or observed during the interviews, was used to assess the accuracy of respondents' understanding of their loan terms.

Almost all respondents brought at least some of their documents to the interview. Most allowed key documents to be copied, and almost all allowed the documents to be used and examined during the course of the interview. Few respondents, however, brought all of their key documents. About one half of the respondents brought their GFEs, and about two-thirds brought their TILA statements.

The moderator followed an interview guide that detailed the questions to be asked during the course of the interview.[35] However, the qualitative interview methodology allowed the interviewer to modify or add questions during each interview, based on the respondent's answers to previous questions, in order to elicit fully and understand each respondent's experience obtaining a mortgage and their understanding of mortgage terms and disclosures. This flexibility is an advantage of the qualitative method, and allows for the collection of information that might not be obtained through a more structured survey.

The interviews began with questions about the background of the respondent and the respondent's experience shopping for and deciding on a mortgage. This included questions about why respondents had sought a mortgage, what concerns they had about obtaining a loan, whether and how they gathered information about mortgages, whether they compared loans from different lenders, what terms they compared, whether making such comparisons were easy, how they selected their originator, how they decided on their particular loan, whether they considered particular terms in their decisions, what would make obtaining and understanding mortgages easier, and how they obtained information about the terms of their mortgage.

The interviews focused next on the respondent's use and understanding of current mortgage disclosures, first on the disclosures provided in the GFE form, and then on the disclosures provided in the TILA statement. The questions were based on a review of the GFE and TILA forms from the respondent's own recently obtained mortgage if the respondent had brought the forms to the interview and allowed their use. Otherwise, respondents were shown sample GFE and TILA forms for a hypothetical mortgage loan.[36]

Respondents were asked a number of general questions about each disclosure form, including if they remembered receiving the document, when they received it, whether it was received at a reasonable time to be useful, how they would rate the understandability of the document on a scale from "one" to "ten," how useful the document was in helping them to understand and make decisions about their loans, and what other information, if any, they would like to see in the document to help them make decisions on their loans.[37] Respondents also were asked about the meaning, usefulness, and clarity of several specific terms in each document. For the GFE, respondents were asked about the "loan origination fee," "loan discount fee," and "total estimated settlement charges" disclosures. For the TILA form, respondents were asked about the "annual percentage rate," "finance charge," "amount financed," "total of payments," and "pre-payment penalty" disclosures.

The interviews concluded with questions about a draft of the prototype disclosure form that was being developed for the study. Respondents were provided a copy of the prototype, with disclosures for a hypothetical loan, and asked their impressions of the form and how it compared to the GFE and TILA forms they had just reviewed. Respondents then were asked questions similar to those asked about the other forms, including a question that asked them to rate the understandability of the prototype on a scale from "one" to "ten."

2.6. Analysis of the Interviews

The interviews were examined for an understanding of each respondent's experiences, knowledge, and beliefs. For respondents who had agreed to share their mortgage documents or loan terms, this information was compared to the respondents' reported understanding of their mortgage terms. Comparisons were made across interviews to identify patterns of similarities and differences. The results of this analysis are presented as a series of observations about the various patterns, similarities, and differences observed in the interviews. Except for the few quantitative, closed-ended questions included in the interviews, the frequencies of particular types of responses across respondents are not quantified. The analysis instead presents the observations in more qualitative manner that is standard for these types of interviews.

Consumer Interview Observations

The in-depth interviews of recent mortgage customers yielded a number of observations on consumer experiences shopping for and obtaining mortgages, their understanding of the terms of their recently obtained mortgages, their understanding of current mortgage disclosures, and their reactions to prototype disclosures developed for the study. Many of the observations are unlikely to have been obtained through a more structured survey, but were revealed through the in-depth, open-ended format of the interviews, used in conjunction with a review of the loan documents received by respondents in their recent mortgages.

Most respondents began the interviews with positive views of their experience obtaining a mortgage. But as the interviews progressed, it became clear that many respondents were unaware of, did not understand, or had substantial misunderstandings about important features of their recently obtained loans. Many respondents also did not understand some of the key terms used in the current disclosure forms, including the loan discount fee, APR, and amount financed, and many had misunderstandings about these terms that could lead to the selection of inappropriate or overly costly loans. These observations suggest that current mortgage disclosures are not effectively conveying important costs and terms to many consumers.

Respondent reaction to the prototype disclosures was overwhelmingly positive and enthusiastic. Respondents praised the clarity, appearance, organization, and apparent usefulness of the prototype, and viewed it as a substantial improvement over current disclosures. These observations suggest that disclosures along the lines of the prototype may lead more consumers to read the disclosures they receive while shopping for their mortgages, and make it easier for them to understand the key costs and terms of their loans.

Although interviews were conducted with only 36 recent mortgage customers, located in a single county, in a suburban area adjacent to Washington, D.C., a remarkable number of the interview observations, in particular, those concerning both consumer confusion with current disclosures and the potential effectiveness of the prototype disclosures, correspond to the findings of the quantitative consumer testing, described below in Chapter 6, which was conducted with a much larger sample of respondents, and in multiple locations across the country.

3.1. General Observations on the Interviews

The interviews yielded three general observations that have broad implications for the interpretation of respondent accounts of their experiences obtaining mortgages, as well as the research design of the interviews, the quantitative consumer testing, and future studies of financial disclosures:

- Most respondents began the interview with a positive assessment of their recent experience obtaining a mortgage, suggesting that this was not a sample of complainers.
- The attitudes of many initially happy respondents deteriorated during the interview, as many recalled problems with their loans or realized that they did not understand their loans as well as they had thought, suggesting that the in-depth interviews yielded insights that may not have been uncovered through a more structured survey.
- Respondents who obtained their mortgages from subprime lenders were more likely to be experiencing financial difficulties than respondents who obtained their mortgages from prime lenders, suggesting that the HUD subprime lender list was an effective method for identifying a sample of subprime borrowers.

3.1.1. Most Respondents Began the Interview Happy with their Mortgage Experience

During the early stages of the interviews, almost all of the respondents expressed satisfaction with their recent mortgage transactions, mortgage lenders, and loan originators, with the latter including both loan officers and brokers. Many noted that their transactions were smooth and easy, and that the mortgage originators were helpful in providing the loans and explaining the terms. Several respondents mentioned problems with prior mortgage experiences, but thought that the most recent transactions went smoothly. Some respondents contrasted their satisfactory experiences with their experiences with other lenders who had either denied them loans or from whom they had obtained previous loans. Few respondents began the interviews with complaints about their most recent loans, lenders, or originators.

The initial satisfaction of almost all respondents, and the general lack of complaints, suggests that the procedures used to identify and recruit a sample of recent mortgage customers did not produce a sample of disgruntled borrowers, unhappy with their loans, and eager to complain to a government agency sponsoring interviews. Such a sample would have raised concerns that the experiences reported by respondents represented only the worst cases of consumer borrowing experiences, and were not typical of most borrowers. Instead, the sample consisted of consumers generally happy with their experiences and not particularly eager to complain.

3.1.2. Many Respondents' Attitudes Deteriorated During the Interview

Although most respondents began the interview happy with their recent mortgage experience, the attitudes of many respondents deteriorated during the course of the interviews. The change in attitudes typically arose in one of three ways. First, when respondents' own loan documents were reviewed during the interviews, many respondents found significant costs, terms, or potential problems that they had not recognized previously. Second, the highlighting of particular loan terms in the interview script, such as balloon payments and prepayment penalties, appeared to lead many respondents to realize that they knew much less about the features of their loan than they had thought. Third, the overall breadth and depth of the interviews seemed to trigger memories about problems that respondents had not relayed in their initial accounting of their experiences, often about aspects of their transactions unrelated to the immediate question. When such memories were triggered, the open-ended structure of the interviews enabled respondents to relay the experiences to the interviewer, and allowed the interviewer to explore the experiences with additional, unscripted questions.

An example of the deterioration in the attitudes of many respondents is provided by a respondent who initially expressed satisfaction with her experience and her loan originator, but began to recall problems with a possibly premature rate lock as the interview progressed. Later review of the respondent's loan documents led her to believe that the lock-in agreement may have been back-dated at the loan closing, resulting in an interest rate that was higher than the rates prevailing at the closing date. These revelations led her to question her initial satisfaction with the transaction. Other respondents discovered substantial points, prepayment penalties, or other loan features of which they had been unaware. In some cases, respondents specifically sought loans without these features, and had been strongly certain and pleased that they were successful, only to discover during the interviews that they were wrong.

Many of the problems discovered in the respondents' experiences are unlikely to have been found with a more structured survey. Such a survey may have elicited only the apparent satisfaction that respondents relayed at the beginning of the interviews. The in-depth, open-ended structure of the interviews, however, combined with a review of the respondents' own loan documents, provided a much fuller picture of respondents' experiences and knowledge.

3.1.3. Subprime Respondents were More Likely to be Experiencing Financial Difficulties

Respondents who obtained their mortgages from subprime lenders were more likely to be experiencing financial difficulties than respondents who obtained their mortgages from prime lenders, suggesting that the HUD subprime lender list was an effective method for identifying a sample of subprime borrowers, for both the in-depth interviews and the quantitative consumer testing. Subprime respondents exhibited a wide range of financial and other difficulties, including unemployment, recent divorce, and problems with a family-run business. A number of subprime respondents had refinanced their existing mortgage in order to consolidate and pay off other debts. Others were stretching their finances as much as possible to purchase a home.

Many of the subprime respondents had been turned down by several lenders before obtaining their loan, suggesting some type of problem in their recent credit history. One such respondent, for example, reported that:

> Friends give us some mortgage companies to call for refinancing. I called them and nothing happened. This is the only one [lender] that gave us the opportunity. (Interview 5)

In another example, a respondent sought a home equity loan in order to raise cash for a small business and other purposes:[38]

> We did just about everything that we could. Went through all of the telephone book and all that calling the lenders one at a time. . . . we were running out of time to keep my business and things running with the funds we had on hand. (Interview 9)

Many subprime respondents were aware of and acknowledged that they had some type of problem with their recent credit history. Further, many realized that this was the reason that they did not qualify for the best rates and may have had trouble being approved for a loan.

While most subprime respondents appeared to have some type of financial difficulty, there were exceptions. One respondent, for example, a lawyer by training, appeared to have a solid financial situation but chose a mortgage with a subprime lender because he had a personal connection to the mortgage originator, with whom he had prior satisfactory experiences obtaining loans. At least two other respondents, one with a professional background, refinanced with a subprime lenders because they were approached by acquaintances, working for the lenders, who offered to improve their overall financial situations, purportedly by providing loans with lower monthly payments. But these cases were exceptions. Subprime respondents generally appeared to have more difficult financial circumstances than prime respondents, as one might expect for borrowers obtaining loans in the subprime, rather than prime, loan market.

3.2. Mortgage Shopping

Given the wide range of respondent backgrounds, and their reasons for obtaining mortgages, it was not surprising to find a variety of shopping behaviors and decision strategies. The interviews yielded several observations concerning respondent shopping behavior:

- Respondents differed substantially in the extent and nature of their shopping behavior.
- Although both prime and subprime respondents contacted multiple lenders before obtaining their loans, subprime respondents were often seeking loan approval after being turned down by other lenders.
- A number of respondents relied primarily on the reputation of the lenders, their trust in the loan originators, or the recommendations of friends, rather than carefully reading and understanding their loan disclosures themselves to learn the costs and terms of their loans, and to ensure that the features of the loan fit their needs and circumstances.

3.2.1. Extent and Nature of Shopping

Almost all respondents sought general information from newspapers or the Internet, and many used both. Respondents used these sources to find information on prevailing mortgage rates, and to assess whether their mortgage terms seemed reasonable. Most respondents also contacted more than one lender or mortgage broker, either in-person, over the telephone, or through an Internet site. A few respondents contacted as many as four or five lenders. At least one respondent prepared a detailed chart of the loan terms offered by different lenders.

Many of the respondents who did not contact multiple lenders relied on the recommendations of friends to identify a lender, and a couple of respondents merely contacted their prior lenders (in one case, the prior mortgage was with a prime lender, who suggested that the respondent go to its subprime affiliate to refinance, though the respondent continued to refer to the subprime affiliate with the prime affiliate's name throughout the interview). Only a few respondents obtained their loans from lenders who had contacted them through unsolicited calls, and nearly all of these few respondents had already been in the market for a refinance, either actively looking or preparing to begin. One such respondent, for example, had just learned that her prior mortgage was an interest-only loan (her father realized this when he was helping her prepare her taxes), and wanted to refinance to a more traditional loan, when she received the solicitation call.

3.2.2 Prime and Subprime Respondents

The wide range of shopping behaviors and intensities appeared in both the prime and subprime borrower interviews. Both groups included respondents who did not shop at all, who shopped a little, and who shopped extensively. The experiences of borrowers with loans from subprime lenders, however, were often qualitatively different from the experiences of borrowers with loans from prime lenders. Subprime borrowers were more likely to contact multiple lenders out of necessity, because they had been turned down by several lenders prior to being approved for their loans. A few other subprime respondents searched extensively to find lenders that would assume the level of risk that the respondents wished to assume. This included the case of a first time home buyer who wanted to stretch her finances as much as possible to get into the market. A few subprime respondents, however, obtained quotes from multiple lenders and compared terms to find the better deal.

3.2.3. Reliance on Reputation and Trust as a Substitute for Understanding Disclosures

A number of respondents relied primarily on the reputation of the lenders, their trust in the loan originators, or the recommendation of friends or financial advisors, rather than reading and understanding their loan disclosures to learn the costs and terms of their loans themselves, and to ensure that the features of the loan fit their needs and circumstances.[39] In some cases, this strategy seemed to work well, particularly when a respondent returned to their original mortgage company for a refinance. In other cases, undue reliance on personal relationships left the respondents with undesirable or inappropriate loan terms that they might not have otherwise chosen.

3.3. Respondent Understanding of their Recently Obtained Mortgages

The types of loans recently obtained by respondents varied widely, and included fixed-rate, adjustable-rate, interest-only, balloon, bi-weekly payment, payment option, and combination (piggy-back) loans. Most respondents appeared to understand the general types of mortgages they had obtained, including whether the loans had fixed- or adjustable-rates. Some respondents also had clearly matched the loan type to their circumstances, choosing, for example, adjustable-rate or interest-only loans, and stating that the future monthly payment increases or balloon payments were not a concern because they intended to stay in their current homes for only a few years. Most respondents also knew the maturity of their loans and their initial interest rates.

Although most respondents understood many of the key features of their loans, many respondents were either unaware of, did not understand, or misunderstood some important cost or feature of their loans. The misunderstandings involved loan features that had substantial impacts on the overall cost of the loans, the future payments, or the ability to refinance with other lenders. The misunderstandings included confusion over whether up-front points and fees had been paid, whether the monthly payments included escrow for taxes and insurance, whether the loan contained a large balloon payment, whether the interest rate had been locked, whether the interest rate was adjustable, and whether the loan contained a prepayment penalty. These types of misunderstandings were present among both prime and subprime respondents, and both respondents who had done extensive comparison shopping and those who had not done any.

Some respondents first learned of these loan features at or after their loan closings, or only a few days prior to their closings. Others became aware of the loan features only during the course of the interviews, or while preparing for the interviews. Others continued unaware of the features after the interviews.

One respondent, for example, obtained loan offers from three different lenders and compared them intently:

> I looked at all of the break downs, the disclosure form that itemizes all of the costs involved, not so much the rate only, but to look at the whole picture, with the filing fees what your closing costs are, your points all of that. . . . I looked at the total cost involved in obtaining that loan. Not so much the long term but just the initial also. (Interview 8)

Yet despite efforts to read the disclosures and understand the loans, the respondent did not realize until a few days before closing that the stated monthly payments on the loan she had selected did not include escrow for taxes and insurance. Another respondent reported a similar misunderstanding with a previous mortgage.

At least a couple of respondents had loans with balloon payments of which they were unaware at the time of the interviews. Another respondent did not realize that her loan contained a balloon payment until her father noticed it at the loan closing:

> I wasn't aware until settlement, and then I heard it. Then my dad said, whoa, wait. What happened? At that point I was just too overwhelmed to really understand it and never got back to asking my dad what it really meant. (Interview 32)

Another respondent had a loan that adjusted in such a way that the future monthly payments might not be sufficient to cover the interest charges, which would result in negative amortization, and either increases in future payments or the imposition of a balloon. The respondent did not understand the nature of the loan, and was unaware of the possibility of negative amortization and its consequences. Further, the day before the interview, while reviewing her loan papers, the respondent was surprised to learn that her monthly payments were scheduled to increase significantly in three years.

At least one other respondent, a couple interviewed jointly, also was unaware that their loan had an adjustable rate. But even respondents who understood that they had adjustable rates did not understand the potential increases they could incur. Respondents generally did not know the maximum possible interest rates that were allowed by their loans.

Several other respondents believed that their settlement fees were significantly lower than indicated in their loan documents. The settlement fees in these loans were usually financed and rolled into the loan principal. One respondent, for example, did not realize before closing that she had been charged $10,000 in up-front points and fees, and that the charges had been rolled into her loan principal and financed:

> I think it was a mild misunderstanding. It's called I didn't read over the papers nearly as well as I should have, but if I did, I think I would have been a lot happier. (Interview 33)

Another respondent, who had contacted a number of lenders and had created detailed charts to compare the various loan offers, believed that a $4,700 discount fee that he paid on the loan was a discount that he had received off his loan fees, rather than a charge that he had paid. The respondent believed that he received the discount because he had other financial accounts with the lender.

Several respondents believed mistakenly that their loans did not contain prepayment penalties, and were surprised during the course of the interviews to find that their loan documents indicated that such penalties were included in the loans. One such respondent indicated surprise when he was directed to the TILA statement disclosure during the interview:

> [reading the disclosure] ". . . the borrower will not be entitled to a refund part of the finance charge and may have to pay a penalty." Wait a second. I thought I didn't have to pay it. This is interesting. You caught me off guard on that. I'm going to have to talk to them

about that. They said I wouldn't have to pay a penalty. . . . I'm glad you pointed this out, because I intend to pay it off ahead of time. (Interview 22)

Another respondent continued to insist her loan did not contain a penalty even after the moderator pointed to the TILA disclosure that indicated that it did. One respondent who thought that he did not have a prepayment penalty was surprised to see that his disclosure failed to indicate whether a penalty applied:

Son of a gun. Excuse me, as you are talking about this, and saying do I have prepayment penalty, I don't think so, but none of the boxes are checked off. I hope I don't. I'm sorry go ahead. . . . I wonder how useful it is when it's blank.

It's not checked off. . . . It's clear that I should have looked at it more closely, yes it is. (Interview 48)

Another respondent refinanced her mortgage after being solicited by a friend who was working as an originator for a subprime lender, and was left completely confused about the nature of the new loan and whether it had been in her interest to refinance. The new loan had a 30 year term, but was intended to be paid off in 22 years using bi-weekly payments. The loan also had an interest rate that was substantially higher than the old loan. The respondent was confused about the loan term and the interest rate, and whether the loan had been prudent:

. . . the only thing I question was why would I be going from a 4.75 [interest rate] to an eight [8.34 interest rate]. They just kept—I'm a little naive when it comes to it—but they just kept telling me it was better because more money would be going to the principal doing it this way, because they take it out twice a month versus the other. I just believed them. I hope it's true. (Interview 51)

When asked if there was anything that she wished the lender had done differently, she responded:

Take time to explain what I was signing. . . . [when filling out] the application, I was just told, "sign here, sign here," and they did most of, [the lender] did most of the application. They just kind of had me sign it. Then the closing, it literally took half an hour. It was just one page after another, "sign here, sign here."

They told me what it was, but there wasn't any time to really explain it. . . . (Interview 51)

These various misunderstandings about key terms of recently obtained mortgages suggest that current mortgage disclosures do not effectively convey important loan features to many consumers, or that many borrowers do not carefully read their disclosures, or perhaps both. Any lack of careful reading, however, may not entirely reflect the interest and diligence of the respondents, but may be at least partially due to disclosures that may be difficult to read and understand, which may intimidate some borrowers and deter them from even attempting to read the forms, and which may lead some of the borrowers who do read them to misunderstand their loans. The various misunderstandings also suggest that loan originators, at least in some cases, may have misled borrowers about the features of their loans, and that the current disclosures were not sufficient to overcome these deceptions.

3.4. Use and Understanding of Current Disclosures

When asked for their views on the GFE and TILA forms, most respondents said that they liked and understood the documents. The interviews revealed, however, that many respondents did not understand the disclosures as well as they believed. Many respondents clearly had not carefully read and understood their forms prior to the interviews. As discussed in the previous section, many were either unaware of, did not understand, or misunderstood some important cost or feature of their recently obtained loans, even though most of these costs and features were disclosed in their GFE or TILA forms. Further, many respondents said that they initially were not able to understand the disclosures on their own, but relied on their originators to explain the disclosures and their loan terms. Finally, when respondents were asked about the meaning of specific key terms in the disclosures, many did not understand the terms, were confused, or had substantial, and potentially harmful, misunderstandings. The observations on respondent understanding of current disclosures included:

- Many respondents were not able to understand the disclosures on their own, but relied on their originators to explain the disclosures and their loan terms.
- Many respondents did not understand the meaning of many of the fees itemized on the GFE form, or did not understand how the fees differed from one and other.
- Many respondents were particularly confused by the discount fee disclosure, and many mistakenly believed that it was a discount they were receiving rather than a charge they were paying.
- Few respondents understood the APR disclosure, and many mistakenly believed that the APR was simply the interest rate.
- Few respondents understood the "amount financed" disclosure, and many mistakenly believed that it was the loan amount (loan principal).
- A number of respondents were confused by the prepayment penalty disclosure.

3.4.1. Many Respondents Relied on their Originators to Explain the Disclosures

Many of the respondents who said that they understood the disclosures reported that they had not been able to understand the disclosures on their own, but had relied on their originators or closing agents to explain them. Many of these respondents appreciated the time and efforts undertaken to help them understand the disclosures. Many reported that they had asked numerous questions about the meanings of the terms in the form, and about the costs and features of their loans. One respondent, for example, noted that:

> When I originally got the form it didn't mean a whole lot to me. There were a few things that I understood. And that was where the broker came in. He was able to come in and sit down with me and explain to me what the different things meant. Now do I remember them all? No. I just know at the time when he explained them to me, they made sense to me. But did I keep them in my mind? No. (Interview 39)

Although many respondents were comfortable with the explanations provided by their originators, at least one respondent noted that the originator's explanations were not sufficient:

> Well they offered to explain everything, but that doesn't mean I understood it. Nobody likes to feel like an idiot. They offered to explain everything, and they went through it, but probably like all salesmen, they speak fast. And they haven't got time to sit around and go over all of that for you and everything that you don't understand. (Interview 22)

Although one would expect originators to be helpful in explaining loan terms, reliance on their explanations, rather than understanding the disclosures on one's own, can leave borrowers susceptible to incomplete explanations, and at worst, deceptive lenders. If a borrower only understands what the originator explains about the disclosures, they may learn only what the originator wants them to know. Unfavorable aspects of the loan may be downplayed, while more favorable aspects are highlighted. At worst, unscrupulous originators may orally misrepresent loan terms.

3.4.2. Many Respondents were Confused by Various Fees Itemized on the GFE Form

Many respondents did not understand the meaning of many of the fees itemized on the GFE form, or did not understand the difference between the various fees. Other respondents were confused about how the various fees summed to the total. Even some respondents who otherwise seemed well informed and diligent indicated that much of the terminology was difficult to understand. Examples of respondent confusion over GFE fees include:

> A lot of these charges it's fine to say, yes I can read, and I can see that the processing fee is this much, or the lender's inspection fee is this much, but like my
>
> wife said, when you go in-depth you don't really understand what you are paying for. (Interview 34)
>
> Everything's there, but I don't know what everything means. I didn't pay any Loan Origination Fee. That's great, but what is a Loan Origination Fee? (Interview 22)
>
> The biggest, I don't know if it's a con but just the biggest trouble was looking at these fees because some are up top, some are hidden. They just seem to be all different, as far as the application fees, the attorney fees, those are all different. (Interview 35)
>
> I have 13-years of college, Master Degrees, and they were perplexing me. . . .
>
> [The GFE] was only useful in breaking things down, but not in terms of meaning. Some of it was meaningless. For example Appraisal Fee, that one I don't understand. This Tax Related Service Fee didn't make any sense to me. It was $75 so I overlooked it for the convenience of signing the papers there. The Processing Fee, I didn't know what [that] was. The Underwriting Fee, I assumed that whoever was writing the loan desired some form of payment. I said okay
>
> $500 was reasonable. The Wire Transfer Fee, I don't know what was wired. I don't know what was transferred. Closing Escrow Fee, these were not clear at all. Document Preparation Fee, I felt that should have been included here. I think I mentioned that at settlement. Attorney Fees, Title Insurance, that I can understand. Recording Fees, that I can understand. And this interest for two-days I know its interest on the original loan for the extra days. These taxes, I can understand that. . . . It is very useful. But its utility is shrouded in confusion because things were not clearly defined in detail. (Interview 52)

Several respondents mentioned a need for a glossary to explain the different fees. One respondent noted that he did not realize how confused he was until the moderator asked questions about various fees during the interview.

> I think the fact that you've asked me some questions that I really had to think about. It didn't just off the page and say this is what it is. It would be great if maybe they had some kind of—I don't know if you call it glossary or key or something, on the back it says define some of these terms. (Interview 13)

Many respondents, as noted above, relied on their loan originators or closing agents to explain the disclosures to them. A few other respondents indicated that they did not understand the fees the first time they obtained a mortgage, and only understand them now because of their subsequent experience. As noted by one such respondent:

> . . . It's understandable. I've seen them before. I've walked through them several times. So, because it's the third or fourth time that I've looked at it I thought it was relatively straightforward because I had seen it before. The first time I had looked at one, I needed to have somebody walk me through it and tell me what is the bottom line and why. . . . I think that every single line ought to have an explanation like lines on a tax form. (Interview 23)

Although some respondents said that they liked the itemization of numerous fees, many were confused by the detailed information, including even some of those who said that they liked it. A few indicated that they would prefer disclosures that focused on the total cost, rather than the individual fees:

> I'm the kind of guy that doesn't like to be nickeled and dimed. I'm like, give me a price and that is it. He could have added up all of the fees, and said this is your price, and I would have said okay, and would have probably been happier. (Interview 12)
>
> . . . when you go to [a furniture store] and buy a piece of furniture. The chair is $575. The delivery fee is $55. Fine. I don't want to pay the $55 for delivery. May I pick it up? No. You mean to tell me that I have to pay the delivery fee? Yes. Then why isn't it just part of the cost of the thing? Why don't you just tell
>
> me up-front that the chair costs $630? That is sort of my reaction to this. What is a Doc Prep Fee as separate from an Administration Fee? My take on it is that is it is a nickel and diming process. (Interview 21)

Confusion over the numerous fees listed in the GFE, as well as uncertainty over other disclosures, made it difficult for some respondents to use the disclosures to compare loan offers. One respondent, for example, who compared loan offers from different lenders, apparently did not use the GFE and TILA forms because she felt she did not understand the information:

> I was basically matching the interest rates, because that was truly all I really understood on my own. (Interview 32)

Another respondent, already quoted earlier in this section, said that he would have liked to have compared loans from different lenders, but was unable to do so because of the difficulty understanding loan costs:

> It's a process that I would like to engage in. But at times it's so convoluted. . . . because they have different costs that they load on the front-end and the back-end and dazzle the untrained eye easily. I was not prepared to delve too deeply into that kind of territory. (Interview 52)

3.4.3 Many Respondents were Particularly Confused by the Discount Fee Disclosure

The discount fee denotes a charge imposed on the borrower in exchange for a lower interest rate than would otherwise be charged on the loan. The term "discount" refers to the lowered interest rate, not lowered fees. The discount fee is one of the required itemized settlement charges that must be disclosed in the GFE, if such a charge is included in the loan. Most respondents did not have any idea of what was meant by the term "discount fee." Much worse, roughly a third of the respondents misunderstood the term to indicate a discount received by the borrower, rather than a charge paid, and believed that settlement fees were being discounted by the stated amount. Examples of respondent comments on the discount fee disclosure are presented in Table D.1 of Appendix D.

Such a misunderstanding was held even by some respondents who had incurred a discount fee in their loan, and who were pleased that they had "received a discount" and saved money. One respondent, for example, with a loan from a subprime lender, misinterpreted a disclosed $4,700 discount fee as a discount that he had received:

> "Loan discount fee" of one and a half percent to me means that they are giving me a discount of one and a half percent off the value of the loan. And I'm guessing it is because I do have other accounts with them. (Interview 55)

Another respondent, who obtained a loan from a subprime lender, discovered the true meaning of the term at her loan settlement. When the moderator asked about the discount fee disclosure in her GFE, her comments illustrated borrower confusion and frustration over the disclosure:

> That's the one that is tricky. . . To me it means that I saved something. But that is not really what it means. It means that I have to pay extra. . . . I asked them. I said where is my discount? It says I'm getting a $2,600 discount where is it?
>
> They said no that is what you have to pay. So, it's a trick. It's misleading is what it is. (Interview 51)

Such misunderstandings of the discount fee can lead confused borrowers to dramatically poor choice of loans and the payment of excessive fees.

3.4.4. Few Respondents Understood the APR

Most respondents were confused by the APR disclosure in the TILA statement and did not understand its meaning. Nearly half of the respondents appeared to believe mistakenly that the APR was the same as the interest rate (note rate). A few respondents explained how they had been confused at their loan closings when they noticed that the disclosed APR was not the same as the interest rate that they had been quoted. At least a of couple of other respondents noticed the difference between their note rate and the APR during the course of the interview and were quite surprised and confused by the discrepancy. Examples of respondent comments on the APR disclosure are presented in Table D.2 of Appendix D.

Although some respondents knew that the APR and the interest rate were different, only two or three respondents had a fairly complete and correct understanding of the APR and the reason for the difference between the two rates. Others who recognized a difference between the two rates had misconceptions about the reason. A few respondents, for example, believed that the difference was caused by the compounding of interest. At least one respondent believed that it was because the APR took into account future rate changes in an adjustable rate loan. In several instances, it was difficult to discern how respondents interpreted the APR. Many were just confused in unspecified ways.

3.4.5. Few Respondents Understood the Amount Financed

Most respondents did not understand the "amount financed" disclosure in the TILA statement, and many mistakenly believed that it was the loan amount (loan principal). The amount financed, by definition under TILA, is the loan amount minus prepaid finance charges. The latter include charges such as any origination fee, discount fee, mortgage broker fee, mortgage insurance premium, or other charge related to the extension of credit. As a result, the amount financed disclosed on the TILA statement is generally less than the loan amount. The rationale for this formulation is that it represents the net amount of proceeds the borrower receives from the loan, after the prepaid finance charges, which are paid to obtain the loan, are deducted. Although this figure may make sense for some financial analyses, and is needed to calculate the APR, these purposes, and the meaning of the term, were lost on most respondents. Instead, most were confused, and many misinterpreted the figure for what it facially appears to be, which is the loan amount. Examples of respondent comments on the amount financed disclosure are presented in Table D.3 of Appendix D.

Borrowers who believe that the amount financed is the full loan amount may be susceptible to confusion about the amount of points and fees paid on the loan, particularly if those fees are financed into the loan principal rather than paid in cash at closing. For example, a lender that charges $15,000 in prepaid finance charges on a $200,000 mortgage refinance, and rolls the fees into the loan principal, resulting in a $215,000 total loan amount, would provide a TILA statement indicating that the amount financed was $200,000. Some borrowers may misinterpret the $200,000 as the loan amount, which is the loan amount they had applied for, and fail to realize that the loan principal is actually higher, and includes $15,000 in fees. This may result in borrowers paying loan fees of which they are unaware. Instances of such confusion appeared to be present in the interviews of a number of respondents with financed fees, who did not understand the extent of the fees they had paid.

3.4.6. A Number of Respondents were Confused by The Prepayment Penalty Disclosure

A number of respondents misinterpreted the prepayment penalty disclosure. Although most respondents appeared to understand the general concept of a prepayment penalty, some appeared to believe that the penalty was relevant only if they paid off their entire loan in cash, perhaps from a sudden windfall. They did not seem to understand that the penalties also would be incurred if they refinanced their loans.

Several respondents also were confused by the ambiguous language of the disclosure, which merely provides two check boxes labeled "may have a prepayment penalty" and "will not have a prepayment penalty," or in the case of some TILA statements, the even more confusing "may" and "may not."

One respondent, who had believed that her loan did not contain a prepayment penalty, was surprised during the interview to see that her TILA disclosure indicated a penalty was included, but she was confused by the wording:

> . . . well the word "may" is kind of sketchy. It doesn't really say when you get a penalty . . . . The word "may" I guess is a little misleading. (Interview 35)

Another respondent also noted the ambiguity of the "may" language when asked whether the disclosure could be made clearer:

> Well, actually it could be because they know in advance whether it's going to be prepayment or not. So, this whole business of if you pay it off early you may have to pay a penalty, that is the wrong word. It should be you will have to pay a penalty or will not. Because that is what got me stuck that first time [in a previous loan]. Once you are burnt you try to make sure. (Interview 11)

The disclosure language also was confusing to at least one respondent who had a loan without a prepayment penalty. When directed to the disclosure and asked whether the loan contained a penalty, the respondent noted:

> It says "may not." If you payoff early you may or you may not have to pay a penalty, and I may not. . . . That means that if I decide to pay the loan off in less than the specified period of time I don't have to pay a penalty for that. . . . "May not" means that it might and it might not. "Will not" is what it should say, if in fact that is what it means. (Interview 21)

Most of the respondents who appeared to have prepayment penalties in their loans seemed to be aware of this prior to the interviews, but, as noted earlier, a few respondents were surprised during the interviews to find that their loans did contain prepayment penalties, including one respondent who continued to believe she did not have a prepayment penalty even after the moderator pointed to the disclosure that indicated she did. Also, at least one respondent received a TILA form in which neither prepayment penalty box was checked, making it impossible to discern if the loan had a prepayment penalty.

3.4.7. A Number of Respondents were Confused by the Finance Charge Disclosure

A number of respondents misinterpreted the finance charge disclosure to indicate the sum of the interest payments over the life of the loan. In fact, the finance charge also includes prepaid finance charges, such as loan origination fees, discount points, and other loan-related charges. Many respondents provided somewhat ambiguous explanations, such as "what I pay for the loan" or "what the loan costs," which implied a general understanding of the term, but did not indicate whether the respondent understood that prepaid finance charges were included in the figure. Examples of respondent comments on the finance charge disclosure are presented in Table D.4 of Appendix D.

3.5. Reaction to the Prototype Disclosures

The final segment of the interviews examined respondents' reactions to an initial version of the prototype disclosure form that was being developed for the study. Although the initial version of the prototype was developed prior to the interviews, it attempted to address many of the same problems that interview respondents had with either the current disclosures or their understanding of their recently obtained loans. This included confusion over a variety of mortgage costs and disclosures, including settlement fees, APR, amount financed, prepayment penalties, escrow payments, balloon payments, and optional charges, as well as the overall format, readability, and organization of the disclosures.

Respondents were given a copy of the prototype form, with disclosures for a hypothetical loan, and told that it was a possible alternative document for providing information about mortgage costs that might be used instead of the GFE and TILA forms they had just examined. Respondents were asked to examine the form carefully and think about its clarity and usefulness. Respondents then were asked a series of questions, including what they thought of the form, how it compared to the current GFE and TILA documents, and how they would rate its understandability and usefulness.

Respondent reaction to the prototype form was overwhelmingly positive. Nearly all of the respondents viewed the prototype favorably and considered it a significant improvement over current forms. Respondents also commented favorably on a number of specific attributes of the prototype, including its clarity, readability, appearance, organization and usefulness. Several respondents said they wished that they had the prototype form when shopping for their mortgage, and believed it would have helped their decisions. The enthusiasm expressed over the form by many respondents was quite remarkable. Examples of respondent comments on the prototype disclosures are presented in Table D.5 of Appendix D.

A few of the respondents who praised the prototype form said they would have liked it to have included an itemization of the individual settlement fees. The prototype provided only the total settlement costs, not an itemization. These comments, however, were made by only a small minority of the respondents.

The reaction of respondents also was favorable when they were asked to rate the understandability of the prototype on a scale from "one" to "ten," with "one" being "extremely difficult to understand" and "ten" being "extremely easy to understand." Respondents earlier had been asked to rate the current GFE and TILA forms in the same way. The average ratings were 9.2 for the prototype form, 8.3 for the current TILA form, and 7.0 for the current GFE form. The differences in the ratings between the prototype form and each of the current forms was statistically significant at the one percent level. The results were very similar when the responses of prime and subprime respondents where examined separately.

The differences between the ratings of the prototype and current forms is likely to understate respondents' views of the differences between the forms. Respondents rated the current forms before they had seen the prototype. As most respondents initially believed that they understood the current forms fairly well, they gave fairly high understandability ratings to the forms. This left little room to distinguish the prototype form on the one-to-ten scale. Respondent comments about the prototype form suggest that the difference in the ratings would have been much larger if respondents had viewed all three forms before applying the ratings.

The fairly high ratings given to the current forms also must be viewed in light of the respondents' actual understanding of the forms. Although most respondents believed that they understood the forms, many actually misunderstood key information, believing, for example, that the amount financed was the loan amount, the APR was the interest rate, and the discount fee was a discount.

The strongly positive reaction to the prototype form suggests that it has the potential to improve consumer understanding of mortgage costs, and perhaps lead to better consumer mortgage shopping and loan choices. One must be somewhat careful, however, in the conclusions one reaches from these observations. The interviews provide only the respondents' opinions on the prototype form. The interviews do not provide a systematic assessment of how effectively consumers would be able to use the form, or how effectively the form conveys key mortgage costs to consumers. These issues are examined by the quantitative consumer testing, described in the following chapters of this chapter. As will be seen, however, the observations of the qualitative interviews are confirmed by the findings of the quantitative testing, which show that the prototype form does convey key mortgage costs to consumers more effectively than do current disclosure forms.

Although the interview responses do not provide a systematic assessment of the actual effectiveness of the prototype form in conveying loan costs, the overwhelmingly favorable reaction, and the extensive praise of the form's clarity, readability, organization, and usefulness, suggests that, in real-life settings, borrowers may be more likely to read and use the disclosures, because the form appears readable and manageable, rather than intimidating and overwhelming. Getting borrowers to believe that they will be able to understand the disclosures and find them useful may be half the battle. Borrowers must be willing to read and use the disclosures if they are to be effective. This aspect of the potential effectiveness of the current and prototype forms could not be easily assessed in the context of the quantitative testing, but becomes clear in the in-depth interviews.

Consumer Testing Methodology

The quantitative consumer testing used a controlled experiment to examine the extent to which consumers could understand and use the current mortgage cost disclosures and whether better disclosures could improve consumer understanding of mortgage costs. The study was conducted through one-on-one, in-person tests with over 800 recent mortgage customers in 12 locations across the country. Respondents were given cost disclosure forms for two hypothetical mortgage loans and asked a series of questions about the costs and terms of the loans. The tests were conducted with two different loan-cost scenarios, one of which included more complicated loan features such as optional credit insurance, a large balloon payment in an interest-only loan, monthly payments that did not include escrow for taxes and insurance, and prepayment penalties. About half of the study participants had obtained a recent mortgage from a subprime lender and the other half had obtained mortgages from prime lenders.

4.1. Current and Prototype Disclosure Forms

Two alternative versions of mortgage cost disclosure forms were tested in the study. One version consisted of the currently required federal cost disclosures, presented in forms similar to those used by many lenders. The second version consisted of prototype disclosures developed for this study. Approximately half of the respondents were tested with the current forms and half were tested with the prototype form. This study design allowed for direct comparisons of the performance of the current and prototype forms and provided a benchmark and control for evaluating the results of each alternative form.

The current forms consisted of the Truth-in-Lending ("TILA") statement and the Good Faith Estimate of Settlement Costs ("GFE").[40]They were presented in a two-page format, with one page for each form. The forms were obtained from a large commercial vendor that supplies these and other forms to numerous lenders. The forms used in the tests are presented in Appendix G.

The GFE used in tests was an enhanced version that included a great deal of information not required by current regulations but which reflects the information provided in the GFE forms used by many lenders. Many lenders use some variation of an enhanced GFE that goes beyond the regulatory requirements.[41] The additional information in the tested GFE that is not required by regulation included the amount of money borrowed, the interest rate, the total monthly payment amount (including taxes and insurance), an itemization of the monthly payment, the cash due at closing, and the total sum of the various individual settlement charges. The TILA statement used in the tests did not include any significant information not required by the relevant regulations.[42]

The enhanced version of the GFE provides a better basis for conclusions if significant problems are found with the current forms. If a more "bare-bones" regulatory version of the GFE had been used, any finding that the current forms do not successfully convey key mortgage costs to consumers might have been dismissed as irrelevant and unimportant because the form tested did not correspond to the forms that many consumers actually receive in the marketplace. The enhanced version of the GFE avoids this criticism because it more closely represents the forms that many consumers actually receive. This means, however, that any problems found with consumer understanding of loan costs under the enhanced GFE will likely understate the problems consumers would have with a GFE that merely complied with the regulations, because many of the key mortgage costs examined in the tests, including all of the items listed in the previous paragraph, would not have been present anywhere in the current disclosure forms.

The prototype form used in the study was developed to test whether better disclosures could improve consumer understanding of loan costs. The form combines all of the cost information into a single form, adding important information not required by the current regulations, eliminating currently required information that is less important or confusing, and presenting the information in easy-to-understand language and in an easy-to-use format. The disclosures were presented in a three-page form, with the first page providing a summary of the loan costs and the following two pages providing additional detail. Appendix H presents the prototype form disclosures for the test loans used in the study. A more detailed discussion of the development of the prototype form and its content and organization is presented in Chapter 5.

The inclusion of both current and prototype disclosure forms in the tests greatly increases our ability to understand and evaluate the test results. Each version of the form acts as a benchmark and control for the testing of the other. If only the current forms were tested, one would not know, regardless of the results, whether it was possible to improve consumer understanding of the information. A seemingly poor performance by the current disclosures may be the best performance possible given the limits of consumer comprehension, and a seemingly good performance might still be significantly improved. These questions can only be answered through the testing of possible alternatives. Similarly, if only the prototype form were tested, one would not know whether it provided any improvement over the current forms. A seemingly mediocre performance by the prototype may still represent a substantial improvement over the current disclosures, and an excellent performance may not differ significantly from the performance of the current forms. The study design used here, which tests both current and prototype disclosure forms, provides for direct comparisons of the two alternatives and an informed assessment of the performance of both.

4.2. Test Procedure and Questions

The cost disclosure forms were tested through one-on-one, in-person interviews conducted by a consumer research firm. Study participants ("respondents") were given disclosure forms for two hypothetical mortgage loans and asked a series of questions about the costs and terms of the loans. The forms consisted of two to three pages for each loan. The loans were identified by single letters, such as "Loan M" and "Loan V." The tests took about 30 minutes to complete for each respondent. The experimental setting allowed for a controlled environment, a standardization of the loan cost information viewed by the respondents, and comparisons of the effect of different cost disclosure formats.

The test consisted of two main parts. A different set of loans was used in each. The first part of the test, which included only two questions, focused on a comparison of the overall cost of the loan. The second part, which included more than two dozen questions, focused on various individual loan costs. Table 4.1 summarizes the questions asked in each part of the test.

The tests began with a series of questions asking about the respondent's demographic background and mortgage experience. Respondents then were given disclosure forms for the first set of loans and instructed to look at the information as if they were shopping for a mortgage. When they were ready, respondents were asked to identify which of the two loans would "cost them less," that is, which loan was less expensive.[43] The loan costs were specified so that one loan had higher settlement costs than the other loan, but all other loan terms, including the interest rates, were identical. This made one loan unambiguously less expensive than the other, avoiding any trade-off between lower rates and lower up-front costs over which consumers may have different preferences.[44] A follow-up question asked respondents which of the two loans they would choose if they were shopping for a mortgage. For both questions, respondents could continue to examine the forms while they were answering the questions.

After respondents completed the first two questions, the disclosure forms were removed and replaced with forms for a second pair of loans which were used for the remainder of the test.

Table 4.1. Summary of Test Questions

Question topic	Question summary
I. Overall loan-cost comparison questions	Which loan would cost you less? Which loan would you choose if shopping for a mortgage?
II. Individual loan cost questions	
Loan amount	• Which loan has the lower loan amount? How much is the loan amount in Loan V(T)? Does that include money to pay for settlement costs?
Settlement charges	• Which loan has the lower settlement charges? How much are the settlement charges in Loan M(K)?
Optional charge	• Any charges for optional products or services in Loan V(T)? What products or services are the optional charges for? How much do the optional products and services cost?
Total up-front charges	• Which loan has the higher total up-front charges? How much are the total up-front charges in Loan V(T)?
Interest rate	• Which loan has the lower interest rate? How much is the interest rate in Loan M(K)?
APR	• Which loan has the lower APR? How much is the APR in Loan M(K)? Why is the APR sometimes higher than the interest rate?
Cash at closing	• Which loan would require less cash at closing? How much cash at closing is required in Loan V(T)?
Monthly payment	• Which loan has the lower monthly payment? How much is the monthly payment in Loan M(K)?
Escrow payment	Does the monthly payment include property taxes and insurance in Loan M(K)? How much would you have to pay for property taxes and insurance?
Balloon payment	• Would the last payment in Loan V(T) be the same as other monthly payments? How much is the last monthly payment be in Loan V(T)? Would you still owe anything after making the last monthly payment? How much would you still owe?
Prepayment penalty	If you refinanced after 2 years, would you have to just pay off remaining balance to get out of Loan M(K), pay the balance plus some additional fees, or pay less than the balance. How much less/more would you have to pay? If you refinanced after 6 years, would you have to just pay off remaining balance to get out of Loan M(K), pay the balance plus some additional fees, or pay less than the balance.

Notes: For the full text of each question, see the questionnaire presented in Appendix F. Loan identifiers, such as "Loan V(T)," indicate the loan to which the question referred, with the first letter ("V" in this example) corresponding to one of the loans in the simple-loan scenario and the second letter, which is in parentheses ("T" in this example), to one of the loans in the complex-loan scenario.

Respondents again were instructed to look at the information as if they were shopping for a mortgage and, when ready, they were asked a series of questions about various individual costs and terms of the loans. Respondents could continue to examine the forms throughout the questioning.

The second part of the test included 28 questions on 11 different costs and terms of the loans. As summarized in Table 4.1, the costs and terms addressed by the questions included the loan amount, settlement charges, charges for optional products and services (credit insurance), total up-front charges, interest rate, APR, cash due at closing, monthly payment, escrow for property taxes and homeowner's insurance, balloon payment, and prepayment penalties.

The questions can be categorized into four main types. One type of question asked respondents to identify which of the two loans was better or worse on a particular cost margin (which loan, for example, had the lower interest rate). A second type directed respondents to one of the loans and asked them to identify the amount of a particular loan cost (how much, for example, were the settlement charges). A third type directed respondents to one of the loans and asked whether a particular cost was present (were there any charges, for example, for optional products or services not required for the loan; did the loan include money borrowed to pay for settlement costs). A fourth type of question, used only once, examined the general knowledge of the respondents about a particular cost term (why the interest rate and APR of a loan sometimes differ).

4.3. Loan-Cost Scenarios

The first part of the test consisted of two questions in which respondents were asked to compare the overall cost of two loans. A single loan-cost scenario was used for all respondents for these questions. As noted above, one of the two loans had higher settlement costs than the other, but all other loan costs, including the interest rate and monthly payments, were identical. The two loans were identified as "Loan G" and "Loan R" in the disclosure forms provided to respondents. Table 4.2 presents the various costs that were specified for these loans.[45]

The second part of the test asked respondents about various individual costs and terms of the loans. Two different loan-cost scenarios were used for these questions so that the disclosure forms could be tested under two different sets of conditions. One scenario was a relatively simple, straightforward loan for a home purchase. The other scenario was a more complex loan for a refinancing that included debt consolidation and cash removed from the home equity.

Approximately half of the respondents were given disclosure forms for the simple-loan scenario and the other half were given disclosure forms for the complex-loan scenario. This was done in both the current and prototype form groups, so that approximately one-quarter of the respondents used the current forms with the simple-loan scenario, one quarter used the current forms with the complex-loan scenario, one-quarter used the prototype form with the simple-loan scenario, one quarter used the prototype form with the complex-loan scenario.

Table 4.2. Loan Cost Figures for the Overall Loan-Cost Comparison Questions

	Loan G	Loan R
Loan amount	$176,000.00	$176,000.00
Loan purpose	Purchase	Purchase
Loan term	30 years	30 years
Loan type	Fixed rate	Fixed rate
Interest rate	5.87%	5.87%
Total settlement charges	8,052.05	7,026.05
Charges for optional items	0.00	0.00
Total up-front charges	8,052.05	7,026.05
Annual percentage rate (APR)	6.03%	6.03%
Home price	220,000	220,000
Down payment	44,000	44,000
Amount of home price financed	176,000	176,000
Earnest money credit	2,000	2,000
Financed up-front costs	0.00	0.00
Cash due at closing	50,052.05	49,026.05
Monthly payment	1,268.88	1,268.88
Property taxes and hazard insurance included in monthly payment	Yes	Yes
Balloon payment		
Prepayment penalty	None	None
Late fee	None	None
	5%	5%

Table 4.3.Loan Cost Figures for the Individual Loan Cost Questions

	Simple-loan scenario		Complex-loan scenario	
	Loan M	Loan V	Loan K	Loan T
Loan amount	$160,000.00	$167,066.04	$175,425.00	$189,313.43
Loan purpose	Purchase	Purchase	Refinance	Refinance
Loan term	30 years	30 years	30 years	10 years
Loan type	Fixed rate	Fixed rate	Fixed rate	Fixed rate, interest-only, balloon
Interest rate	5.75%	5.90%	6.20%	6.65%
Total settlement charges	6,606.64	7,066.04	5,303.39	7,658.43
Charges for optional credit insurance	0.00	0.00	0.00	6,230.00
Total up-front charges	6,606.64	7,066.04	5,303.39	13,888.43
Annual percentage rate (APR)	5.88%	6.02%	6.38%	6.88%
Home price	200,000.00	200,000.00	n/a	n/a
Down payment	40,000.00	40,000.00	n/a	n/a
Amount of home price financed	160,000.00	160,000.00	n/a	n/a

Earnest money credit	2,000.00	2,000.00	n/a	n/a
Refinanced amount	n/a	n/a	150,000.00	150,000.00
Cash paid to borrower	n/a	n/a	20,000.00	20,000.00
Consolidation of debts	n/a	n/a	5,425.00	5,425.00
Financed settlement charges	0.00	7,066.04	0.00	7,658.43
Financed optional charges	0.00	0.00	0.00	6,230.00
Cash due at closing	44,606.64	38,000.00	5,303.39	0.00
Monthly payment	1,160.38	1,237.60	1,074.42	1,254.95
Property taxes and hazard insurance included in monthly payment	Yes	Yes	Yes	No
Additional charges for property taxes and hazard insurance	None	None	205.83	None
Monthly payment with all charges for property taxes and hazard insurance	1,160.38	1,237.60	280.26	1,254.95
Balloon payment	None	None	None	190,568.38
Prepayment penalty	None	None	4% of balance, 7,017.00 if refinanced immediately	None
Late fee	5%	5%	5%	5%

The two loans were identified as "Loan M" and "Loan V" in the simple-loan scenario and as "Loan K" and "Loan T" in the complex-loan scenario. The loan costs specified in each of these scenarios are presented in Table 4.3.

Both loans in the simple-loan scenario were fully amortizing, thirty-year, fixed-rate, purchase loans. Charges for credit insurance or other optional products were not present in either loan and the monthly loan payments in both included escrow for property taxes and homeowner's insurance. The only feature that was slightly complicated was that in one of the loans the settlement charges were rolled into the loan amount and financed.

The loans in the complex-loan scenario included a number of complicating features that sometimes occur in prime loans, often occur in subprime loans, and quite commonly occur in loans marketed with deceptive tactics. These features, which were present in at least one of the two loans, included substantial charges for optional credit insurance, a large balloon payment in an interest-only loan, substantial prepayment penalties, and monthly loan payments that did not include escrow for property taxes and homeowner's insurance. One loan also rolled the settlement and credit insurance charges into the loan amount.

Both loans in both cost scenarios were fixed-rate loans. Fixed-rates were used so that the prototype disclosures developed for the study could concentrate on trying to improve consumer understanding of this simpler case first. If successful, further development of the disclosures could extend to adjustable-rate loans. Nearly all of the disclosures for fixed-rate loans would apply equally well to loans with adjustable-rates. The main difference would be the addition of disclosures on the variable-rate features.

4.4. Sample

The tests were conducted in October through early December of 2005 with 819 recent mortgage customers at 12 interview sites across the country. The sites included Boston, Westchester County (New York), Akron, Chicago, Nashville, Atlanta, Denver, Dallas, Phoenix, Las Vegas, Portland, and Seattle.

Participants were recruited from lists of consumers who had recently obtained a mortgage and who lived in proximity to one of the twelve interview sites. The lists were obtained from a commercially available database of mortgage transactions that is compiled primarily from public records available from county recorders and which should reflect all mortgages recorded in those locations. Potential respondents were contacted by telephone and recruited for the study. Those agreeing to participate were paid $30 after the completion of the interview.

Respondents were qualified if they had obtained a mortgage of any type within approximately two and a half years of the study.[46] Mortgages included purchase money loans, refinances of existing mortgages, second mortgages, and home equity loans. Respondents also were required to have been either the principal or joint decision maker on the mortgage transaction for the household.[47] This ensured that respondents had relatively recent experience obtaining a mortgage and would be at least somewhat familiar with mortgage cost information and terminology. The sample also was selected so that approximately half of the respondents had obtained their mortgage from a prime lender and the other half from a subprime lender.[48]

Table 4.4. Sample Groups

Group	Disclosure form	Loan-cost scenario	Borrower type	Sample size
1	Current forms	Simple loan	Prime borrowers	100
2	Current forms	Simple loan	Subprime borrowers	105
3	Current forms	Complex loan	Prime borrowers	104
4	Current forms	Complex loan	Subprime borrowers	102
5	Prototype form	Simple loan	Prime borrowers	102
6	Prototype form	Simple loan	Subprime borrowers	99
7	Prototype form	Complex loan	Prime borrowers	109
8	Prototype form	Complex loan	Subprime borrowers	98
Total				819

The two types of borrowers used in the study (prime and subprime), combined with the two alternative cost disclosure forms tested (current and prototype), using two different loan-cost scenarios (simple and complex), yielded eight sample groups of approximately 100 respondents. The eight groups are summarized in Table 4.4. The demographic characteristics and mortgage experience of the sample are summarize in Tables 4.5 and 4.6, at the end of this chapter.

Some care must be taken in interpreting the study sample. The sample is not nationally representative, because it was drawn from mortgage customers in only 12 particular locations. This limitation is somewhat ameliorated, however, through the use of multiple locations in geographically diverse areas of the country.

Some care also must be taken in interpreting the division of respondents into prime and subprime groups. The classifications were not based on whether the loans were prime or subprime, but whether the respondents had obtained the loans from prime or subprime lenders[49]

The HUD subprime lender list was used to classify whether respondents' lenders were prime or subprime.[50] Lenders were classified as subprime if they were on the HUD list, and were classified as prime if they were not on the list.

Using the HUD subprime lender list to classify lenders has several limitations that likely result in the incorrect classification of some respondents. One limitation arises because the list classifies lenders as subprime if their loans are primarily subprime, and omits lenders from the list if their loans are primarily prime. But some lenders have significant volumes of both prime and subprime loans. Some primarily-subprime lenders also make prime loans, and some primarily-prime lenders also make subprime loans. A respondent who obtained a prime loan from a primarily-subprime lender, if present in our sample, would have been classified as subprime. Similarly, a respondent who obtained a subprime loan from a primarily-prime lender would have been classified as prime. This implies that our subprime respondent group may contain some prime borrowers, and our prime respondent group may contain some subprime borrowers. If that is the case, comparisons of prime and subprime respondents may understate the actual differences between prime and subprime borrowers.

Another limitation of the HUD list is that it only includes lenders who are required to report loan data to the federal government under the Home Mortgage Disclosure Act ("HMDA"). Relatively small lenders, however, are not required to report under HMDA, and would not appear on the HUD list, even if they are exclusively subprime.[51] Thus, respondents with loans from small lenders, if present in our sample, would have been classified as prime, regardless of whether their loans were prime or subprime. This also implies that comparisons of prime and subprime respondents may understate the actual differences between prime and subprime borrowers.

Although the use of the HUD list is likely to have resulted in the incorrect classification of some respondents, overall, the classifications appear to have been largely successful in differentiating prime and subprime borrowers. As discussed more fully in the presentation of the in-depth interview findings, subprime interview respondents were more likely to be experiencing some type of financial difficulty when they sought their loans, many had been turned down by several lenders before being approved for their loans, and many acknowledged problems with their recent credit histories. Similarly, in the consumer testing samples, as shown in Tables 4.5 and 4.6, prime and subprime respondents differed significantly on a number of demographic and experience characteristics, including their racial compositions, income levels, types of loans obtained, and whether they had previously done business with their lenders. The differences between prime and subprime respondents, in both the in-depth interviews and consumer testing, suggest that even though the sample classifications are unlikely to be perfect, they seem to have worked fairly well.

Table 4.5. Demographic Characteristics of the Sample

Demographic category (N)	(1)All respondents (819)	Disclosure form group		Borrower group	
		(2) Current forms (411)	(3) Prototype form (408)	(4) Prime borrowers (415)	(5) Subprime borrowers (404)
Gender					
Male	35.0%	35.8%	34.3%	33.3%	36.9%
Female	65.0	64.2	65.7	66.8	63.1
Age					
18-24	0.4	0.5	0.3	0.0	0.7
25-34	11.1	11.2	11.0	11.3	10.9
35-44	31.0	29.2	32.8	32.5	29.5
45-54	32.6	32.6	32.6	29.4	35.9
55-64	17.2	19.0	15.4	17.1	17.3
65+	7.6	7.5	7.6	9.6	5.5
Don't know	0.1	0.0	0.3	0.0	0.3
Education					
Less than high school	1.6	0.7	2.5	1.7	1.5
High school graduate	18.2	17.3	19.1	17.1	19.3
Technical or trade school	6.1	4.6	7.6	7.2	5.0
Some college / Associates degree	29.2	30.2	28.2	26.8	31.7
College graduate	30.8	31.6	29.9	32.5	29.0
Graduate or professional school	13.6	15.1	12.0	13.7	13.4
Refused	0.6	0.5	0.7	1.0	0.3
Race / ethnicity *†					
White (non-Hispanic)	79.6%	78.6%	80.6%	83.9%	75.3%
African American (non-Hispanic)	13.6	14.1	13.0	9.6	17.6
Hispanic	4.2	4.1	4.2	3.4	5.0
Asian	1.5	2.4	0.5	1.9	1.0

American Indian / Alaska Native	0.2	0.0	0.5	0.0	0.5
Hawaiian or Other Pacific Islander	0.4	0.0	0.7	0.2	0.5
Multiple race (non-Hispanic)	0.2	0.5	0.0	0.2	0.3
Inconsistent response	0.1	0.2	0.0	0.2	0.0
Refused	0.2	0.0	0.5	0.5	0.0
Income †					
Less than $25,000	4.3	4.1	4.4	3.6	5.0
$25,000–49,999	21.3	21.9	20.6	16.6	26.0
$50,000–74,999	33.1	33.8	32.4	34.9	31.2
$75,000–99,999	20.8	19.7	21.8	21.5	20.1
$100,000+	16.6	16.3	16.9	19.0	14.1
Don't know	0.4	0.2	0.5	0.5	0.3
Refused	3.7	3.9	3.4	3.9	3.5

Notes: Percentages may not sum to 100 because of rounding. * indicates that the difference between the disclosure form groups is statistically significant at the five percent level; † indicates the same for the difference between borrower groups. Two-tailed t-tests were used to test the differences between means; two- tailed chi-square tests were used to test the differences between distributions. The difference in the age distributions of the two borrower groups was marginally significant at the six percent level.

Table 4.6. Mortgage Experience of the Sample

Mortgage experience category (N)		Disclosure form group		Borrower group	
	(1) All respon dents (819)	(2) Current forms (411)	(3) Prototype form (408)	(4) Prime borrowers (415)	(5) Subprime borrowers (404)
Decision-maker on mortgage †					
Main decision-maker in household	46.8%	48.2%	45.3%	41.2%	52.5%
Shared in decision-making	53.2	51.8	54.7	58.8	47.5
Date of most recent mortgage					
Less than six months ago	16.4	15.8	16.9	15.2	17.6
Six months but less than one year	28.7	29.7	27.7	28.9	28.5
One year but less than two years	37.0	36.7	37.3	37.4	36.6
Two years or more	17.6	17.8	17.4	18.3	16.8
Don't know	0.1	0.0	0.3	0.0	0.3
Refused	0.2	0.0	0.5	0.2	0.3

Table 4.6. (Continued)

Mortgage experience category (N)		Disclosure form group		Borrower group	
	(1) All respon dents (819)	(2) Current forms (411)	(3) Prototype form (408)	(4) Prime borrowers (415)	(5) Subprime borrowers (404)
Type of most recent mortgage[1]					
Purchase †	18.8	19.0	18.6	21.5	16.1
Refinance †	63.7	64.5	63.0	56.6	71.0
Cash-out / debt consolidation †	17.8	16.6	19.1	14.2	21.5
Home equity line-of-credit (HELOC) †	15.5	16.3	14.7	22.2	8.7
Cash-out or HELOC[2]	1.2	1.0	1.5	1.2	1.2
Other type	1.1	0.5	1.7	0.7	1.5
Don't know	0.1	0.0	0.3	0.2	0.0
Refused	0.1	0.0	0.3	0.0	0.3
Previous business with lender †					
Yes	44.9%	45.0%	44.9%	56.4%	33.2%
No	54.3	54.7	53.9	42.9	66.1
Don't know	0.7	0.2	1.2	0.7	0.7
Number of lenders/brokers shopped	2.8	2.9	2.7	2.7	2.9
Average number[3]					
Total number of mortgages in lifetime	4.2	4.2	4.2	4.4	4.1
Average number[3]					

Notes: Percentages may not sum to 100 because of rounding. * indicates that the difference between the disclosure form groups is statistically significant at the five percent level; † indicates the same for the difference between borrower groups. Two-tailed t-tests were used to test the differences between means; two-tailed chi- square tests were used to test the differences between distributions.

1 Percentages may sum to greater than 100 percent for the type of mortgage because some respondents reported more than one type (for example, refinance and cash-out). The statistical significance of the results was tested for each mortgage type individually using two-tailed t-tests of the difference between proportions.

2 The category "Cash-out or HELOC" consists of responses in which the two mortgage types could not be distinguished.

3 Averages exclude "don't know" and "refused" responses.

4.5. Method of Analysis

The heart of the analysis is the comparison of the performance of current and prototype disclosure forms. The analysis also compares the performance of prime and subprime borrowers. For both, the analysis focuses on the percentage of respondents who were able to answer the various test questions correctly. The results are examined both in the aggregate and for individual test questions.

The aggregate analysis combines the results of the individual test questions and examines the average percentage of questions answered correctly by the respondents. This average is compared across the two disclosure-form groups or two borrower groups. The analysis of individual questions makes similar comparisons with the percentage of respondents who answered each question correctly. Where it provides useful insight, the analysis also examines the responses provided by respondents who did not answer correctly.

For some of the questions concerning the monthly and balloon payments, ambiguities in the question wording that made it difficult to categorize whether responses were correct. The ambiguities were eliminated when the results of several questions were combined and analyzed jointly. Two questions concerning the monthly payment were combined, as were four questions concerning the balloon payment, thereby reducing the results of these six questions to two combined results. One additional question concerning the monthly payment was excluded entirely because of unresolved ambiguities in the interpretation of the results. Together, this left 25 results that were examined in the individual-question analysis.[52]

The aggregate analysis for the complex-loan scenario includes these 25 results. The aggregate analysis for the simple-loan scenario includes 21 results. Four questions were omitted from the latter, because they asked about the details of cost features that were not included in the simple-scenario loans.[53]

Prototype Mortgage Cost Disclosures

5.1. Development of the Prototype Disclosures

A prototype mortgage cost disclosure form was developed to test whether better disclosures could improve consumer understanding of mortgage costs. The objective was to design a disclosure form that enabled consumers to more easily recognize loan costs, more easily comparison shop for the least expensive loan that fits their needs, and more readily recognize and avoid deceptive lending practices.

The principles followed in designing the form were simple and straightforward. The key mortgage costs that consumers need to understand when obtaining a loan were included in the form. Information that is less important or confusing was excluded. Costs were conveyed in simple, easily-to-understand language. The form was organized and formatted so that the various costs could be easily recognized and identified. The consumer testing examined how well we implemented these principles.

In designing the content and language of the form, we started by imagining that the current federal mortgage cost disclosures did not exist and asked what should be done if we started anew. We were guided by a general financial analysis of the key costs of a mortgage, the types of consumer problems encountered in the deceptive lending cases investigated by the FTC, our experience in designing and evaluating consumer disclosures, and the insights gained from the in-depth consumer interviews conducted in the first part of the study.

We also sought to consolidate all key costs in a single disclosure document, rather than providing separate disclosures for financing and settlement costs, as in the current TILA and GFE disclosures. This is consistent with recommendations made by the FRB and HUD in a 1998 report to Congress.[54]

We sought to keep the prototype form as short as possible but not at the expense of comprehensiveness or clarity. The form uses clear headings for each section and loan cost, and incorporates a substantial amount of "white space" to make each figure easy to locate, identify, and read. The organization and formatting present a less intimidating appearance than many consumer financial disclosures, making it more likely that consumers will both want to read the form and be able to use it productively in their decisions.

The content and format considerations resulted in a three-page disclosure form. A one- or two-page form might have been possible but would have required either the omission of some of the cost information or the use of smaller type-fonts and less white space. These alternatives were rejected. The former would make the form less informative and the latter would result in a denser, contract-like appearance that is more difficult to read and use, perhaps deterring many consumers from even trying.

Appendix H presents the prototype disclosure form for the six loans tested in the study. The first four loans (Loans "G," "R," "M," and "V") are relatively simple purchase loans. The last two loans (Loans "K" and "T") are more are complex refinance loans that contain complicating features such as cash paid to the borrower, consolidation of other debts, financed settlement costs, charges for optional credit insurance, interest-only monthly payments, exclusion of property taxes and homeowner's insurance from the monthly payments, a large balloon payment, and a prepayment penalty during the first five years of the loan.[55] The various loans illustrate the ability of the prototype to provide relatively simple disclosures for simple loans but more comprehensive disclosures for more complicated loans.

5.2 Comparison of the Prototype to the Current TILA and GFE Forms

The design of the prototype disclosure form was not restricted to include all of the disclosures currently required in the TILA statement and GFE form. In designing the form, we attempted to start anew, as if the current disclosures did not exist, and ask what mortgage cost information was most important to provide to consumers. We included the information from current disclosures that we considered most important and omitted the information that we considered less important.

The prototype form includes, as does the current TILA statement, disclosures of the APR, payment schedule, and optional credit insurance charges, although the prototype uses different language for the latter two disclosures and expands the last to include all optional products and services. The prototype form does not, however, incorporate the TILA disclosures of the "amount financed," finance charge, and total of payments. We considered these disclosures to be less important to consumers shopping for a mortgage, potentially confusing, and sometimes misleading.[56]

The prototype form also includes, as does the GFE, disclosure of the cost of settlement services. The prototype, however, presents the total cost for all settlement services, which is not required in the GFE. The prototype does not present an itemization of the individual costs of two-to-three dozen different settlement services, as required in the GFE. We considered the overall cost, rather than how that cost is distributed across various individual categories, to be more important for consumer understanding of the cost of the loan and for comparing loan offers from different lenders. We considered the detailed itemization to be less useful for consumers and potentially overwhelming when presented in the form.[57]

The prototype form provides a number of cost disclosures not required in the current TILA and GFE forms, including:

- Disclosure of the total loan amount, rather than the "amount financed," and an itemization that divides the total into the categories of money borrowed to purchase or refinance a home, cash for debt consolidation or a home equity loan, financed settlement charges, and financed charges for optional products or services.
- Disclosure of the total charges for settlement services.
- Stronger disclosure of charges for optional credit insurance, and expansion of the disclosure to include all types of optional products and services, with clearer notice that the optional items are not required for the loan, and that charges should not be included if the consumer does not want to purchase the items.
- Disclosure of total up-front charges, and an itemization that divides the total into two categories: settlement and optional charges.
- Disclosure of the amount of cash due at closing, and an itemization that divides the total into the categories of down payment, payments for settlement services,
- Disclosure of whether the monthly payment includes property taxes and homeowner's insurance, and if not, the additional monthly amounts that must be paid by the borrower.
- Consumer tips and warnings on the benefits of comparison shopping, not relying on oral promises, and verifying costs at closing.

5.3. Description of the Prototype Form

As can be seen in the examples shown in Appendix H, the first page of the prototype form provides a summary of key loan costs. This allows consumers to easily review the overall cost of the loan and compare the costs of different loan offers. The second and third pages provide additional details on the costs. This allows consumers to more fully understand the details of the loan costs. The third page also presents several consumer tips and warnings.

5.3.1. Page One – Summary of Key Loan Costs

The first page of the form summarizes the key costs and features of the mortgage, including the nature of the loan, the charges assessed by the lender, the payments required of the borrower, and any penalties and fees assessed for late and prepayments. The page consists of four sections titled "Your Loan," "Our Loan Charges," "Your Loan Payments," and "Penalties and Late Fees."

The "Your Loan" section describes the type of loan offered (for example, "30-year, fixed- rate" or "10-year, interest-only, balloon"), the loan amount, and the length of the loan term. The loan amount equals the total initial loan principal, including the amount borrowed to purchase or refinance the home, any debt consolidation or home-equity borrowing added to the loan, any financed settlement costs, and any financed charges for optional products or services such as credit insurance. The loan amount is typically larger than the "amount financed" disclosed on the current TILA statement, because the latter deducts any prepaid finance charges, such as origination fees (points), from the loan amount to obtain the disclosed "amount financed."

The "Our Loan Charges" section summarizes all of the charges assessed in connection with the loan. This includes the interest rate, the total up-front charges, and any monthly billed charges. Up-front charges are divided into two categories, settlement charges and charges for optional products and services, in order to highlight charges for any add-on products or services not required for the loan. Monthly billed charges include items such as monthly billed mortgage or credit insurance, if included in the loan. The section concludes with a disclosure and explanation of the APR. The APR and interest rate are disclosed in close proximity in order to highlight the difference between the two.

The "Your Loan Payments" section summarizes all of the payments that the borrower is obligated to make under the loan, including the amount of cash due at closing, the monthly payment schedule, and any balloon payment due at the end of the loan. The monthly payment disclosure also indicates whether the stated payment amount includes required payments for property taxes and homeowner's insurance. The juxtaposition of the "Payments" and "Charges" sections highlights to consumers the difference between the two sets of figures.

The "Penalties and Late Fees" section discloses any prepayment penalty and late fee included in the loan. The prepayment penalty disclosure indicates whether a penalty is included in the loan and, if so, provides both the penalty amount and the period during which it applies. The penalty amount is presented both in general form that shows how the penalty will be calculated, such as "A penalty of four percent of the prepaid loan balance will be charged if the loan is paid off during the first five years," and in specific numerical form, calculated for an immediate prepayment of the full loan amount, such as "An immediate refinancing of the loan would result in a penalty of $7,017.00." The latter clearly conveys the financial consequences of the penalty to consumers if they should accept the offer and then wish to refinance.[58]If the loan does not contain a prepayment penalty, the prepayment section of the form would simply state "None."

5.3.2. Page Two – Details of the Home Purchase, Loan Amount, Optional Charges, Cash Due at Closing, and Initial Monthly Payment

The second page of the form presents details of the home purchase (for purchase loans), loan amount, optional charges (if applicable), cash due at closing, and initial monthly payment. The page consists of five sections titled "Home Purchase Details," "Loan Amount Details," "Optional Charges Details," "Cash Due at Closing Details," and "Monthly Payment Details."

The "Home Purchase Details" section presents the price of the home, the down payment, and the amount of the price being financed. The section is omitted for refinance loans.

The "Loan Amount Details" section presents an itemization of the total loan amount. The itemization includes the amount of the home price being financed (if a purchase), the amount of existing mortgage being refinanced (if a refinance), any financed settlement charges, any financed charges for optional products or services, any cash paid to the borrower (if a cash-out refinance or home equity loan), and any financing to consolidate other debts. These figures, along with the total presented both here and on the first page, represent the actual total loan amount rather than only the "amount financed" figure that is disclosed in the current TILA form. As noted above, the "amount financed," as defined by the TILA regulations, is typically smaller than the total loan amount.

The "Optional Charges Details" section provides an itemization of the charges for optional products or services that will be included in the loan if the consumer agrees to their purchase. The section also provides a notice stating that the optional items are not required for the loan, and that consumers who do not wish to purchase the optional items should ask the loan provider for a revised disclosure form that excludes the charges. If the loan does not contain any charges for optional items, this section of the form would simply state "None."

The prototype form does not require that the borrower sign or initial an affirmative written request that indicates agreement to purchase the optional products, as is currently required under TILA for optional credit insurance and related products such as debt cancellation coverage.[59] The prototype, however, makes the disclosures of the amount and optional nature of the charges more prominent than is currently required, both here and on the first page of the form, includes and identifies the optional charges in the disclosure of the total amount of up-front charges that appears on the first page of the form, and, if the optional charges are financed and added to the loan principal, includes and identifies the charges in the loan amount detail that appears on the second page. One might consider adding a signature requirement, which borrowers would sign if they choose to purchase the insurance, similar to that currently required for optional insurance by TILA, if a form such as the prototype were adopted. This would further protect borrowers by requiring that they take an affirmative action to approve the purchase of the optional items.[60]

The "Cash Due at Closing Details" section provides an itemization of the total amount of cash due at closing. The itemization includes any down payment (if a purchase loan), any cash paid at closing for settlement charges, any cash paid at closing for optional products or services, and any credit to the borrower for purchase earnest money.

The "Monthly Payment Details" section presents an itemization that divides the initial monthly payment into the categories of principal and interest, property tax escrow, hazard insurance, mortgage insurance, and monthly billed, optional products or services. In addition to the itemization, the section includes a separate statement that indicates whether the monthly payment includes the required payments for property taxes and hazard insurance. If these are not included in the monthly payment, the section states that:

Property taxes and hazard insurance are NOT included in your monthly loan payment. You will be responsible for paying these additional required costs yourself.

This is followed by a disclosure of the additional monthly costs that the borrower will incur for each item.

5.3.3. Page Three – Details of the Settlement Charges; Consumer Tips and Warnings

The third page of the form provides details of the settlement charges and several consumer tips and warnings. The main section of the page is titled "Settlement Charges Details."This section provides an itemization that divides settlement charges into the categories of charges for the settlement services package, the interest charge for a partial initial month, any prepaid items, and any reserves deposited with the lender. Total settlement charges are presented at the bottom of the section.

The settlement services charges are not further itemized into the numerous individual categories listed in the current GFE. Instead, the form simply presents the total cost for all settlement services, and provides a list of the services included. A notice at the top of the section states that all of the settlement services required for the loan are included in the stated charge. The form omits the itemization of individual settlement costs in order to make it easier for consumers to focus on the overall total cost, and compare the total costs of loan offers from different lenders, rather than getting lost in the overwhelming detail of the itemization.[61]

The second section on page three, titled "How to Protect Yourself," provides three tips and warnings for consumers. The first tip reminds consumers of the benefits of comparison shopping:

> COMPARISON SHOP TO FIND THE BEST DEAL — The lender or broker providing this loan is not necessarily shopping on your behalf or providing you with the lowest cost loan.

The obvious intent is to encourage consumers to comparison shop for the best loan that fits their needs. This is the best way for consumers to make sure they are getting a good deal. The statement also reminds consumers that all loan providers, both lenders and brokers, may be seeking their own benefit rather than the consumer's.

The second tip warns consumers not to rely on oral promises and to get all changes to the loan terms in writing:

> DO NOT RELY ON ORAL PROMISES TO CHANGE THESE TERMS — Obtain all changes in writing.

The third tip reminds consumers to compare the closing documents to the offer sheet to verify that the loan costs have not be increased:

> SAVE THIS OFFER SHEET AND COMPARE TO DOCUMENTS AT CLOSING — Before you sign any papers at your loan closing (loan settlement), make sure that the costs have not been increased.

Ensuring that costs have not been changed would be made easier if at closing the final costs were presented in a form identical to the offer sheet. Consumers could then place the two side-by-side and easily scan for differences.

A final notice at the bottom of the prototype form notes that federal law requires the offer sheet be provided to the borrower within three business days after the borrower has applied for a loan (or whatever deadline would be in effect if such a form were implemented through regulation), instructs consumers to obtain a revised offer form if the loan terms are changed, and instructs consumers to notify the FTC if the lender does not abide by the terms set forth in the offer or does not provide the offer sheet within the required deadline.[62]

One feature not included in the tested prototype, but would need to be added if such a form were adopted, is signature lines to indicate acceptance of the loan offer by the consumer and acknowledgment of the consumer's acceptance by the loan provider. As noted above, a separate signature line also could be added, in the optional charges section of the form, that consumers would sign if they wished to purchase any optional products or services not required for the loan.

5.4. Adjustable-Rate, Hybrid, and Payment Option Loans

The prototype disclosures developed and tested in this study are for fixed-rate loans, including those with interest-only and balloon payments. Adjustable-rate, hybrid, and payment option loans would require additional disclosures that described how the interest rate, monthly payment, or both, may change over the course of the loan. We focused on fixed-rate loans in order to first test whether better disclosures could be designed for these relatively simpler loan products. If the prototype disclosures are shown to be more effective than current disclosures for these simpler loans, additional disclosures for adjustable-rate, hybrid, and payment option loans could be added. An additional page that described the adjustable-rate and option features, and their potential impact on the interest rate and payments of the loan, could be added to the form.

A prominent disclosure also could be added to the first page to direct consumers to the additional disclosures, and perhaps provide the maximum monthly payment possible in the loan.

Additional disclosures for adjustable-rate and hybrid loans would likely include the rate index, margin, current fully indexed rate, first adjustment date (initial fixed-rate period), subsequent adjustment periods, limits on the size of the periodic rate adjustments, the maximum lifetime interest rate, and the impact of the periodic and maximum lifetime rate adjustments on the monthly payment amount. Additional disclosures for payment option loans would describe the potential impact of the payment option on the outstanding loan balance (including any possible negative amortization), the monthly payments, and any balloon payment. Additional consumer testing could be used to examine the effectiveness of the disclosures in conveying these loan terms to consumers.

Disclosures for interest-only loans could be handled within the prototype disclosure form developed here for fixed-rate loans. If the interest-only feature results in a balloon payment at the end of the loan, that can be disclosed in the payment schedule and balloon payment sections of the form, as was done for one of the loans tested in the study. If the interest-only payment converts to a fully amortizing payment at some point during the loan, the resulting higher payment level would be disclosed in the payment schedule. Additional cautions about the payment increase also might be added to a fourth page of the disclosures.

Consumer Testing Results

The consumer testing produced four major findings: (1) current mortgage cost disclosures failed to convey key mortgage costs to many consumers; (2) prototype disclosures developed for the study significantly improved consumer recognition of mortgage costs, demonstrating that better disclosures are feasible; (3) both prime and subprime borrowers failed to understand key loan terms, and both benefitted from the improved disclosures; and (4) improved disclosures provided the greatest benefit for more complex loans, where both prime and subprime borrowers had the most difficulty understanding loan terms. The findings are apparent in both the aggregate and individual-question results.

6.1. Aggregate Results

6.1.1. Comparison of Current and Prototype Cost Disclosure Forms

The aggregate results clearly show that the current mortgage cost disclosure forms fail to convey key mortgage costs to many consumers and that the prototype disclosure form designed for this study significantly improved consumer understanding of mortgage costs. Table 6.1 presents the average percentage of questions answered correctly by respondents in the current- and prototype-form groups. As shown in the first row of the table, on average, respondents viewing the current forms answered 61 percent of the questions correctly. In contrast, respondents viewing the prototype form answered 80 percent of the questions correctly, a 19 percentage point improvement over the current-forms group.[63] The difference between the two groups is statistically significant.

Table 6.1. Percentage of Questions Answered Correctly With Current and Prototype Disclosure Forms

Loan scenario and borrower type N (current forms / prototype form)	Percentage of questions answered correctly		Difference between forms (prototype – current)	
	(1) Current forms	(2) Prototype form	(3) Percentage point difference	(4) Percentage change
Both loans combined				
All borrowers (41 1/408)	60.8%	79.7%	19.0**	31.3%
Prime borrowers (204/211)	62.0	80.6	18.6**	30.0
Subprime borrowers (207/197)	59.6	78.8	19.2**	32.2
Simple purchase loan				
All borrowers (205/201)	65.9	81.9	16.0**	24.3
Prime borrowers (100/102)	67.0	82.6	15.6**	23.3
Subprime borrowers (105/99)	65.0	81.2	16.2**	24.9
Complex refinance loan				
All borrowers (206/207)	55.7	77.7	22.0**	39.5
Prime borrowers (104/109)	57.2	78.8	21.6**	37.8
Subprime borrowers (102/98)	54.0	76.4	22.4**	41.5

Notes: Percentages are based on the aggregate results of 21 questions for the simple purchase loan and 25 questions for the complex refinance loan. Percentages may not sum to 100 because of rounding. Figures in parentheses are the number of current- and prototype-form respondents

in the indicated group. Asterisks indicate statistically significant differences in the proportions of respondents giving the correct response. Two-tailed t-tests were used to test the differences. * indicates significance at the five percent level and ** indicates significance at the one percent level

Both disclosure-form groups had lower accuracy rates in the complex-loan scenario, but the difference was larger in the current-forms group. Current-forms respondents answered an average of 66 percent of the questions correctly in the simple-loan scenario, compared to 56 percent in the complex-loan scenario, a difference of 10 percentage points. Prototype-form respondents answered an average of 82 percent of the questions correctly in the simple-loan scenario, compared to 78 percent in the complex-loan scenario, a difference of four percentage points.[64]

Table 6.2. Percentage of Respondents Answering a High Percentage of the Questions Correctly when Viewing Current and Prototype Disclosure Forms

Percentage of questions answered correctly N (current forms / prototype form)	Percentage of respondents		(3) Percentage point difference
	(1) Current forms	(2) Prototype form	
Both loans combined (411/408)			
90% or more correct	1.7%	30.1%	28.4**
80% or more correct	10.9	64.0	53.0**
70% or more correct	29.4	80.1	50.7**
Simple purchase loan (205/201)			
90% or more correct	3.4	39.8	36.4**
80% or more correct	15.6	67.2	51.6**
70% or more correct	43.9	84.1	40.2**
Complex refinance loan (206/207)			
90% or more correct	0.0	20.8	20.8**
80% or more correct	6.3	60.9	54.6**
70% or more correct	15.0	76.3	61.3**

Notes: Percentages are based on the aggregate results of 21 questions for the simple purchase loan and 25 questions for the complex refinance loan. Percentages may not sum to 100 because of rounding. Figures in parentheses are the number of current- and prototype-form respondents in the indicated group. Asterisks indicate statistically significant differences in the proportions of respondents giving the correct response. Two-tailed t-tests were used to test the differences. * indicates significance at the five percent level and ** indicates significance at the one percent level.

The prototype form provided a greater improvement, however, in the complex-loan scenario, where it scored 22 percentage points higher than the current forms, compared to 16 percentage points higher in the simple-loan scenario.[65]

The difference in the performance of the two forms is even more dramatic if one examines the percentages of respondents in each group who answered relatively a high percentage of the questions correctly. As shown in Table 6.2, across both loan scenarios combined, 80 percent of the respondents viewing the prototype form were able to answer 70 percent or more of the questions correctly, compared to only 29 percent of the respondents viewing the current forms, an improvement of 51 percentage points. As shown in the table, large improvements also are found in the percentage of respondents that answered 80 and 90 percent of the questions correctly. All of the differences between the forms were statistically significant.

Table 6.3. Percentage of Questions with Various Types of Responses — Current Versus Prototype Disclosure Forms

Type of response N (current forms / prototype form)	Percentage of questions		Difference between forms	
	(1) Current forms	(2) Prototype form	(3) Percentage point difference	(4) Percentage change
Simple purchase loan (205/20 1)				
Correct	65.9%	81.9%	16.0**	24.3%
Incorrect	28.7	14.0	– 14.7**	– 51.2
"Don't know"	3.8	2.4	– 1.4*	– 36.8
"Not enough information / can't tell"	2.5	1.8	– 0.7	– 28.0
Refused	0.2	<0.1	– 0.1	– 50.0
Skipped	n/a	n/a	n/a	n/a
Complex refinance loan (206/207)				
Correct	55.7	77.7	22.0**	39.5
Incorrect	30.4	14.7	– 15.7**	– 51.6
"Don't know"	4.0	2.4	– 1.6**	– 40.0
"Not enough information / can't tell"	5.8	1.4	– 4.4**	– 75.9
Refused	0.1	0.0	– 0.1	---
Skipped	6.0	3.9	– 2.1**	– 35.0

Notes: Percentages are based on 19 questions for the simple purchase loan and 23 questions for the complex refinance loan. Two questions that consisted of multi-question sequences were excluded. Percentages may not sum to 100 because of rounding. "Skipped questions" indicates follow-up questions that were contingent on the responses to the initial questions and which were skipped because incorrect responses were given on the initial question. Figures in parentheses are the number of current- and prototype-form respondents in the indicated group. Asterisks indicate statistically significant differences between the current and prototype groups. Two-tailed t-tests were used to test the differences. * indicates significance at the five percent level and ** indicates significance at the one percent level.

When respondents did not answer a question correctly they most often provided an incorrect answer rather than merely saying that they "did not know" or "could not tell from the information shown." As shown in Table 6.3, prototype-form respondents had a significantly lower incidence of incorrect responses than did current-forms respondents, which mirrored the significantly higher level of correct responses achieved by the group. On average, respondents viewing the current forms provided incorrect answers to about 30 percent of the questions in each loan scenario. In contrast, respondents viewing the prototype form provided incorrect answers to slightly less than 15 percent of the questions, a statistically significant reduction of slightly more than 50 percent.[66] Prototype-form respondents also had lower average levels of "don't know" and "not enough information / cannot tell" responses than did current-forms respondents.[67]

6.1.2 Comparison of Prime and Subprime Borrowers

The aggregate results show that both prime and subprime borrowers had significant difficulty recognizing and identifying key loan costs when viewing current disclosure forms, and both groups benefitted significantly from the improved disclosures. Subprime borrowers were less likely than prime borrowers to accurately recognize and identify mortgage costs, but the difference between the two groups was quite small. As shown in Table 6.4 (which rearranges the figures from Table 6.1 to better highlight the differences between the two borrower groups), subprime borrowers answered a lower percentage of questions correctly than did prime borrowers, but the difference was very small. Among respondents who viewed current disclosures, across both loan scenarios, prime borrowers answered an average of 62.0 percent of the questions correctly, compared to 59.6 percent for subprime borrowers, a difference of only 2.4 percentage points. Similar results were found in the prototype-form group and in each loan- cost scenario.[68]

The prototype form provided similar benefits to both prime and subprime borrowers. As shown in the second and third rows of each section of Table 6.1, the difference between the prototype and current forms was about the same for both types of borrowers. In the complex-loan scenario, for example, the prototype form performed 21.6 percentage points better than the current forms among prime borrowers and 22.4 percentage points better among subprime borrowers. Similar results were found in the simple-loan scenario.[69]

It is important to note that these comparisons of prime and subprime borrowers hold constant the complexity of the loans. Relatively equal numbers of prime and subprime borrowers viewed simple loans, and relatively equal numbers viewed complex loans. In actual market transactions, however, subprime loans may be more likely to be complex, because they may be more likely to contain features such as optional credit insurance, balloon payments, prepayment penalties, and the exclusion of escrow from the monthly payments. As shown in Table 6.1 and noted in the text, above, respondents had more difficulty recognizing and identifying mortgage costs in the complex-loan scenario.[70] This implies that borrowers in the subprime market may have more difficulty understanding their loan terms than borrowers in the prime market.[71] The difference in understanding, however, would be due largely to differences in the complexities of the loans, rather than the capabilities of the borrowers. For the same reason, the improved disclosures presented in the prototype form may have a larger beneficial impact in the subprime market than in the prime market. [72]

Table 6.4. Percentage of Questions Answered Correctly by Prime and Subprime Borrowers

Loan scenario and disclosure form N (prime! subprime)	Percentage of questions answered correctly			Difference between borrower groups (subprime – prime)	
	(1) All borrowers	(2) Prime borrowers	(3) Subprime borrowers	(4) Percentage point difference	(5) Percentage change
Both loans combined					
Both forms (415!404)	70.2%	7 1.5%	69.0%	– 2.5*	– 3.5%
Current forms (204!207)	60.8	62.0	59.6	– 2.4	– 4.0
Prototype form (211!197)	79.7	80.6	78.8	– 1.8	– 2.2
Simple purchase loan					
Both forms (202!204)	73.8	74.8	72.9	– 2.0	– 2.7
Current forms (100!105)	65.9	67.0	65.0	– 2.0	– 3.0
Prototype form (102!99)	81.9	82.6	81.2	– 1.4	– 1.7
Complex refinance loan					
Both forms (213!200)	66.7	68.3	65.0	– 3.2	– 4.7
Current forms (104!102)	55.7	57.2	54.0	– 3.2	– 5.6
Prototype form (109!98)	77.7	78.8	76.4	– 2.4	– 3.0

Notes: Percentages are based on the aggregate results of 21 questions for the simple purchase loan and 25 questions for the complex refinance loan. Percentages may not sum to 100 because of rounding. Figures in parentheses are the number of prime and subprime borrowers in the indicated group. Asterisks indicate statistically significant differences in the proportions of respondents giving the correct response. Two-tailed t-tests were used to test the differences. * indicates significance at the five percent level and ** indicates significance at the one percent level.

6.2. Individual Question Results 6.2.1 Overview

As with the aggregate results, the individual question results clearly show that the current mortgage cost disclosure forms fail to convey key mortgage costs to many consumers and that the prototype disclosure form significantly improves consumer understanding of mortgage costs. In most of the questions, the prototype form performed better than the current forms, that is, the percentage of respondents providing the correct answer was higher in the prototype-form group than in the current-forms group. In many of the questions, the prototype outperformed the current forms by quite a large margin.

As shown in Table 6.5, the prototype form performed better than the current forms in 17 of the 21 questions in the simple-loan scenario and 23 of the 25 questions in the complex-loan scenario.[73] Many of the improvements provided by the prototype form were quite large. In the complex-loan scenario, for example, the prototype outperformed the current forms by more than 10 percentage points in 15 questions, more than 30 percentage points in eight questions and more than 50 percentage points in four questions.

Table 6.5. Number of Questions in Which Each Disclosure Form Performed Better than the Other

Number of questions in which the form performed better than the other

	Simple-loan scenario	Complex-loan scenario
Total number of questions	21	25
Prototype form performed better than the current forms	17	23
Difference greater than 10 percentage points	13	15
Difference greater than 30 percentage points	4	8
Difference greater than 50 percentage points	2	4
Difference greater than 60 percentage points	0	2
Current forms performed better than the prototype form	4	2
Difference greater than 10 percentage points	0	0
Difference greater than 30 percentage points	0	0
Difference greater than 50 percentage points	0	0
Difference greater than 60 percentage points	0	0

Notes: Performance is measured as the percentage of respondents correctly answering the question, with better performance for a form implying that a higher percentage of respondents in that group provided the correct answer. In the questions in which the prototype form performed better than the current forms, the difference between the forms was statistically significant in 13 questions in the simple-loan scenario and 16 questions in the complex-loan scenario. In the questions in which the current forms performed better than the prototype form, none of the differences were statistically significant.

The current forms performed better than the prototype in only four questions in the simple-loan scenario and two questions in the complex-loan scenario, and all of the differences were quite small—less than five percentage points in the simple-loan questions and less than 10 percentage points in the complex-loan questions. None of the differences were statistically significant.

The results provide substantial evidence that current mortgage cost disclosures fail to convey key mortgage costs to many consumers. This was evident across a wide range of loan terms and for substantial proportions of respondents. As shown in Table 6.6 and discussed in detail in the individual loan-cost sections below, about a fifth of the respondents viewing the current disclosure forms could not correctly identify the APR of the loan, the amount of cash due at closing, or the monthly payment (including whether it included escrow for taxes and insurance). Nearly a quarter could not identify the amount of settlement charges. About a third could not identify the interest rate or which of two loans was less expensive, and a third did not recognize that the loan included a large balloon payment or that the loan amount included money borrowed to pay for settlement charges. Half could not correctly identify the loan amount. Two-thirds did not recognize that they would be charged a prepayment penalty if in two years they refinanced with another lender (and a third did not even recognize that they "may" be charged such a penalty). Three-quarters did not recognize that substantial charges for optional credit insurance were included in the loan. Almost four-fifths did not know why the interest rate and APR of a loan sometimes differ. And nearly nine-tenths could not identify the total amount of up-front charges in the loan.

Table 6.6. Percentage of Respondents Viewing the Current Disclosure Forms Who Could Not Correctly Identify Various Loan Costs

Loan cost	Percentage of current-forms respondents
APR amount	20%
Cash due at closing amount	20
Monthly payment (including whether it included taxes and insurance)	21
Settlement charges amount	23
Balloon payment (presence and amount)	30
Interest rate amount	32
Whether loan amount included financed settlement charges	33
Which loan was less expensive	37
Loan amount	51
Presence of prepayment penalty for refinance in two years	68
Presence of charges for optional credit insurance	74
Reason why the interest rate and APR sometimes differ	79
Property tax and homeowner's insurance cost amount	84
Total up-front charges amount	87
Prepayment penalty amount	95

Notes: All figures are combined results for both loan scenarios, with the following exceptions: results for "balloon payment (presence and amount)," "property tax and homeowners's insurance cost amount," "presence of prepayment penalty for refinance in two years," "prepayment penalty amount," and "presence of charges for optional credit insurance" are from the complex-loan scenario, which included these terms in the loans; the result for the "settlement charges amount" is from the simple-loan scenario, which provides a better indication of respondent performance on this question (see the discussion of the settlement charges results in Section 6.2.3).

The results also provide substantial evidence that better disclosures can significantly increase consumer understanding of key mortgage costs. This was evident across a wide range of loan terms and for substantial proportions of respondents. As shown in Table 6.7 and discussed in detail below, the prototype form produced a 66 percentage point increase in the proportion of respondents correctly identifying the total amount of up-front charges in the loan, a 43 percentage point increase in the proportion of respondents recognizing that the loan contained charges for optional credit insurance, a 37 percentage point increase in the proportion correctly identifying the amount borrowed, a 24 percentage point increase in the proportion recognizing that a prepayment penalty would be assessed if the loan was refinanced in two years, a 21 percentage point increase in the proportion correctly identifying why the APR and interest rate may differ in a loan, a 16 percentage point increase in the proportion correctly identifying the APR, a 15 percentage point increase in the proportion correctly identifying the amount of settlement charges, a 13 percentage point increase in the proportion correctly identifying which of two loans was less expensive, a 12 percentage point increase in the proportion correctly identifying the interest rate, and a nine percentage point increase in the proportion recognizing that settlement charges were financed and included in the loan amount. The prototype form also conveyed the correct prepayment penalty amount to 59 percent of the respondents and the correct amounts of property taxes and homeowner's insurance charges for a loan in which the charges were not included in the monthly payment to 79 percent of the respondents—information that is not included at all in the current forms.

Table 6.7.Improvements Provided by the Prototype Disclosure Form in the Percentage of Respondents Correctly Identifying Various Loan Costs

Loan cost	Percentage point improvement
Total up-front charges amount	66
Property tax and homeowner's insurance cost amount	62
Prepayment penalty amount	53
Presence of charges for optional credit insurance	43
Loan amount	37
Presence of prepayment penalty for refinance in two years	24
Reason why the interest rate and APR sometimes differ	21
APR amount	16
Settlement charges amount	15
Which loan was less expensive	13
Interest rate amount	12
Whether loan amount included financed settlement charges	9

Notes: All figures are combined results for both loan scenarios, with the following exceptions: results for "property tax and homeowners's insurance cost amount," "presence of prepayment penalty for refinance in two years," "prepayment penalty amount," and "presence of charges for optional credit insurance" are from the complex-loan scenario, which included these terms in the loans; the result for the "settlement charges amount" is from the simple-loan scenario, which provides a better indication of respondent performance on this question (see the discussion of the settlement charges results in Section 6.2.3).

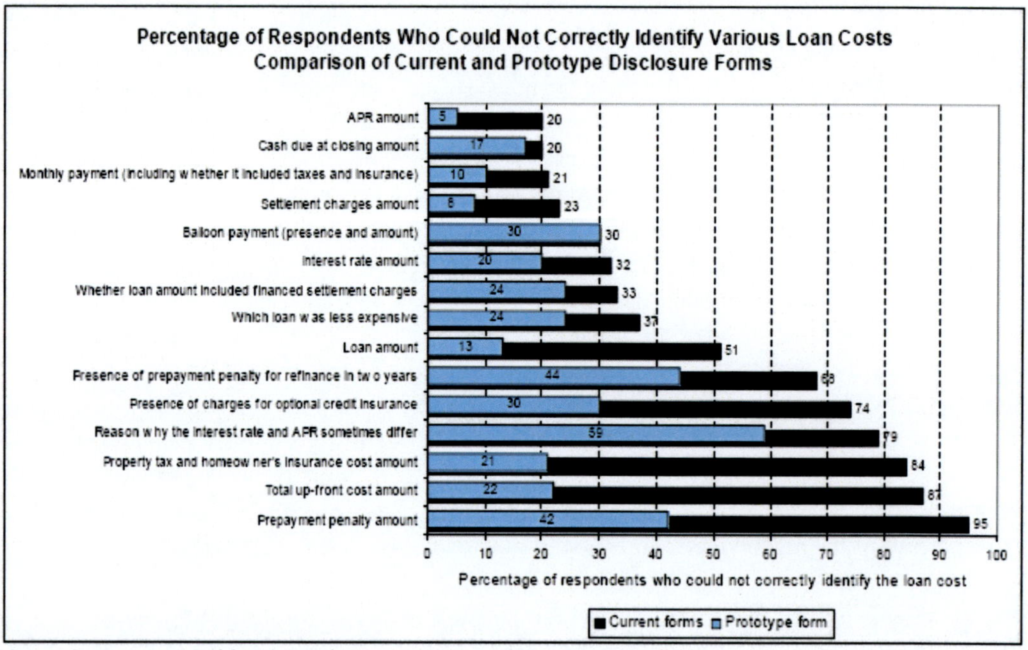

Notes: See notes to Tables 6.6 and 6.7.

Figure 6.1. Percentage of Respondents Who Could Not Correctly Identify Various Loan Costs Comparison of Current and Prototype Disclosure Forms.

Figure 6.1 compares the percentage of respondents viewing the current and prototype forms who could not correctly identify various loan costs and illustrates the improvements provided by the prototype form. As the figure and the above summary show, the prototype form provided significant improvements in consumer understanding of many loan terms, and substantial improvements in some. But significant problems remained in some areas, particularly in consumer awareness that a balloon payment, prepayment penalty, optional credit insurance charges, and financed settlement costs were included in the loan, as well as consumer understanding of the APR and how it differs from the interest rate. As discussed, below, further refinement and development of the disclosures is needed to find the best way to convey this important information to consumers.

6.2.2. Overall Loan Cost Comparison and Loan Choice Questions

Table 6.8, located at the end of this chapter, presents the percentage of current- and prototype-form respondents who provided correct answers to the 25 individual loan-cost questions. The first two test questions asked respondents about the overall cost of the loan. Respondents were given disclosure forms for two loans (labeled "Loan G" and "Loan R") and instructed to look at the information as if they were shopping for a mortgage. After they had time to examine the forms, respondents were asked to identify which of the two loans would cost them less. This was followed by a question that asked which loan they would choose if they were shopping for a mortgage.[74]

The loan costs were specified so that one loan had higher settlement costs than the other, but all other loan terms, including the interest rates, were identical. This made one loan unambiguously less expensive than the other, avoiding any trade-off between lower rates and lower up-front costs over which consumers may have different preferences.[75]

The results are shown in the first section of Table 6.8. Only one set of results are shown because, unlike the questions that follow, these questions used only one scenario with a single pair of loans.[76]

The prototype disclosure form performed significantly better than the current forms in both questions. In the loan-cost question, 63 percent of the respondents viewing the current disclosure forms correctly identified the less expensive loan, leaving more than a third of the group unable to do so. In contrast, 76 percent of the respondents viewing the prototype form correctly identified the less expensive loan, an improvement of 13 percentage points.[77] Even with the significant improvement, however, a quarter of the prototype group did not correctly identify the less expensive loan, leaving room for further improvement of the disclosures.[78]

The prototype form also performed better than the current forms, although by a smaller margin, in the follow-up question that asked which of the two loans respondents would choose if they were shopping for a mortgage. Seventy-six percent of the respondents viewing the current forms correctly chose the loan that was less expensive, compared to 84 percent of the respondents viewing the prototype form, a difference of 8 percentage points.[79] In both questions, most of the respondents not providing a correct answer provided an incorrect one rather than simply saying that they did not know or did not have enough information.[80]

6.2.3. Individual Loan-Term Questions

The remaining questions in the study asked about individual loan terms. The disclosure forms used for the overall-cost questions were removed and replaced with forms for a second pair of loans. These were used for the remainder of the test. As with the first set of loans, respondents were instructed to look at the information as if they were shopping for a mortgage. After respondents had the opportunity to examine the forms, the various individual loan-term questions were asked. Respondents could continue to examine the forms throughout the questioning. The results for each individual question are presented below, grouped by topic area.

Loan Amount

The loan amount in a mortgage may include financed settlement charges and perhaps additional financed charges for optional items such as credit insurance. Although consumers are likely to know how much money they sought from the lender to purchase a home or refinance an existing loan, they may not recognize that the loan amount has been increased to cover financed settlement and other charges. Failure to recognize that such charges have been added to the loan amount may leave some consumers unaware that they are paying substantial points and other charges for the loan.

The first three individual loan-term questions examined the ability of consumers to recognize the loan amount. Respondents first were asked to identify the loan with the lower loan amount, that is, in which loan would they be borrowing less. Respondents then were directed to one of the loans and asked to identify the size of the loan amount. They then were asked whethern that loan included money borrowed to pay for settlement costs or other up-front charges.[81]

With perhaps one exception, the current disclosure forms left substantial proportions of respondents unable to correctly answer the loan amount questions. The prototype form provided improvements in all three questions in both loan-cost scenarios, although one was not statistically significant. The prototype provided particularly large improvements when respondents were asked to identify the size of the loan amount, a question that half of the current-forms respondents failed to answer correctly.

The first question asked respondents to identify the loan with the lower loan amount. In the simple-loan scenario, 82 percent of current-forms respondents provided the correct answer, compared to 93 percent of prototype-form respondents, an improvement of 11 percentage points. Both groups performed significantly worse in the complex-loan scenario, but the improvement provided by the prototype form was larger. In this scenario, 60 percent of the current-forms respondents correctly identified the loan with the lower loan amount, compared to 81 percent of the prototype-form respondents, an improvement of 21 percentage points.[82]

The second question directed respondents to one of the loans and asked them to identify the size of the loan amount. About half of the current-forms respondents correctly identified the loan amount (50 and 48 percent in the simple- and complex-loan scenarios, respectively), leaving half unable to do so. In contrast, 86 and 87 percent of the prototype-form respondents identified the correct amount, improvements of 36 and 38 percentage points.

Much of the difference in the performance of the two disclosure groups was accounted for by the large proportions of current-forms respondents (36 and 43 percent in the simple- and complex-loan scenarios, respectively) who instead of providing the loan amount provided the "amount financed" figure shown on the TILA statement. This suggests that the TILA "amount financed" disclosure causes consumer confusion over the loan amount.[83] This confusion could result in some consumers being unaware that they are paying a large amount of points and other charges for the loan.[84]

Half of the current-forms respondents failed to correctly identify the loan amount even though the amount was disclosed at the top of the GFE.[85] This disclosure was one of the "enhanced" features of the GFE used in the study, and is included in the forms used by many lenders but is not required by the regulations governing the GFE. If a GFE had been used that merely followed the regulatory requirements, it is likely that none of the current-forms respondents would have provided the correct loan amount, because the figure is not required in either the GFE or the TILA statement.

The final loan amount question asked whether the loan included money borrowed to pay for settlement costs or other up-front charges. The loan amount included financed settlement costs in both loan scenarios, and in the complex-loan scenario, also included financed charges for optional credit insurance.

Approximately two-thirds of the current-forms respondents (65 and 70 percent in the simple- and complex-loan scenarios, respectively) recognized that settlement and other up-front charges were financed and included in the loan amount, leaving about a third of the group unaware that these charges were financed.[86] Across both loan scenarios, 21 percent of the group incorrectly said that the costs were not financed and 11 percent said that they either did not know or could not tell from the information provided.

The prototype form performed better than the current-forms, with 74 and 79 percent of the respondents in the two loan scenarios recognizing the charges were financed, improvements of about 9 percentage points in each scenario, although the difference was statistically significant only in the complex-loan scenario. About 20-25 percent of the prototype-form respondents still failed to recognize that financed charges were included in the loan amount, indicating room for further improvement of the disclosures.

The results of the loan amount questions show that the current disclosure forms fail to convey the correct loan amount to about half of the consumers using the form, and fail to alert a significant proportion of consumers that the loan amount contains financed settlement and other charges. The prototype form provided significant improvements in both areas, but room for further improvement of the disclosures remains.

Settlement Costs

Settlement costs represent the mandatory up-front charges assessed in the loan, which together with the monthly interest charges (and any optional charges), determine the overall cost of the mortgage. Consumers must be able to recognize the amount of settlement costs in order to properly evaluate the cost of the loan and to compare the costs of different loan offers. Recognizing the amount of settlement costs is particularly important when the costs are financed rather than paid in cash at closing. In these circumstances, the failure to recognize the settlement costs may lead consumers to wrongly believe they are not paying any points or other up-front charges for the loan.

Two questions in the study examined the ability of consumers to recognize settlement costs. The first asked respondents to identify the loan with the lower settlement costs. The second directed respondents to one of the loans and asked them to identify the amount of settlement costs.[87] Significant proportions of current-forms respondents were unable to correctly answer the settlement cost questions. When asked to identify which loan had lower settlement charges, 73 and 76 percent of the current-forms respondents (in the simple- and complex-loan scenarios, respectively) correctly identified the loan with the lower charges, leaving about a quarter of the respondents in each scenario unable to answer correctly.[88] The prototype form performed significantly better in both scenarios, with 85 and 94 percent of the group able to correctly identify the loan with lower charges, improvements of 12 and 18 percentage points.

Similar results were found when respondents were directed to one of the loans and asked to identify the amount of settlement costs, but some care must be taken in examining the results. In the simple-loan scenario, 77 percent of the current-forms respondents correctly identified the amount of settlement charges, leaving about a quarter of the group unable to identify these costs. In contrast, 92 percent of the prototype-form respondents correctly identified the amount of settlement charges, an improvement of 15 percentage points.

Most of the difference in the performance of the two groups is due to the significant proportion of current-forms respondents who confused settlement costs with cash due at closing. Three-quarters of the current-forms respondents who did not provide the correct settlement cost figure instead provided the amount of cash due at closing. These respondents amounted to 17 percent of the entire current-forms group.[89] Eighty-six percent of these respondents, amounting to 15 percent of the entire group, also chose the wrong loan when asked, in the previous question, to identify the loan with the lower amount of settlement costs. Interestingly, the loan they chose had higher settlement costs but less cash due at closing, providing further evidence that these respondents confused the two terms.[90]

The same confusion was not apparent among current-forms respondents in the complex-loan scenario. Ninety-two percent of the group provided the correct amount of settlement charges—15 percentage points higher than in the simple-loan scenario.[91] The better performance, however, appears to be an anomaly arising from the fact that, in the complex-loan scenario, settlement costs and cash due at closing were the same. Thus, respondents who confused the two terms still would have provided the correct answer, even though they had been looking at the wrong figure in the forms. This explanation is supported by the similarity of the two results: in the scenario in which it is possible to detect the confusion, 17 percent of current- forms respondents confused the two terms; in the scenario in which it is not possible to detect the confusion because the two terms are the same, the proportion of respondents appearing to provide the correct answer is 15 percentage points higher.

Additional evidence is provided by a comparison of the results of the two settlement cost questions in the complex-loan scenario. Although 92 percent of the current-forms provided the correct amount of settlement costs in the second question, only 76 percent correctly identified the loan with lower settlement costs in the first question—a difference of 16 percentage points. Almost all (90 percent) of the respondents who got the second question right but the first question wrong appeared to confuse the two loan terms in the first question, choosing the loan that had higher settlement costs but less cash due at closing. These respondents were able to provide the correct settlement cost figure on the follow-up question because the amount was the same as the cash due at closing.

All of these results suggest that the better performance of the current-forms group in the complex-loan scenario was due to anomalies in the loan cost specifications rather than a better understanding of the cost disclosures. The simple-loan scenario provides a better indicator of the performance of the current-forms group. These results show that about a quarter of the respondents viewing the current disclosure forms were unable to identify the amount of settlement costs, including 17 percent who confused the cash due at closing with settlement costs. This suggests that the current disclosure forms either lead to or fail to correct significant consumer confusion between these loan terms. The prototype form provided significant improvements in the understanding of settlement charges.

Charges for Optional Products and Services

Charges for additional products and services sold with the loan, such as credit-life and disability insurance, can substantially increase the cost of a mortgage. These products are often sold as optional add-ons which are not required for the loan. Consumers who fail to recognize the presence of such charges, or fail to recognize that the products are not required, but pay for them nonetheless, pay more for their loans than necessary and obtain products or services they may not have purchased if more fully informed.[92]

Three questions examined whether consumers could recognize that optional charges were included in the mortgage costs. Respondents were directed to one of the loans and asked whether there were any charges for optional products or services that were not required for the loan. Respondents who answered "yes" were then asked to identify the optional items and the amount of the optional costs.[93]

Optional charges were not present in either loan in the simple-loan scenario. Charges of $6,230 for optional credit-life and disability insurance were included in the costs of one of the loans in the complex-loan scenario. Thus, the correct answer to the initial question was "no" in the simple-loan scenario but "yes" in the complex-loan scenario.[94] Accordingly, in Table 6.8, the results for all three questions are presented for the complex-loan scenario, but the results of only the first question are presented for the simple-loan scenario.

The key issue in these questions is whether respondents in the complex-loan scenario recognized that optional charges were included in the loan costs. In response to the initial question, 57 percent of current-forms respondents recognized that optional charges were included in the loan; more than 40 percent of the group did not.[95] In contrast, 79 percent of prototype- form respondents recognized that such charges were included, an improvement of 22 percentage points.

Current-forms respondents performed significantly worse in the follow-up questions. Only 26 percent of the group correctly identified the optional items as credit insurance and only 34 percent correctly identified the amount of the charges. This left two-thirds or more of the group unable to identify the optional items and charges.[96] In contrast, 69 percent of the prototype-form group correctly identified the optional items and 78 percent correctly identified the charges, improvements of 43 and 44 percentage points.[97] These improvements, which more than doubled the proportion of respondents who recognized the optional items and charges, were some of the largest achieved by the prototype form in the study.[98]

The results of the two follow-up questions appear to more closely reflect the ability of consumers to identify optional credit insurance charges using the current disclosure forms. Fifty- five percent of the current-form respondents who correctly noted that optional charges were included in the loan (in response to the first question) failed to correctly identify the optional items in the follow-up question.[99] Nearly all of these respondents incorrectly identified some other loan item which was not optional.[100]Thus, their responses to the first question provide a misleading picture of their understanding of the optional charges in the loan.

Consumer groups have criticized the inclusion of credit insurance in mortgage loans, arguing that consumers often pay for the insurance without realizing that it is not required for the loan.[101] The FTC and other agencies have filed legal complaints and obtained orders against a number of subprime lenders, alleging that the lenders engaged in deceptive practices designed to conceal the charges or misled consumers into believing that the insurance was required for the loan.[102] The test results, which found that two-thirds or more of the consumers viewing the current forms failed to recognize that optional credit insurance was included in the loan, suggests that many subprime borrowers may have paid for credit insurance without realizing that the charges were optional.

In actual mortgage transactions, some consumers, who did not earlier recognize that charges for optional insurance were included in the loan, may become aware of the charges during the loan closing, because they may have to sign the TILA statement to indicate their agreement to purchase the insurance.[103] The failure of most consumers to recognize the charges on their own, however, raises the possibility that many may miss the disclosure at closing as they are inundated with multiple papers they are asked to quickly sign, or perhaps distracted or misled by deceptive lenders attempting to conceal the charges.

The prototype form provided substantial improvements that more than doubled the proportion of consumers who correctly identified the optional items and costs. The disclosures would allow consumers to recognize the optional charges on their own, early in the transaction, before the loan was even accepted. One-quarter or more of the respondents, however, still failed to recognize the optional charges, indicating room for further improvement of the disclosures.

The proportion of consumers who fail to recognize optional charges might be reduced further through the addition of a signature requirement to the prototype form, similar to that currently required by TILA. A signature requirement would further protect borrowers by requiring that they take an affirmative action to indicate that they wish to purchase the optional items. Requiring a signature might also reduce the possibility that lenders could overcome the disclosures through deception.[104]

Total Up-Front Charges

Total up-front charges include the sum of settlement and optional charges. These charges, along with the monthly interest payments, are the costs that borrowers are obligated to pay if they accept the loan. The up-front charges may be paid in cash at closing or added to the loan amount and financed. Either way, consumers must correctly recognize the charges in order to properly evaluate the loan offer. As noted in regard to settlement costs, recognition of up-front charges is particularly important when the charges are financed, because the lack of payments at closing may otherwise lead some consumers to wrongly believe that they are not paying points or other charges for the loan. Although information on the total amount of up-front charges is somewhat redundant if consumers already recognize the settlement and optional charges separately, examining consumer recognition of the total provides another test of how well these costs are understood.

Two questions examined respondent understanding of the amount of total up-front charges in the loans. Respondents first were asked to identify which loan had the higher total upfront charges and then were directed to one of the loans and asked to identify the amount of upfront charges.[105]

Respondents viewing the current disclosure forms produced some of the lowest levels of correct responses found in the tests. The prototype form performed substantially better, yielding some of the largest improvements. In the simple-loan scenario, only 17 percent of current-forms respondents correctly identified the loan with higher up-front costs and only 21 percent correctly identified the amount of up-front costs. In contrast, 74 and 79 percent of prototype-form respondents were able to do so, improvements of 57 and 59 percentage points. These differences were the two largest found for any question in the simple-loan scenario.

Similar results were found for the complex loan. Only 34 percent of current-forms respondents correctly identified which of the two loans had higher up-front costs and only five percent correctly identified the amount of up-front costs, compared to 86 and 78 percent of prototype-form respondents, improvements of 53 and 72 percentage points. These differences were two of the three largest found for any question in the complex-loan scenario.

The large differences between the forms may be partly due to the question wording. The term "up-front charges" was used explicitly in the prototype form but not in the current forms. This may have left some current-forms respondents unsure of what was being asked.

The most common figure provided by current-forms respondents was the amount of cash-due-at-closing rather than the amount of up-front charges (62 and 45 percent in the simple- and complex-loan scenarios, respectively). This may indicate confusion about what was being asked, but it also may indicate that many consumers confused up-front charges with cash due at closing. The latter confusion would be consistent with results found in the settlement cost questions, discussed above, and the cash-due-at-closing questions, discussed below. Confusion of these loan terms could be particularly harmful to consumers in which all of the up-front charges are financed and no cash is due at closing (as in the complex-loan scenario), if the confusion leads them to believe that they are not paying any points or other up-front charges for the loan.

Thirty-three percent of current-forms respondents in the complex-loan scenario incorrectly provided the amount of settlement charges rather than the sum of settlement and optional charges. This is consistent with results from the optional-charges questions, discussed above, that found a large proportion of current-forms respondents did not recognize the optional charges included in the loan. This type of mistake also could be particularly harmful to consumers with loans such as the one in the complex scenario, because the omitted optional charges nearly doubled the total amount of up-front charges assessed in the loan.

Although the question wording may have had some effect on the responses to this set of questions, the results still appear to indicate that consumers have significant problems recognizing total up-front charges in the current disclosure forms, even if the magnitude of the problem is not quite as large as found here. The prototype form produced substantial improvements in consumer recognition of the charges. Even with the substantial improvements, however, about a fifth of the prototype group still failed to identify the amount of total up-front charges, indicating room for further improvement.

Interest Rate

The ability to correctly recognize the interest rate of a loan is obviously important to consumer borrowing decisions. The interest rate, along with any up-front charges, determines the costs consumers pay for the loan. Comparison of the interest rates and up-front charges of different loan offers is fundamental in determining which loan is least expensive and which best fits the borrower's needs.[106] Failure to recognize the interest rate can only lead to poor borrowing decisions.

Two questions examined respondents' ability to identify the interest rate. As in earlier series of questions, respondents first were asked to identify which of the two loans had the lower interest rate and then were directed to one of the loans and asked to identify the interest rate amount.[107]

The first interest rate question yielded the highest level of correct responses achieved by the current-forms group in any question in the study, and was among the highest achieved (along with the APR questions that follow) by the prototype-form group. The loan with the lower interest rate was correctly identified by 96 and 95 percent of the current-forms group in the simple- and complex-loans, respectively, and by 97 and 96 percent of the prototype-form group.[108]

The high level of accuracy seems to suggest that the disclosure forms accurately convey the interest rate to almost all consumers. The responses to the next question, however, in which respondents were directed to one of the loans and asked to identify the amount of the interest rate, show that such a conclusion is not warranted.

Although nearly all of the current-forms respondents correctly identified the loan with the lower interest rate, only about two-thirds of the group (65 and 70 percent in the simple and complex-loan scenarios, respectively) correctly identified the interest rate amount in the follow- up question. This left about a third of the group unable to provide the correct rate. Prototype- form respondents performed significantly better. In both scenarios, 80 percent of the prototype group correctly identified the interest rate, improvements of 14 and 10 percentage points.

Twenty percent of the group, however, was unable to provide the correct rate.

Nearly all of the respondents who did not correctly identify the interest rate confused the interest rate with the APR. Thirty and 28 percent of current-forms respondents in the simple and complex loans, respectively, and 19 and 18 percent of prototype-form respondents, incorrectly provided the APR amount rather than the interest rate amount. These respondents performed better on the first question, which asked them to identify which loan had the lower interest rate, only because the same loan had both the lower interest rate and the lower APR. Any consumer confusion of the two rates would not have been detected.

The better performance of the prototype form may be due to the juxtaposition of the two rates in the form. Placing the two figures in close proximity may more clearly convey that the rates are not the same and help consumers distinguish the two. The current TILA form, in contrast, contains a very prominent disclosure of the APR but does not mention the interest rate. The regulatory requirements for the GFE do not require the disclosure of either, although the enhanced version used in the study disclosed the interest rate. If the minimum-regulatory version of the GFE had been used, the confusion found in the current-forms group likely would have been much greater, because the interest rate would not have appeared anywhere in the forms.

The results of the study indicate significant consumer confusion about interest rates, APRs, and the difference between the two, particularly with the current disclosure forms. This confusion is troubling given the centrality of these figures to consumer borrowing decisions, their prevalence in advertising, and the more than three decades of consumer experience with required APR disclosures. The prototype form performed significantly better than the current forms but still left 20 percent of respondents who could not correctly identify the interest rate.

Annual Percentage Rate (APR)

The APR combines the ongoing interest payments with the up-front points and other finance charges to provide a measure of the overall cost of a loan. The rate is useful for comparing the costs of loans with different combinations of interest rates and points.[109] The ability to recognize the APR and use it to compare different loan offers is important for consumer borrowing decisions. Consumers who fail to understand the APR or confuse it with the interest rate may choose loans that are inappropriate for their borrowing circumstances or more costly than other alternatives.

Three questions examined the ability of consumers to recognize and understand APRs. As in the questions about the interest rate and other loan terms, the first asked respondents to identify which loan had the lower APR and the second directed them to one of the loans and asked them to identify the APR amount. The third question asked respondents to explain why the APR is sometimes higher than a loan's interest rate.[110]

As in the interest rate questions, the percentage of respondents who were able to correctly identify the loan with the lower APR was among the highest found for any question in the study. Ninety-two percent of the current-forms respondents in both loan scenarios, and 96 and 95 percent of the prototype-form respondents (in the simple- and complex-loan scenarios, respectively) identified the correct loan.[111]

As also in the interest rate questions, the percentage of current-forms respondents who provided the correct answer declined when they were directed to one of the loans and asked to identify the APR amount. Although 92 percent of the group correctly identified the loan with the lower APR, only 79 and 80 percent correctly identified the APR amount (in simple and complex loan scenarios, respectively).[112] This left about 20 percent of the current-forms group unable to identify correctly the APR. In contrast, 95 and 96 percent of the prototype-form group correctly identified the APR, an improvement of 16 percentage points in both scenarios.[113]

The current-forms result is largely due to the significant proportion of current-forms respondents, about 16–17 percent in each scenario, who incorrectly provided the interest rate rather than the APR. This confusion of the interest rate with the APR was not apparent when respondents were asked to identify the loan with the lower APR because the same loan had both the lower APR and the lower interest rate.

Consumer confusion over interest rates and APRs is shown further in the third question, which asked respondents why the APR of a loan is sometimes higher than its interest rate. The correct answer is that the APR includes prepaid and other finance charges as well as interest payments in its calculation, whereas the interest rate includes only the interest payments. Respondents were counted as providing the correct answer if they said anything indicating that the APR included additional costs, regardless of how they characterized the additional costs.[114]

Even with this broad criteria, only a little more than a fifth of the current-forms respondents were able to provide a correct explanation of why the APR is sometimes higher than the interest rate. The prototype form provided significant improvement, approximately doubling the percentage of respondents providing a correct answer, but still left more than half of the group unable to explain the difference between the two rates.[115]

Together, the results of the interest rate and APR questions indicate substantial consumer confusion about the meaning of the APR and how it differs from the interest rate. Such confusion may impact consumer understanding of mortgage costs and distort comparison shopping for the best terms. Although the results did not show distortions in the loan-to-loan comparisons, that was only because the same loan had both the lower interest rate and the lower APR, allowing respondents who confused the two rates to still obtain the correct answer. The result likely would have been different if the loan with the lower interest rate had the higher APR. Overall, the results indicate that much work is needed to educate consumers on the meaning of the APR and its relation to the interest rate.

Cash Due at Closing

The cash paid at closing is the first payment that borrowers make on the loan (assuming that the up-front charges are not financed and rolled into the loan amount), and often determines, along with the monthly payment amounts, whether borrowers can afford the loan. Correctly recognizing the amount of cash due at closing is important for borrowers considering a loan offer or comparing the offers of different lenders. Recognizing the amount of cash due at closing, and distinguishing it from the amount of up-front charges, also is important to prevent consumer misunderstandings when all or part of the up-front charges are financed.

Two questions examined the ability of consumers to recognize the amount of cash due at closing. The first asked respondents to identify which loan required them to pay less cash at closing. The second directed respondents to one of the loans and asked them to identify the amount of cash required at closing.[116]

Respondents in both disclosure-form groups performed relatively well in the simple-loan scenario. Eighty-eight and 85 percent of the respondents in the current- and prototype-form groups, respectively, correctly identified which loan required less cash due at closing. When directed to one of the loans, 84 and 89 percent of the two groups correctly identified the amount of cash due.[117]

Both groups performed significantly worse in the complex-loan scenario. Seventy-seven and 69 percent of the current- and prototype-form groups, respectively, correctly identified which loan required less cash due at closing, and 75 and 78 percent correctly identified the amount of cash due.[118] About one-quarter of the respondents in both groups were unable to identify the amount of cash due at closing.

The disclosure of the amount of funds needed at closing was a feature of the enhanced GFE used in the study but is not required by the regulations that govern the form. If a GFE had been used that merely complied with the regulations, the performance of the current-forms group would have been much worse in both scenarios, because the amount of cash due at closing would not have appeared anywhere in the forms.

The greater difficulty identifying the amount of cash due at closing in the complex scenario may have been related to the fact that, in this scenario, all settlement and up-front charges were financed, leaving zero cash due at closing and a "zero" dollar amount disclosed.[119] Most of the complex-loan respondents who did not correctly identify the amount of cash due at closing (80 and 96 percent in the current and prototype groups, respectively) instead provided an amount related to the settlement and other up-front charges, even though these charges were financed.[120] This is consistent with other results, above, that show significant consumer confusion between settlement (and other up-front charges) and the amount of cash due at closing, that is, between up-front charges and up-front payments. Further refinement of the disclosures is needed to reduce the remaining confusion.

Monthly Payment and Escrow

The monthly payment amount is central to the borrowing decision of many consumers obtaining a mortgage. Consumers must assess whether the payment is affordable given their income and expenses, and may compare the payments required in different loan offers to find the loan that best fits their needs. Consumers refinancing a mortgage also may compare the payment to the one in their current loan to assess whether a refinancing is worthwhile.

When assessing and comparing monthly payments, consumers must understand what the payment includes. The monthly payment in many loans includes payments for property taxes and homeowner's insurance, while the monthly payment in other loans may include only principal and interest payments, leaving taxes and insurance to be paid separately by the borrower. Some lenders may quote payments that include property taxes and homeowner's insurance, while others may quote payments that include only principal and interest. Unscrupulous lenders have made misleading comparisons of consumers' current monthly payments, including taxes and insurance, with refinanced payments that excluded these items, in an effort to convince consumers that refinancing would reduce their monthly expenses.[121] Failure to correctly recognize the monthly payment amount and understand what it includes may lead some consumers to inadvertently choose loans with higher payments.

Several questions examined whether consumers could correctly identify the monthly loan payments and recognize whether the payments included taxes and insurance. Respondents first were asked to identify which loan had the lower monthly payment, then were directed to one of the loans and asked to identify the amount of the monthly payment. They then were asked whether that monthly payment amount included payments for property taxes and homeowners insurance, or whether the borrower would have to pay for those separately. Respondents who said that they would have to pay for those items separately were asked how much they would have to pay each month.[122]

In the simple-loan scenario, the monthly payment for both loans included payments for property taxes and homeowner's insurance. In the complex-loan scenario, the monthly payment for one of the loans did not include payments for taxes and insurance.

In the current forms, the TILA statement does not require that the disclosed monthly payment amount include taxes and insurance, even when taxes and insurance are included in the monthly payment to the lender. Disclosure of the monthly payment amount, in any form, is not required in the GFE. The enhanced version of the GFE used in the study, however, disclosed the total monthly payment paid to the lender, including any taxes and insurance, and provided an itemization that detailed the amounts of principal and interest, taxes, and insurance. Although not required by the regulations governing the GFE, this type of disclosure is included in the forms used by many lenders. The prototype form also disclosed the total amount paid to the lender, including any payments for taxes and insurance, and provided an itemization. In addition, the prototype included a separate disclosure that stated whether the monthly payment included taxes and insurance, and if it did not, what additional monthly costs would be incurred by the borrower for these items.

Drafting question wording that clearly signaled that respondents should examine the full monthly payment, rather than only the payment made to the lender, was difficult without explicitly stating this and seemingly giving away the answer and invalidating the test. In the end, the wording remained somewhat ambiguous, allowing different respondents to possibly interpret the questions differently. The correct responses to the questions differed depending on whether the respondent interpreted the questions as asking about the total monthly payment or the payment to the lender. One can combine several questions, however, to test whether the pattern of responses indicates a correct understanding of the payments.

The importance of the combined analysis is evident in the results in the complex-scenario, where the payment to the lender did not include payments for taxes and insurance. When asked to identify the monthly payment amount, nearly all of the respondents in both disclosure groups (98 and 95 percent in the current- and prototype-forms groups, respectively) provided the amount of the principal and interest payment only, which corresponded to the payment to the lender that was disclosed in both disclosure forms. In response to the next question, however, the large majority of these respondents correctly recognized that taxes and insurance were not included and would be paid separately by the borrower (84 and 88 percent in the current and prototype groups, respectively). These respondents were classified as providing a correct response.

A few respondents in each group provided a monthly payment amount that included principal, interest, taxes, and insurance, but most of these also said that the taxes and insurance would be paid separately by the borrower. These respondents also were classified as providing a correct response, because they understood both the total payment amount and the obligation to pay the taxes and insurance separately.

Overall, 84 and 87 percent of the respondents in the two groups, respectively, provided responses that indicated a correct understanding of the monthly payment amount. Although the prototype form performed slightly better than the current forms, the difference was small and not statistically significant.

A much larger difference between the forms, with the prototype group performing substantially better, was found when respondents who had recognized that taxes and insurance had to paid separately were asked to identify the amount they would have to pay each month for those items. Seventeen percent of the current-forms respondents correctly identified these costs, compared to 79 percent of the prototype-form respondents, a difference of 62 percentage points.[123]

The large difference between the groups is not surprising because the tax and insurance costs did not appear in the current forms for this loan.[124] The current-forms respondents who provided a correct answer may have obtained the figures either from the form for the other loan in the pair they were examining (which had the same tax and insurance costs) or from inappropriately overseeing the pre-coded responses listed on the interviewer's computer screen. Either explanation implies that the 62 percentage points understates the true difference between the disclosure groups.

The prototype form also performed significantly better than the current forms in the simple-loan scenario. Here, the monthly payments for both loans included payments for taxes and insurance. Respondents were counted as correct if they either provided the correct total payment, including taxes and insurance, and said that the payment included taxes and insurance, or if they provided the correct principal and interest portion of the payment and said that it did not include taxes and insurance. By this criteria, 74 percent of current-forms respondents correctly understood the monthly payment amount, leaving about a quarter of the group unable to do so. In contrast, 93 percent of prototype-form respondents correctly identified the monthly payment, an improvement of 19 percentage points.[125]

The results from one of the monthly payments questions is not presented in Table 6.8 or included in the aggregate analysis presented earlier in this chapter. This is the first question in the sequence, which asked respondents to identify which of the two loans had the lower monthly payment. These results are excluded because it is not clear whether they present an accurate picture of respondent understanding or are an unintended artifact of the loan costs specified in the test forms. The large majority of respondents in both the current- and prototype-form groups (90 and 94 percent, respectively) correctly identified the loan with the lower monthly payment in the simple-loan scenario, but the large majority in both groups (81 and 92 percent, respectively) incorrectly selected the loan with the higher payment in the complex-loan scenario. The reason for this is not clear. One could conclude that the complex-loan respondents were unaware that one loan included taxes and insurance in the payment and the other loan did not and, therefore, wrongly compared "apples and oranges" (or more precisely, compared principal, interest, taxes, and insurance with principal and interest). But this explanation is inconsistent with the results, presented above, that find that most respondents correctly understood that taxes and insurance were not included in the payment for one of the loans.

An alternative explanation is that the incorrect responses may have been due to the presence of a large balloon payment in the loan that had the lower regular monthly payment. Respondents may have focused on the large balloon payment and concluded that the other loan had the "lower monthly payment," even though its regular monthly payment was higher. If this explanation were correct, the results would be an artifact of the cost specifications rather than an indication of consumer misunderstanding. On the other hand, it is possible that respondents did not understand the monthly payment amount and it was only the prompting of the later question that made them aware that the taxes and insurance were not included.

Because there is no conclusive way, at this point, to determine which of these explanations is correct, the proper interpretation of the results is uncertain, and the results are omitted from Table 6.8 and the aggregated analysis.

In the end, this sequence of questions provides somewhat mixed results. The results show that the large majority of respondents in both disclosure groups, when asked about the monthly payment of one of the loans, correctly understood the amount of the payment and whether it included property taxes and homeowner's insurance. However, when asked to compare the monthly payments of two loans, one of which did not include taxes and insurance, the large majority of both groups incorrectly identified the loan with the higher payment as having the lower payment. It is not clear if these responses were due to the exclusion of taxes and insurance in this loan, which made the payment appear lower, or to the presence of a large payment amounts is needed to fully clarify these issues.

Balloon Payment

Loans with a balloon payment contain a final payment that is substantially larger than the regular monthly payment. In some loans, where the regular monthly payments cover only the interest on the loan, the balloon may equal the entire original loan principal. Consumers facing a balloon payment must have sufficient cash to pay the balloon, which may be unlikely in most cases; refinance with a new loan, perhaps at less favorable terms if interest rates have risen or their credit rating has fallen; or face default, and the possible loss of their homes, if they cannot obtain or qualify for refinancing. Failure to recognize that a loan contains a balloon payment may cause substantial harm to a borrower's finances when it becomes due.[126]

Several questions examined the ability of consumers to recognize whether a loan contained a balloon payment. The questions did not use the phrase "balloon payment" but instead asked respondents to compare the amount of the last payment to the other monthly payments. Because there was some uncertainty over whether respondents would view the "last payment" as the balloon or the last regular monthly payment, the question was asked in two ways. First, respondents were directed to one of the loans and asked whether the last payment would be the same as the other monthly payments. If the respondent said that the last payment would be different, they were asked to identify the amount of the last payment. All respondents then were asked if they would still owe anything on the loan after making the last payment. Respondents who answered "yes" were asked how much they would still owe.[127]

The loan in the simple-loan scenario did not contain a balloon. The loan in the complex-loan scenario contained a large balloon payment equal to the original loan principal plus the interest payment for the final month. Respondents were counted as correctly recognizing the balloon payment if they provided the balloon amount in response to either the question asking for the amount of the last payment or the question asking how much they would still owe after the last payment.[128]

In the complex-loan scenario, 70 percent of the respondents in both disclosure groups correctly recognized that the loan contained a large balloon payment.129 This left 30 percent of the respondents in both groups not recognizing that the last loan payment would be substantially higher than the regular monthly payment. The prototype form did not provide any improvement over the current forms' performance.[130]

The substantial proportion of respondents who were unaware of the balloon payment is somewhat surprising given the prominence of the payment schedule disclosure in both the current and prototype forms, and the explicit use of the term "balloon payment" and the explanation "[you] will have to pay this amount at the end of the 10 year loan term" in the prototype.[131] The results indicate the need for further development of disclosures that might more effectively convey the presence of a balloon payment to consumers.

Prepayment Penalty

Prepayment penalties are common in the subprime mortgage market. The penalties impose costs on consumers who refinance their loans within a specified period early in the loan term. The penalties may make refinancing prohibitively expensive for consumers who do not have sufficient cash on hand.

Lenders use prepayment penalties to deter prepayments and to ensure that their expenses are recouped if borrowers refinance early and end ongoing interest payments. Similar loans without a prepayment penalty, if made to borrowers with similar credit risks, may contain higher interest rates or higher up-front charges to offset the higher risk of prepayment losses. Thus, loans with prepayment penalties may be more affordable if a borrower stays in the loan, but more costly if the borrower wishes to refinance to take advantage of lower interest rates or an improved credit rating.

Consumers who fail to recognize the presence of a prepayment penalty may obtain loans that are inappropriate for their circumstances, and may be subject to unpleasant surprises if they attempt to refinance the loan to obtain a better interest rate. Unscrupulous lenders may attempt to misrepresent that a loan does not contain a prepayment penalty in order to deceive borrowers into believing that they could easily refinance if they later find better terms elsewhere.[132]

The last three questions in the study directed respondents to one of the loans and examined their ability to recognize the presence and amount of prepayment penalties in the loan. Two questions asked whether they would have to pay additional fees, on top of paying off the remaining loan balance, if they wanted to refinance the mortgage with a different lender to get a better interest rate.[133] One of the questions asked about refinancing two years after taking out the loan and the other about refinancing after six years. Respondents who correctly answered that additional fees would be required for a refinancing two years after taking out the loan were asked to identify how much they would have to pay in additional fees.[134]

In the complex-loan scenario, the loan contained a substantial prepayment penalty, equal to four percent of the prepaid amount, during the first five years of the loan. In the simple-loan scenario, the loan did not contain a prepayment penalty.

In the complex-loan scenario, 32 percent of the respondents viewing the current disclosure forms recognized that they would have to pay additional fees on top of the outstanding loan balance if two years after taking out the loan they wanted to refinance with a different lender. Respondents viewing the prototype form performed significantly better, with 56 percent of the group recognizing that they would have to pay a penalty, an improvement of 24 percentage points. Even with the large improvement, however, nearly half of the prototype-form group still failed to recognize the presence of the penalty.

The difference between the two disclosure groups is eliminated if, in addition to counting as correct responses stating that the borrower would have to pay additional fees, one also counted as correct responses stating that the borrower may have to pay such fees. Under this criteria, an identical 65 percent of the respondents in both groups recognized at least the possibility of having to pay a prepayment penalty.

The "may" responses reflect the language of the TILA statement, which has only two check-box disclosures for the prepayment penalty, one to indicate that borrowers "may" have to pay a prepayment penalty and one to indicate that they "will not."[135] The "may" language is used in the TILA statement even when it is certain that a prepayment penalty will be assessed. Although the TILA disclosure alerts consumers of the possibility that a penalty may be assessed, it does not clarify whether, or under what conditions, this will occur. In the loan specified in the study, a borrower refinancing two years after taking out the loan would unambiguously have to pay a substantial prepayment penalty. Thus, the narrower definition of correct responses—only those that said that additional fees "would" have to paid—is more appropriate and reflective of what a borrower should know about the loan. The less informative wording is a significant shortcoming of the current disclosures.

Further illustration of the limitations of the current disclosure is found when respondents were asked about refinancing the loan after six years. The prepayment penalty specified in the test loan was applicable only during the first five years, so no additional fees over the loan balance would be assessed for a refinancing in the sixth year. But only 30 percent of the respondents in the current-forms group recognized this, undoubtably because the current TILA disclosure says only that the borrower "may" have to pay a penalty and does not provide any further detail. Thirty percent of current-forms respondents incorrectly said that they would have to pay additional fees, and another 25 percent said that they may have to pay such fees. In contrast, 71 percent of the respondents in the prototype-form group correctly recognized that they would have to pay only the remaining loan balance to refinance after six years, an improvement of 40 percentage points over the current-forms result. As in the previous question, however, this still left a sizeable proportion (30 percent) of the prototype group unable to correctly recognize

The key finding is not affected by the different possible classifications of correct responses. Even if one counts as correct responses indicating that a penalty "may" have to be paid, which in complex-loan scenario essentially doubles the percentage of current-forms respondents counted as providing a correct answer, the results still show that 35 percent of the respondents in both disclosure groups failed to recognize even the possibility of a prepayment penalty, even though one was certain in the first five years of the loan.[136]

A large difference between the disclosure forms is found in the follow-up question that asked respondents to identify the amount of additional fees they would have to pay if the loan was refinanced after two years. Only 5 percent of current-forms respondents were able to provide the correct amount, compared to 59 percent of prototype-form respondents, a margin of 53 percentage points.[137] The large difference is not surprising given that the current forms do not disclose any information on the amount of the prepayment penalty.[138]

Although the prototype form provided substantial improvements over the current forms, 41 percent of prototype-form respondents still did not correctly identify the amount of the prepayment penalty. Eighty-five percent of these were respondents who answered the initial question incorrectly, not even recognizing that additional fees would be imposed. Nearly 90 percent of the prototype respondents who answered the initial question correctly, recognizing that additional fees would be imposed, correctly identified the amount of the fees in the follow-up question.

Respondent confusion about the presence of a prepayment penalty also was evident in the simple-loan scenario. Seventy and 65 percent of the current- and prototype-form respondents, respectively, correctly recognized that they would need to only pay off their loan balance if they wanted to refinance with another lender after two years.[139] About a third of the respondents in both groups failed to recognize that the loan did not contain a prepayment penalty.[140] Identical results were obtained when respondents were asked about refinancing after six years. This is somewhat surprising given that for these loans the current forms clearly states: "Prepayment: If you pay off early you will not have to pay a penalty;" and the prototype form states: "Prepayment penalty: None."

Overall, the results of the prepayment penalty questions indicate that the current disclosure forms fail to convey important information about prepayment penalties. This is due in large part to the lack of specificity in the current disclosures, which at most say that the borrower "may" have to pay a prepayment penalty, even if the assessment of a prepayment penalty is certain. The prototype form provided substantial improvements. More than 40 percent of prototype-form respondents, however, still could did not recognize that a penalty would be assessed, indicating the need for further refinement of the disclosures.

6.2.4. Comparison of Prime and Subprime Borrowers

As discussed earlier in this chapter in the analysis of the aggregate results, both prime and subprime borrowers had significant difficulty recognizing and identifying key loan costs when viewing current disclosure forms, and both groups benefitted significantly from the improved disclosures. Subprime borrowers were less likely than prime borrowers to accurately recognize and identify mortgage costs, but the difference was small. Similar results are found when the performance of prime and subprime borrowers is compared in the various individual loan-term questions.

The percentage of prime and subprime borrowers correctly answering each question is presented in columns 7–9 of Table 6.9.[141] As can be seen in the table, prime borrowers perform better than subprime borrowers in most of the questions, but the differences are almost always small and, with only two exceptions, not statistically significant.

The table also shows that the improvements achieved by the prototype form were similar for both prime and subprime borrowers. Columns 1–3 present the percentages of prime borrowers in the current- and prototype-forms groups that provided the correct answer in each question, and the difference between the two forms. Columns 4–6 present the same results for subprime borrowers. Examination of the results shows that in the 23 questions in which the prototype form performed better than the current forms, prime borrowers obtained a larger percentage point improvement in 11 of the questions and subprime borrowers obtained a larger improvement in 12 of the questions, virtually an even split.

As also noted above in the discussion of the aggregate results, these comparisons of prime and subprime borrowers hold constant the complexity of the loans. The results of the study also show that both types of borrowers had more difficulty understanding the terms of more complex loans, and improved disclosures had a greater beneficial impact with the complex loans. If loans in the subprime market tend to have more complex features than loans in the prime market, borrowers in the subprime market may have greater difficulty understanding their loan terms than borrowers in the prime market, and improved disclosures may provide a greater beneficial impact to borrowers in the subprime market.

Table 6.8. Performance of the Current and Prototype Disclosure Forms

Percentage of respondents giving the correct response, by loan cost scenario and disclosure form version

Question(N)	Both loan scenarios			Simple purchase loan			Complex refinance loan		
	(1) Current forms (411)	(2) Prototype form (408)	(3) Difference	(4) Current forms (205)	(5) Prototype form (201)	(6) Difference	(7) Current forms (206)	(8) Prototype form (207)	(9) Difference
Overall loan-cost comparison[1]									
Lower cost loan	62.8%	75.7%	13.0**	---	---	---	---	---	---
Loan choice	76.4	84.3	7.9**	---	---	---	---	---	---
Individual loan-term questions									
Loan amount									
Loan with lower loan amount	71.3	86.8	15.5**	82.4%	93.0%	10.6**	60.2%	80.7%	20.5**
Loan amount	48.9	86.3	37.4**	49.8	86.1	36.3**	48.1	86.5	38.4**
Are settlement costs financed	67.4	76.5	9.1**	64.9	73.6	8.8	69.9	79.2	9.3*
Settlement costs									
Lower settlement cost loan	74.7	89.5	14.8**	73.2	85.1	11.9**	76.2	93.7	17.5**
Settlement cost amount	84.7	89.7	5.0*	77.1	92.0	15.0**	92.2	87.4	– 4.8

Table 6.8. (Continued)

Percentage of respondents giving the correct response, by loan cost scenario and disclosure form version

	Both Loan Scenarios			Simple Purchase Loan			Complex Refinance Loan		
Response (N)	(1) Current forms (411)	(2) Prototype form (408)	(3) Difference	(4) Current forms (205)	(5) Prototype form (201)	(6) Difference	(7) Current forms (206)	(8) Prototype form (207)	(9) Difference
Optional costs									
Any charges for optional items	52.1%	82.8%	30.8**	47.3%	86.6%	39.3**	56.8%	79.2%	22.4**
What items are optional	n/a	n/a	n/a	n/a	n/a	n/a	25.7	69.1	43.4**
Optional item cost amount	n/a	n/a	n/a	n/a	n/a	n/a	34.0	77.8	43.8**
Total up-front charges									
Higher total up-front cost loan	25.3	80.1	54.8**	17.1	74.1	57.1**	33.5	86.0	52.5**
Total up-front charge amount	12.9	78.4	65.5**	20.5	79.1	58.6**	5.3	77.8	72.4**
Interest rate									
Lower interest rate loan	95.1	96.1	0.9	95.6	96.5	0.9	94.7	95.7	1.0
Interest rate amount	67.6	79.9	12.2**	65.4	79.6	14.2**	69.9	80.2	10.3*

Percentage of respondents giving the correct response, by loan cost scenario and disclosure form version

	Both Loan Scenarios			Simple Purchase Loan			Complex Refinance Loan		
Response	(1) Current forms	(2) Prototype form	(3) Difference	(4) Current forms	(5) Prototype form	(6) Difference	(7) Current forms	(8) Prototype form	(9) Difference
(N)	(411)	(408)		(205)	(201)		(206)	(207)	
APR									
Lower APR loan	92.2%	95.3%	3.1	92.2%	96.0%	3.8	92.2%	94.7%	2.5
APR amount	79.6	95.1	15.5**	79.0	94.5	15.5**	80.1	95.7	15.6**
Why APR/int rate difference	21.1	42.2	21.0**	20.5	43.8	23.3**	21.8	40.6	18.7**
Cash at closing									
Less cash at closing loan	82.2	76.7	– 5.5*	87.8	85.1	– 2.7	76.7	68.6	– 8.1
Cash at closing amount	79.6	83.3	3.8	83.9	89.1	5.2	75.2	77.8	2.5
Monthly payment and escrow									
Monthly payment amount and inclusion/exclusion of escrow[2]	78.6	89.7	11.1**	73.7	93.0	19.4**	83.5	86.5	3.0
Tax and insurance cost amount	n/a	n/a	n/a	n/a	n/a	n/a	16.5	78.7	62.2**

Table 6.8. (Continued)

Percentage of respondents giving the correct response, by loan cost scenario and disclosure form version

	Both Loan Scenarios			Simple Purchase Loan			Complex Refinance Loan		
Response (N)	(1) Current forms (411)	(2) Prototype form (408)	(3) Difference	(4) Current forms (205)	(5) Prototype form (201)	(6) Difference	(7) Current forms (206)	(8) Prototype form (207)	(9) Difference
	74.0%	71.6%	– 2.4	78.0%	73.1%	– 4.9	69.9%	70.0%	0.1
Balloon payment									
Balloon presence and amount[2]									
Prepayment penalty									
Any prepay penalty at year 2	50.9	60.3	9.4**	69.8	65.2	– 4.6	32.0	55.6	23.5**
Any prepay penalty at year 6	49.9	67.9	18.0**	69.8	65.2	– 4.6	30.1	70.5	40.4**
Prepayment penalty amount	n/a	n/a	n/a	n/a	n/a	n/a	5.3	58.5	53.1**

Notes: Figures in parentheses are the number of respondents in the indicated group. Asterisks indicate statistically significant differences in the proportions of current and prototype form respondents giving the correct response. Two-tailed t-tests were used to test the differences. * indicates significant at the five percent level and ** indicates significant at the one percent level.

[1] The same disclosure forms were used for all respondents for the two overall loan-cost comparison questions. The loan costs in these forms differed from the costs in the simple- and complex-loan scenarios that were used in the individual loan-term questions that followed.

[2] The results for these loan costs reflect the results of several questions that were combined and analyzed jointly. *See* Section 4.5 of the Consumer Testing Methodology chapter and relevant parts of Section 6.2.3 of the Consumer Testing Results chapter.

Table 6.9. Performance of Prime and Subprime Borrowers

Percentage of respondents giving the correct response, by loan cost scenario and borrower type

Response	Prime Borrowers			Subprime Borrowers			Both Disclosure Forms		
	(1) Current forms	(2) Prototype form	(3) Difference	(4) Current forms	(5) Prototype form	(6) Difference	(7) Prime Borrowers	(8) Subprime Borrowers	(9) Difference
(N)	(204)	(211)		(207)	(197)		(415)	(404)	
Overall loan cost comparison									
Lower cost loan	66.2%	76.3%	10.1*	59.4%	75.1%	15.7**	71.3%	67.1%	– 4.2
Loan choice	81.9	87.2	5.3	71.0	81.2	10.2*	84.6	76.0	– 8.6**
Loan amount									
Loan with lower loan amount	73.5	88.2	14.6**	69.1	85.3	16.2**	81.0	77.0	– 4.0
Loan amount	50.0	86.3	36.3**	47.8	86.3	38.5**	68.4	66.6	– 1.8
Are settlement costs financed	71.6	75.8	4.3	63.3	77.2	13.9**	73.7	70.0	– 3.7
Settlement costs									
Lower settlement cost loan	74.5	92.9	18.4**	74.9	85.8	10.9**	83.9	80.2	– 3.7
Settlement cost amount	84.8	90.5	5.7	84.5	88.9	4.3	87.7	86.6	– 1.1

Table 6.9. (Continued)

Percentage of respondents giving the correct response, by loan cost scenario and borrower type

	Prime Borrowers			Subprime Borrowers			Both Disclosure Forms		
Response (N)	(1) Current forms (204)	(2) Prototype form (211)	(3) Difference	(4) Current forms (207)	(5) Prototype form (197)	(6) Difference	(7) Prime Borrow (415)	(8) Subprime Borrowers (404)	(9) Difference
Optional costs									
Any charges for optional items	51.0%	83.4%	32.4**	53.1%	82.2%	29.1**	67.5%	67.3%	– 0.1
What items optional[1]	26.9	73.4	46.5**	24.5	64.3	39.8**	50.7	44.0	– 6.7
Optional item cost amount[1]	31.7	79.8	48.1**	36.3	75.5	39.2**	56.3	55.6	– 0.8
Total up-front charges									
Higher total up-front cost loan	29.4	81.5	52.1**	21.3	78.7	57.4**	55.9	49.3	– 6.6
Total up-front charges amount	12.3	74.9	62.6**	13.5	82.2	68.7**	44.1	47.0	2.9
Interest rate									
Lower interest rate loan	97.1	97.6	0.6	93.2	94.4	1.2	97.3	93.8	– 3.5*
Interest rate amount	71.1	81.1	10.0*	64.3	78.7	14.4**	76.1	71.3	– 4.9

Percentage of respondents giving the correct response, by loan cost scenario and borrower type

	Prime Borrowers			Subprime Borrowers			Both Disclosure Forms		
Response (N)	(1) Current forms (204)	(2) Prototype form (211)	(3) Difference	(4) Current forms (207)	(5) Prototype form (197)	(6) Difference	(7) Prime Borrowers (415)	(8) Subprime Borrowers (404)	(9) Difference
APR									
Lower APR loan	90.7%	95.3%	4.6	93.7%	95.4%	1.7	93.0%	94.6%	1.5
APR amount	80.9	95.3	14.4**	78.3	94.9	16.7**	88.2	86.4	– 1.8
Why APR/int rate difference	22.5	41.2	18.7**	19.8	43.1	23.3**	32.0	31.2	– 0.9
Cash at closing									
Less cash at closing loan	83.8	77.3	– 6.6	80.7	76.1	– 4.5	80.5	78.5	– 2.0
Cash at closing amount	80.9	86.3	5.4	78.3	80.2	1.9	83.6	79.2	– 4.4
Monthly payment and escrow									
Monthly payment amount and inclusion/exclusion of escrow[2]	79.4	91.5	12.1**	77.8	87.8	10.0**	85.5	82.7	– 2.9
Tax and insurance cost amount[1]	16.3	86.2	69.9**	16.7	70.4	53.7**	52.1	43.0	– 9.1

Table 6.9. (Continued)

Percentage of respondents giving the correct response, by loan cost scenario and borrower type

Response (N)	Prime Borrowers (1) Current forms (204)	(2) Prototype form (211)	(3) Difference	Subprime Borrowers (4) Current forms (207)	(5) Prototype form (197)	(6) Difference	Both Disclosure Forms (7) Prime Borrowers (415)	(8) Subprime Borrowers (404)	(9) Differen ce
	74.0%	72.5%	– 1.5	73.9%	70.6%	– 3.4	73.3%	72.3%	– 1.0
Balloon payment									
Balloon presence and amount[2]									
Prepayment penalty									
Any prepay penalty at year 2[1]	34.6	54.1	19.5**	29.4	57.1	27.7**	44.6	43.0	– 1.6
Any prepay penalty at year 6[1]	32.7	67.9	35.2**	27.5	73.5	46.0**	50.7	50.0	– 0.7
Prepayment penalty amount[1]	2.9	60.6	57.7**	7.8	56.1	48.3**	32.4	31.5	– 0.9

Notes: Figures in parentheses are the number of respondents in the indicated group. Asterisks indicate statistically significant differences in the proportions of current and prototype form respondents giving the correct response. Two-tailed t-tests were used to test the differences. * indicates significant at the five percent level and ** indicates significant at the one percent level.

1 These results are only from respondents in the complex-loan scenario because the relevant loan feature did not appear in the simple-loan scenario. (Some of these are presented in this way by necessity, since there was no correct answer in the simple loan scenario, and some are presented in this way to highlight the performance of the forms and borrower types in the scenario with the more problematic loan terms.) For these results, the sample sizes for the prime borrower results in columns (1)-(3) are 104 current forms and 109 prototype form respondents. The sample sizes for the subprime borrower results in columns (2)-(6) are 102 current forms and 98 prototype form respondents. In columns (7)-(9) the sample sizes are 213 prime borrowers and 200 subprime borrowers.

2 The results for these loan costs reflect the results of several questions that were combined and analyzed jointly. *See* Section 4.5 of the Consumer Testing Methodology chapter and relevant parts of Section 6.2.3 of the Consumer Testing Results chapter.

CONCLUSIONS

The study produced four major findings: (1) current mortgage cost disclosures failed to convey key mortgage costs to many consumers; (2) prototype disclosures developed for the study significantly improved consumer recognition of mortgage costs, demonstrating that better disclosures are feasible; (3) both prime and subprime borrowers failed to understand key loan terms, and both benefitted from the improved disclosures; and (4) improved disclosures provided the greatest benefit for more complex loans, where both prime and subprime borrowers had the most difficulty understanding loan terms. These findings were obtained in both the in-depth consumer interviews and the quantitative consumer testing, with the exception that the consumer interviews did not examine the impact of the improved disclosures on particular types of borrowers or for particular types of loans. The study also demonstrates the importance of consumer testing in the development and evaluation of consumer disclosures.

7.1. Current Disclosures Failed to Convey Key Mortgage Costs to Many Consumers

The results of the study show that the current mortgage cost disclosures failed to convey key mortgage costs to many consumers. These findings were obtained in both the in-depth consumer interviews and the quantitative consumer testing.

The in-depth consumer interviews found that many borrowers were confused by the disclosures in TILA statement and GFE form and did not understand key terms, such as the APR, amount financed, and discount fees. Many borrowers also did not understand important costs and terms of their own recently obtained mortgages. Many had loans that were significantly more costly than they believed, or contained significant restrictions, such as prepayment penalties, of which they were unaware. Many of these borrowers did not learn of these costs and terms until at or after the loan settlement, and some appeared to learn for the first time during the study interview. Some of these borrowers reported that they had spent considerable time shopping and comparing loan offers, but still experienced problems or misunderstandings. Others relied primarily on their loan officer or mortgage broker to explain the loan terms, or on the reputation of the lender or the recommendation of a friend or relative, rather than examining and verifying the loan terms themselves.

The quantitative consumer testing, conducted with 819 recent mortgage customers, confirmed and quantified the shortcomings of the current mortgage cost disclosures, and provided much greater detail on the ability of the current disclosures to inform consumers of key loan costs. Approximately one-half of the consumers participating in the testing were provided copies of the current TILA statement and GFE forms for two hypothetical loans and asked a series of questions about various costs of these loans.

The failure to convey key mortgage costs was evident across a wide range of loan terms and among substantial proportions of test participants. About a fifth of the respondents viewing the current disclosure forms could not correctly identify the APR of the loan, the amount of cash due at closing, or the monthly payment (including whether it included escrow for taxes and insurance). Nearly a quarter could not identify the amount of settlement charges.

About a third could not identify the interest rate or which of two loans was less expensive, and a third did not recognize that the loan included a large balloon payment or that the loan amount included money borrowed to pay for settlement charges. Half could not correctly identify the loan amount. Two-thirds did not recognize that they would be charged a prepayment penalty if in two years they refinanced with another lender (and a third did not even recognize that they "may" be charged such a penalty). Three-quarters did not recognize that substantial charges for optional credit insurance were included in the loan. Almost four-fifths did not know why the interest rate and APR of a loan sometimes differ. And nearly nine-tenths could not identify the total amount of up-front charges in the loan.

These findings may be even stronger in real-world transactions. Although in real-world transactions borrowers will have greater incentive to understand loan costs, because their homes and savings are at risk, they also may face a number of factors that make it more difficult to understand their loan costs. The consumer testing was conducted in a quiet, experimental setting. Respondents did not face the time pressure of a loan closing, a large stack of other closing paperwork, or deceptive tactics aimed at obscuring loan costs, all of which are likely to aggravate the difficulties consumers have understanding their loan terms. These difficulties may be especially acute for refinance loans, for which the TILA disclosures need not be provided until closing. Further difficulties are introduced because the settlement costs disclosed earlier in the GFE are subject to change at closing.

The problems with the current disclosures appear to be due to several factors, including the omission of important information, such as when a prepayment penalty will be imposed and how it will be calculated; the provision of confusing or misunderstood information, such as the amount financed and APR disclosures; and pre-existing consumer confusion not corrected by the forms, such as the confusion between up-front charges and up-front payments. Some problems, such as the widespread failure to recognize charges for optional credit insurance, are more puzzling given that the charges are disclosed in the forms. The wording or format of the disclosure may make it difficult for consumers to notice and comprehend the information.

In assessing the extent to which the current forms fail to convey important mortgage costs, it is important to note that the GFE used in the tests was an enhanced version that included information not required by the current regulations. Similar forms are used by many lenders. The enhanced version was used so that, in the event the study found significant problems with the current forms, the results would not be dismissed as irrelevant and unimportant because they did not reflect the information that many consumers actually receive in the marketplace. The level of problems found with the enhanced GFE, however, almost certainly understates the problems faced by consumers who receive a form that merely complies with the regulations. If such a GFE had been used in the study, the proportion of consumers unable to identify key loan costs would have been substantially higher. Many of the key mortgage costs examined in the tests, including the amount of money borrowed, the interest rate, the total monthly payment including taxes and insurance, the cash due at closing, and even the sum of the various individual settlement charges, would not have been disclosed in a form that merely met the regulatory requirements.

Consumers who do not recognize key loan costs can be harmed in a number of ways. They may be unable to fully understand the cost of their loan, assess whether it is a good deal, ensure that the terms are appropriate to their circumstances, and compare loan offers from different lenders. These consumers may pay more for their loans than necessary by unknowingly accepting excessive settlement costs or charges for unwanted optional products. They may become obligated for payments they cannot afford, such as property taxes and homeowners' insurance that are not included in the monthly payment, or a large balloon payment they failed to recognize. They may obtain loan terms that are inappropriate to their circumstances, such as a unknowingly accepting a prepayment penalty when they know they are likely to refinance soon. And they may make inappropriate trade-offs between long- and short-term costs (that is, between interest rates and points) or inappropriate selections of alternative mortgage products (such as interest-only or payment option loans).

Although decisions about cost tradeoffs and loan selections involve more sophisticated judgements than those tested in this study, if consumers cannot recognize the basic costs and terms of a loan, they will be unable to make wise choices in these more complicated decisions. Consumers cannot make informed decisions on the trade-off between a higher interest rate and higher up-front costs, for example, if they do not correctly recognize all of the up-front costs assessed in a loan.

Consumers who do not recognize key loan costs also will be more vulnerable to deceptive lending practices that aim to hide or misrepresent loan costs. The failure of the current disclosures to convey key loan costs to many consumers may make it easier for some lenders to engage in deceptive practices. Many of the FTC's deceptive lending cases have involved loan terms that the current disclosure forms have particular difficulty conveying to consumers, such as optional credit insurance, balloon payments, prepayment penalties, and the financing of high fees and optional charges in the loan amount. Lenders in these cases may have used deceptive practices to take advantage of the inability of many consumers to recognize these terms in the current disclosure forms.

The study results indicate that current mortgage cost disclosures fall far short of their intended goal. The current forms fail to convey important loan costs to significant proportions of consumers. The forms leave substantial room for improved disclosures.

7.2 Prototype Disclosures Developed for the Study Significantly Improved Consumer Recognition of Mortgage Costs, Demonstrating that Better Disclosures are Feasible

In this study, we also examined whether better disclosures could improve consumer recognition of key loan costs. We designed a prototype disclosure form that presented all significant loan costs in a single document using what was intended to be easy-to-understand language and an easy-to-use format. Both the in-depth consumer interviews and the quantitative consumer testing found that the prototype disclosures provided a significant improvement over current disclosures.

After recent mortgage customers in the in-depth interviews had been asked a series of questions about the current mortgage disclosures and their experiences shopping for mortgages, they were shown an initial version of the prototype disclosure form. The recent borrowers were nearly unanimous in their strong positive reaction to the prototype form; most characterized it as a substantial improvement over the current forms in organization and readability.

The quantitative consumer testing, conducted with 819 recent mortgage customers, confirmed, quantified, and provided much greater detail on the improvements provided by the prototype disclosure form. Approximately one-half of the consumers participating in the testing were provided copies of the prototype disclosures for two hypothetical loans and asked a series of questions about various costs of these loans. The tests found that the prototype disclosures significantly increased consumer recognition of loan costs.

Respondents viewing the prototype form in the consumer testing answered an average of 80 percent of the test questions correctly, compared to an average of 61 percent for respondents viewing the current forms, an improvement of 19 percentage points. The improvement was largest in the complex-loan scenario, which included a number of potentially problematic loan terms, such as charges for optional credit insurance, a balloon payment, and a prepayment penalty. In this scenario, respondents viewing the prototype form answered an average of 78 percent of the questions correctly, compared to 56 percent for respondents viewing the current forms, an improvement of 22 percentage points.

The difference in the performance of the two forms is even greater if one compares the proportion of respondents in each group who answered a relatively high percentage of the questions correctly. Across both loan scenarios, 80 percent of the respondents viewing the prototype form were able to answer at least 70 percent or more of the questions correctly, compared to only 29 percent of the respondents viewing the current forms, an improvement of 51 percentage points. Similarly large improvements are found in the percentage of respondents that answered 80 and 90 percent of the questions correctly.

The prototype form performed better than the current forms in 17 of the 21 questions in the simple-loan scenario and 23 of the 25 questions in the complex-loan scenario. (Thirteen and 16 of the differences in the two scenarios, respectively, were statistically significant.) Many of the improvements provided by the prototype form were quite large. In the complex-loan scenario, for example, the prototype outperformed the current forms by more than 10 percentage points in 15 questions, more than 30 percentage points in eight questions and more than 50 percentage points in four questions.

The improvements in consumer understanding provided by the prototype form were evident across a wide range of loan terms and for substantial proportions of respondents. Some of the improvements were quite large. The prototype form produced a 66 percentage point increase in the proportion of respondents correctly identifying the total amount of up-front charges in the loan, a 43 percentage point increase in the proportion of respondents recognizing that the loan contained charges for optional credit insurance, a 37 percentage point increase in the proportion correctly identifying the amount borrowed, a 24 percentage point increase in the proportion recognizing that a prepayment penalty would be assessed if the loan was refinanced in two years, a 21 percentage point increase in the proportion correctly identifying why the APR and interest rate may differ in a loan, a 16 percentage point increase in the proportion correctly identifying the APR, a 15 percentage point increase in the proportion correctly identifying the amount of settlement charges, a 13 percentage point increase in the proportion correctly identifying which of two loans was less expensive, a 12 percentage point increase in the proportion correctly identifying the interest rate, and a nine percentage point increase in the proportion recognizing that settlement charges were financed and included in the loan amount. The prototype form also conveyed the correct prepayment penalty amount to 59 percent of the respondents and the correct amounts of property taxes and homeowner's insurance charges, for a loan in which the charges were not included in the monthly payment, to 79 percent of the respondents—information that is not included at all in the current forms.

Although the prototype form provided significant improvements in consumer understanding of many loan terms, and substantial improvements of some, some consumers still did not recognize important loan costs. Significant problems remained, for example, in consumer awareness that a balloon payment, prepayment penalty, optional credit insurance charges, and financed settlement costs were included in the loan, as well as consumer understanding of the APR and how it differs from the interest rate. Although the prototype form demonstrated that the disclosures can be significantly improved, and provides some guidance on how improvements can be achieved, this was only a first step. Further refinement and development of the disclosures may provide further improvements that better convey these important loan costs to consumers.

7.3. Both Prime and Subprime Borrowers Failed to Understand Key Loan Terms, and Both Benefitted from the Improved Disclosures

The in-depth consumer interviews found that both prime and subprime borrowers were confused by the current mortgage disclosures, and both experienced significant misunderstandings about the terms of their recently obtained loans. The quantitative consumer testing confirmed and quantified this finding. When viewing current disclosure forms, both prime and subprime borrowers had significant difficulty recognizing and identifying key loan costs, and both groups benefitted significantly from the improved disclosures.

Although subprime borrowers were less likely than prime borrowers to accurately recognize and identify mortgage costs, the differences between the two groups were almost always small. Across both loan scenarios in the quantitative testing, among respondents who viewed current disclosure forms, prime borrowers answered an average of 62.0 percent of the test questions correctly, compared to an average of 59.6 percent for subprime borrowers, a difference of only 2.4 percentage points. These results do not imply that subprime borrowers do not have problems recognizing mortgage costs, but that both prime and subprime borrowers have similar problems.

The improvements provided by the prototype form also were similar for prime and subprime borrowers. Across both loan scenarios, the prototype form performed 18.6 percentage points better than current forms among prime borrowers, compared to 19.2 percentage points better among subprime borrowers. Such improvements in consumer recognition of loan costs could help subprime borrowers better protect themselves from deceptive practices, and help all borrowers, prime and subprime, better understand loan offers, and more easily shop for the least expensive loan that fits their needs.

The differences between prime and subprime borrowers may be larger in real-world transactions than found in the study. The study results were obtained holding constant the complexity of the loans. In actual market transactions, subprime borrowers may be more likely to face loans with complex features, which, as found in the study, are more difficult for consumers to understand. Adjustable-rate, hybrid, and payment option loans, which were not tested, are likely to create even greater difficulties. Time pressure at closing, voluminous other paperwork, and any deceptive practices are likely to especially aggravate understanding difficulties for these more complex loans. Many subprime borrowers also face pressures not typically faced by prime borrowers, such as the need to obtain a loan quickly in order to address family financial difficulties, or the experience of being turned down by several lenders before being approved for a loan. All of these considerations suggest that subprime borrowers may face even greater difficulties understanding their loan terms than indicated by the study results, and may be likely to obtain the greatest benefit from improved disclosures.

7.4. Improved Disclosures Provided the Greatest Benefit for More Complex Loans, which Both Prime and Subprime Borrowers Had the Most Difficulty Understanding

Both prime and subprime borrowers had more difficulty recognizing and identifying loan costs in the complex-loan scenario, where the loans included features such as optional credit insurance, balloon payments, prepayment penalties, and the exclusion of escrow from the monthly payments. Prime borrowers who viewed current disclosure forms answered 67 and 57 percent of the questions correctly in the simple- and complex-loan scenarios, respectively. Similarly, subprime borrowers who viewed current disclosure forms answered 65 and 54 percent of the questions correctly in the simple- and complex-loan scenarios.

The improved disclosures provided the greatest benefits in the complex-loan scenario, where borrowers had the most difficulty recognizing and identifying loan costs. Among prime borrowers, the prototype form increased the percentage of questions answered correctly by 15.6 percentage points in the simple-loan scenario, compared to 21.6 percentage points in the complex-loan scenario. Similarly, among subprime borrowers, the prototype form increased the percentage of questions answered correctly by 16.2 percentage points in the simple-loan scenario, compared to 22.4 percentage points in the complex-loan scenario.

As noted in the previous section, if loans in the subprime market tend to have more complex features than loans in the prime market, these results suggest that borrowers in the subprime market may have greater difficulty understanding their loan terms than borrowers in the prime market, even though the two groups of borrowers perform similarly when the complexity of the loans is held constant. These results also suggest that improved disclosures may provide a greater beneficial impact in the subprime market.

7.5. The Importance of Consumer Testing

In addition to documenting problems with the current mortgage cost disclosures and showing that better disclosures can improve understanding of mortgage costs, the study also illustrates the importance of consumer testing in the development and evaluation of consumer disclosure policy. Although some disclosures may be so simple and straightforward that testing is not necessary, for most disclosures, particularly something as complicated and difficult to understand as mortgage costs, testing is essential. Without consumer testing it will be difficult to know whether new or existing disclosures effectively convey the desired information in a way that can be understood and used by consumers.

Developing consumer disclosures is tricky. Although effective disclosures can greatly benefit consumers, faulty disclosures can result in more harm than good. Ill-conceived disclosures can confuse and even mislead consumers, distort their decisions, and lead to worse choices and outcomes. Difficult-to-understand and confusing disclosures, and disclosures that provide too much, irrelevant, or unnecessary information, can make it difficult, time-consuming, and frustrating for consumers to understand what is being conveyed and sort the important points from the minor detail. Such disclosures may induce consumers to ignore the information completely because it is simply too much trouble. Faulty disclosure policy can also impose unnecessary compliance costs on industry, distort seller decisions on product and feature offerings, and, if consumers cannot fully understand product prices or attributes, reduce competition for lower prices and better attributes.

As seen in the testing conducted in this study, disclosures may fail to convey the desired information to many consumers. This can be true for long-mandated disclosures, as well as ones that have been newly developed, and for seemingly clear and prominent disclosures, as well as ones that appear confusing or inconspicuous. Without testing, it is difficult to know what information is conveyed to consumers.

In conducting consumer testing, it is important to isolate the effect of the particular disclosures being considered. This can be accomplished through use of a control group. If revised disclosures are being proposed, for example, the control would be the current disclosures. The impact of the revised disclosures would be found by comparing the results of the two groups. Without the comparison provided by the control group, it can be impossible to interpret the meaning of the results. The tests may show, for example, that a revised disclosure is not understood by a significant proportion of consumers, but a control group might make clear that this is still a substantial improvement over the current disclosure. Conversely, the tests may show that nearly all consumers understand a revised disclosure, but a control group might show that the same also is true for the current disclosures, indicating that the revisions provide little additional benefit. In the testing conducted in this study, the performance of neither the current nor prototype disclosures could have been properly evaluated without the corresponding testing of the other for use as a comparison.

The development of effective consumer disclosures requires careful analysis of what information consumers really need, how consumers will interpret and use the information, how to convey the information in a way that can be easily understood and used by consumers, and, combining all of this, careful analysis of the benefits and costs of the disclosures. Consumer testing is a critical part of this analysis.

Appendix A Consumer Interviews Recruitment Script and Screener

FTC Mortgage Disclosure Study Consumer Interview Screener

INTERVIEWER INITIAL:____________

Quota Criteria:

Recruit at least 18 for 11 to show.

Q2A: Gender – Aim for roughly 50/50 mix, make sure not too imbalanced
Q4: Transaction/Activity

- Purchased a home – 5 to 12 of 18
- Refinanced home – 5 to 12 of 18

Hispanic or Latino origin – Recruit at least 3
Race – Recruit at least 3 who are Black or African American
Education

- Some high school/High school diploma (GED equivalent) – Recruit at least 5
- Master, JD, Doctorate or other advanced degree – Recruit no more than 3

Q9. Age: Aim for a mix, make sure not too imbalanced
A MIX OF JURISDICTIONS (I.E., Cities, Towns) To The Extent Possible
B NO MORE THAN 3 PEOPLE WITH SAME LENDER FOR IDIs

SCREENER

S1. Hello, may I speak to ________ [USE NAME FROM SAMPLE]? This is _______ calling for ________, a local marketing research firm.

1 AVAILABLE [CONTINUE]
2 NOT AVAILABLE [ASK TO SPEAK WITH PERSON IN HOUSEHOLD WHO SHARES OR MAKES DECISIONS ON MORTGAGES – IF NOT AVAILABLE, GET PERSON'S NAME AND SCHEDULE A CALLBACK]
3 NO LONGER AT THIS NUMBER [TERMINATE]

S2. We are conducting research for a government agency that is trying to learn how consumers shop for mortgages. I'd like to ask you a few short questions for research purposes only. Be assured that **we are not selling anything and all of your responses are strictly confidential. [IF ASKED: The government agency is the Federal Trade Commission.]**

1. First, do you or does anyone in your family work in:

1 Market Research [TERMINATE]
2 Financing/Banking [TERMINATE]
3 Real Estate [TERMINATE]
4 NONE OF THE ABOVE [CONTINUE]

2A. When your household got its most recent mortgage, what role did you play in making decisions about that mortgage? Would you say that you were the sole decision-maker, that you shared, equally, in the decision making for your household, or that others were primarily responsible for making decisions on the mortgage?

1 Sole decision-maker
2 Shared equally
3 Others were primarily responsible [ASK TO SPEAK WITH PERSON PRIMARILY RESPONSIBLE– IF NOT AVAILABLE, GET PERSON'S NAME AND SCHEDULE A CALLBACK]
4 DK [THANK & TERMINATE]
5 REFUSED [THANK & TERMINATE]

2B. RECORD GENDER: AIM FOR 50/50 MIX. MAKE SURE NOT TOO IMBALANCED

1 MALE
2 FEMALE

2C. RECORD PERSONID FROM SAMPLE LIST

PERSONID: ______________

3. In the last four months, have you purchased a home, taken out a home equity loan or second mortgage, or refinanced your home?

1	YES	[CONTINUE]
2	NO	[THANK & TERMINATE]
3	DK	[THANK & TERMINATE]
4	REFUSED	[THANK & TERMINATE]

4. Which of the items I mentioned have you done [ALLOW MULTIPLE RESPONSE]? [IF NECESSARY, READ:]

1	Purchased a home	[5-12 of 18]
2	Taken out a home equity loan or second mortgage	
3	Refinanced your house	[5-12 of 18]
4	DK	[GO TO 14A IF Q2B=2]
5	REFUSED	[THANK & TERMINATE]

Now, we would like to ask a few general questions:

5. Have you attended an interview or focus group for market research purposes in the past six months?

1	YES	[THANK & TERMINATE]
2	NO	[CONTINUE]
3	DK	[THANK & TERMINATE]
4	REFUSED	[THANK & TERMINATE]

6. Are you of Hispanic or Latino origin? [TRY TO GET AT LEAST THREE]

1	YES	
2	NO	
3	DK	[THANK & TERMINATE]
4	REFUSED	[THANK & TERMINATE]

7. To which racial group or groups do you belong? Would you say: [READ 1 THRU 5 ON LIST]

1	White,	
2	Black or African American,	[GET AT LEAST 3]
3	American Indian/Native American,	
4	Asian,	
5	Native Hawaiian or other Pacific Islander	
		[DO NOT READ 6 THRU 8 ON LIST]
6	HISPANIC OR LATINO (VOLUNTEERED)	
7	OTHER: [SPECIFY] ______________	
8	DK	[THANK & TERMINATE]
9	REFUSED	[THANK & TERMINATE]

8. What is the highest level of education you have obtained: [GET A MIX]

1	Some high school	[AT LEAST 5 WITH H.S. DIPLOMA OR LESS]
2	High School diploma, GED equivalent	[AT LEAST 5 WITH H.S. DIPLOMA OR LESS]
3	Technical or Trade school	
4	Some college	
5	Associate's or 2 year degree	
6	Bachelor's or 4 year degree	
7	Master, JD, Doctorate or other advanced degree	[NO MORE THAN 3]
8	DK	[THANK & TERMINATE]
9	REFUSED	[THANK & TERMINATE]

9. Please stop me when I reach your age category: [GET A MIX]

1	Under 18	[THANK & TERMINATE]
2	18-34	
3	35-54	
4	55-64	
5	65 or older	
6	DK	[THANK & TERMINATE]
7	REFUSED	[THANK & TERMINATE]

10. We would like to invite you to participate in a one- hour research interview on February 24th in Bethesda. The government agency sponsoring the research is seeking ways to make the mortgage process more understandable to consumers so the discussion will center around the process you went through to find and apply for a mortgage. At the end of the interview, you will be paid $100 for your participation. **[IF ASKED: The government agency is the Federal Trade Commission.]**

I want to stress that the purpose of the interview is strictly for research purposes. We are not selling anything. As a research company, our purpose is to write a report explaining what works or doesn't work about the mortgage process. Are you willing to participate?

[IF ASKED – BETHESDA FACILITY (Shugoll Research) ADDRESS IS 7475 WISCONSIN AVENUE, SUITE 200, BETHESDA, MD 20814; AT INTERSECTION OF WISCONSIN AVENUE AND EAST WEST HIGHWAY IN BETHESDA. EASILY ACCESSIBLE FROM THE BETHESDA METRO STATION]

1	YES	[GO TO Q10A]
2	NO	[GO TO Q12A]
3	DK	[GO TO Q12A]
4	REFUSED	[GO TO Q12A]

11A. Great. Now, as part of the interview our sponsor would like you to bring your loan documents to the interview, so that you and the interviewer can review them together. Please be reassured that everything discussed during the interview is strictly confidential. Are you willing to bring your loan documents, including any documents you received about your loan before closing as well as the documents you received at closing, to the interview and share them with the interviewer?

1 YES [RECORD RECRUITMENT INFORMATION AND SCHEDULE, IF Q2B=2, R. SHARED EQUALLY IN MORTGAGE DECISION, GO TO 11B; OTHERWISE GO TO Q15]
2 NO [THANK & TERMINATE]
3 DK [THANK & TERMINATE]
4 REFUSED [THANK & TERMINATE]

[FORWARD THIS INFORMATION TO ROCKBRIDGE ONCE R. IS RECRUITED]

PARTICIPANT	RECRUITED	CONFIRMED
Name:	By:	By:
Phone: (H): (B):		
Street Address: City: State: Zip:		

11B. [IF Q2A=2] Now, you mentioned that you shared, equally, your decisions about your most recent mortgage. We would like to talk to co-decision makers at the same time to understand how they shopped for mortgages and made their decisions. At the end of the interview you would receive a total of $ 150 in appreciation for your participation. Would your co-decision maker be able to join you for the interview?

1 YES [RECORD CO-DECISION-MAKER INFORMATION AND GO TO Q15]
2 NO [GO TO Q15]
3 DK [ARRANGE TIME FOR FOLLOW-UP PHONE CALL ______ AND GO TO Q15]
4 REFUSED [GO TO Q15]

[FORWARD THIS INFORMATION TO ROCKBRIDGE]

Co-Decision-Maker Participant	RECRUITED	CONFIRMED
Name:	By:	By:
Phone: (H): (B):		
Street Address: City: State: Zip:		

12A. [ASK IF Q10=2]: I'm sorry to hear that. Why is it you won't be able to come? PROBE FOR REASON. MAKE SURE RESPONDENT UNDERSTANDS WE ARE NOT SELLING ANYTHING

[RECORD REASON]: ______________________________

______________________________ [GO TO 13]

REFUSED [GO TO 13]

13. Would there be another person in your household responsible for mortgage decisions?

1 YES [CONTINUE]
2 NO [THANK &TERMINATE]
3 DK [THANK & TERMINATE]
4 REFUSED [THANK & TERMINATE]

14. [IF Q13=1] May I speak with them at this time?

1 YES [START BACK AT Q1 TO RECORD ANSWERS FOR NEW R.]
2 NO [TRY TO ARRANGE CALL BACK DATE AND TIME]
3 DK [TRY ARRANGE CALL BACK DATE AND TIME]
4 REFUSED [TRY TO ARRANGE CALL BACK DATE AND TIME]

[FORWARD THIS INFORMATION TO ROCKBRIDGE]

Alternate Decision Maker Call Back Information
Name:
Phone: (H): (B):
Call back date: ______________ Time of availability: ______________

15. Now, to prepare for your interview, we would like to ask you a few questions about your mortgage transaction.

16A. Sometimes in getting a mortgage, some people get two loans at the same time, with each loan covering part of the total loan amount. Thinking about your most recent mortgage transaction, did you use one loan to cover the whole amount, or did you use more than one loan?"

1 One [GO TO Q17A]
2 More than One [GO TO Q16B]
3 DK [GO TO Q17A]
4 REFUSED [GO TO Q17A]

16B. [IF Q16A=2] How many loans did you use?

1 _______________ LOANS [RECORD ANSWER]
2 DK
3 REFUSED

16C. I want to ask you a few questions about the largest of those mortgages. Thinking about the largest of these mortgages:

17A. What is the term of the mortgage, that is the total number of years you have to payoff the mortgage?

1 ____________ YEARS [RECORD ANSWER & GO TO Q17C]
2 DK [Go To 17B]
3 REFUSED [GO TO Q17C]

17B. [Q17A=2] Would you say that your mortgage is a 30-year mortgage, a 15-year mortgage, a 10-year mortgage, or a mortgage that covers a different time period?

1 30 Year Mortgage
2 15 Year Mortgage
3 10 Year Mortgage
4 Other _______________ YEARS [RECORD]
5 DK
6 REFUSED

17C. What is the total amount that you borrowed, that is, the total loan amount with this mortgage?

1 _______________ DOLLARS [RECORD]
2 DK
3 REFUSED

18A. Is your interest rate fixed throughout the full term of the mortgage?

1	YES	[GO TO Q18B]
2	NO	[GO TO Q19]
3	DK	[GO TO Q19]
4	REFUSED	[GO TO Q19]

18B. [Q18A=1] What is the interest rate on your mortgage? [IF NECESSARY CLARIFY: If R. asks "Do you mean the interest rate or the APR" or "Do you mean the note rate or the APR" say "The note rate."]

1 ___________ PERCENT [RECORD ANSWER] → [GO TO Q22A]
2 DK [GO TO Q22A]
3 REFUSED [GO TO Q22A]

19. [Q18A=2, 3, 4] What is the current interest rate on the mortgage?

1 __________ PERCENT [RECORD ANSWER]
2 DK
3 REFUSED

20A. Can the interest rate on the mortgage increase during the life of the mortgage?

1 YES [GO TO Q20B]
2 NO [GO TO Q21A]
3 DK [GO TO Q21A]
4 REFUSED [GO TO Q21A]

20B. [IF Q20A=1] What is the highest or maximum interest rate you might pay during the life of the mortgage?

1 ____________ PERCENT [RECORD]
2 DK
3 REFUSED

21A. Can the interest rate on the mortgage decrease during the life of the mortgage?

1 YES [GO TO Q21B]
2 NO [GO TO Q22A]
3 DK [GO TO Q22A]
4 REFUSED [GO TO Q22A]

21B. [IF Q21A=1] What is the lowest or minimum interest rate you might pay during the life of the mortgage?

1 ____________ PERCENT [RECORD ANSWER]
2 DK
3 REFUSED

22A. Can your monthly payment increase during the life of the mortgage?

1 YES [GO TO Q22B]
2 NO [GO TO Q23A]
3 DK [GO TO Q23A]
4 REFUSED [GO TO Q23A]

22B. [IF Q22A=1] Under what conditions would your monthly payment increase during the life of the mortgage?

1 WHEN THE INTEREST RATE INCREASES
2 OTHER ______________[RECORD]
3 DK
4 REFUSED

23A. Can your monthly payment decrease during the life of the mortgage?

1 YES [GO TO Q23B]
2 NO [GO TO Q24]
3 DK [GO TO Q24]
4 REFUSED [GO TO Q24]

23B. [IF Q23A=1] Under what conditions would your monthly payment decrease during the life of the mortgage?

1 WHEN THE INTEREST RATE DECREASES
2 OTHER ____________________[RECORD]
3 DK
4 REFUSED

24. If you wanted to pay your mortgage off, say next year, would you have to pay your mortgage company just the remaining balance, or would you have to also pay a penalty in addition to the remaining balance?

1 JUST REMAINING BALANCE
2 REMAINING BALANCE PLUS A PENALTY
3 DK
4 REFUSED

25A. Does the payment schedule for your mortgage require a big payment at the end or will the last payment be about the same amount as your regular monthly payments?

1 BIG PAYMENT REQUIRED AT THE END [GO TO 25B]
2 LAST PAYMENT ABOUT THE SAME
3 DK
4 REFUSED

25B. What is the approximate size of that last payment?

1 ______________ DOLLARS [RECORD]
2 DK
3 REFUSED

26A. [ASK if R. USED MORE THAN ONE LOAN (Q16A=2) OTHERWISE GO TO Q27]: Now, thinking about your smaller mortgage loan, If you wanted to pay your smaller loan off, say next year, would you have to pay your mortgage company just the remaining balance, or would you have to also pay a penalty in addition to the remaining balance?

1 JUST REMAINING BALANCE
2 REMAINING BALANCE PLUS A PENALTY
3 DK
4 REFUSED

26B. Does the payment schedule for your smaller loan require a big payment at the end or will the last payment be about the same amount as your regular monthly payments?

1 BIG PAYMENT REQUIRED AT THE END [GO TO 26C]
2 LAST PAYMENT ABOUT THE SAME
3 DK
4 REFUSED

26C. What is the approximate size of the last payment on your smaller loan?

1 ____________ DOLLARS [RECORD]
2 DK
3 REFUSED

27. And finally, do you usually wear eyeglasses or contact lenses when you read?

1 Yes [READ STATEMENT BELOW]
2 No [CONTINUE TO Q28]

[IF Q27=1, READ:] Please bring your eyeglasses or contact lenses with you when you come to the discussion session. We'll be asking you to look at some information about mortgage loans. [CONTINUE TO Q28]

28. Your participation will be very important to our research. Therefore if, for any reason, you find that you cannot make it to the interview, please call us **AS SOON AS POSSIBLE** so that we can find a replacement for you. The more notice you can give us, the better. Please don't send any one else in your place - you have been recruited for who you are.

[FOR INDIVIDUAL RECRUITS SAY:]

At the end of the session you will receive **$100** in appreciation of your participation in this important research study.

[FOR CO-DECISION-MAKER RECRUITS SAY:]

At the end of the session you and your co-decision maker will receive **$150** in appreciation of your participation in this important research study.

You will be called again before the session to confirm your attendance and to remind you to bring your loan papers to the interview.

I think you will find the session interesting and fun. If you have any questions or concerns at all, please do not hesitate to call us at 1-866-666-9548 x 20 and ask for Mariel Molina. Thank you again for agreeing to participate in this important research study. We look forward to seeing you at the interview.

APPENDIX B
CONSUMER INTERVIEWS INTERVIEW GUIDE

FTC MORTGAGE DISCLOSURE STUDY CONSUMER INTERVIEW GUIDE

Interviewer Initials:
Date and Time:
Respondent Name:
CIRCLE ONE: PRIME or SUB-PRIME

I. WARM-UP (2 minutes)

- I am with a market research firm in Great Falls, Virginia. We work with companies and other organizations to get the candid opinions of consumers in the marketplace. And tonight, for example, we plan to share feedback you give us with decision makers who are trying to make the mortgage lending process more understandable to consumers.
- You have been invited here because you have recently completed a mortgage transaction. I would like to get your views on the mortgage loan process, from shopping for a loan to closing on it.
- Be frank – I am a researcher with no vested interests.

- Note the one-way mirror. We are also audio-taping and video taping, which is standard research practice.
- Everything is confidential and for research purposes only. We put the results into a report that does not identify individuals by name.
- Questions?

II. Introductions and Mortgage Decision Process (5 Minutes)

A. Introductions

1. First, please tell me a little about yourself...

- Your occupation and household: Married? Have kids?
- City/County you live in
- Type of mortgage transaction completed recently (e.g., home purchase or refinance)
- Experience with the loan process (e.g., is this your first mortgage purchase? [PROBE to find out total number of mortgage transactions R. ever had.]

B. Mortgage Decision Process

2. Let's talk about how you got your recent mortgage. First of all, what prompted you to consider buying a home or refinancing?

Probe:

- What other events, if any, encouraged you to get a mortgage?
- Did an advertisement or offer encourage you to get a mortgage? In what way?
- [IF REFINANCE:] In refinancing did you consolidate any of your other bills into your mortgage or take cash out of your home equity? Was this an important reason for you to do the refinancing?

3. What concerns, if any, did you have about getting a mortgage?

Probe:

- Were you concerned about getting approved for a mortgage?
- Were you worried about getting a good deal on your mortgage? What does it mean to get a good deal?

III. Gathering Information on the Mortgage Process (5 Minutes)

4.Thinking back to before you completed your loan application, did you seek information about mortgages or did someone contact you first? What happened?

5. Where did you turn for information on getting a mortgage, the types of loans available, and the features of loans? (PROBE: realtors, mortgage brokers, mortgage lenders, associations, companies, friends and family, direct mail, web sites, newspapers, banks, advertisements)

6. Why did you use these sources? How did they help you? What information did they give you?

7. How did you find a mortgage broker or lender? (PROBE: How did you compare brokers/lenders?)

- Which did you use – a broker or lender? Why?
- (PROBE: Do you view them differently? How?)

8. Did you read the advertisements or offers for mortgages that you received in the mail, on e-mail, or by phone?

- Did you contact the company because of the ad/offer?

IV. Shopping for a Loan (10 Minutes)

9. Did you compare loans from different companies? Why or why not?

- Did you think it would be valuable to compare loans from different companies? Why or why not?
- Did you think it was costly to compare loans from different companies? [IF YES:] In What Way?[IF NO:] Why not?
- What would help you compare loans from different companies more easily?

10. [ASK IF R. COMPARED LOANS FROM DIFFERENT COMPANIES; ELSE SKIP TO Q.11] How did you compare loans from different companies? What did you consider in your decision?

- Did you look at specific terms? Which ones?
- Did you consider the up-front fees and points in your decision? How did you assess them? (PROBE: trade-off between up-front fees/points and interest rates)
- Did you consider other fees and charges in your decision? Pre-payment penalties? Balloon payments?

Were you required to pay for anything else to qualify for the loans, such as credit insurance?

11. How did you end up with the particular loan terms that you got? Did you consider different types of loans or was this the only loan option provided by the lender.

[IF CONSIDERED DIFFERENT TYPES OF LOANS:] What loan terms and options did you consider in your decision?

[EVERYONE:] PROBE: Did you consider:

- The length of the mortgage (15 year, 30 year, etc.)
- Fixed or adjustable interest rate
- Up-front points and fees
- Financing the up-front points and fees
- Prepayment penalty
- Balloon payment

For each: What did you get (OR Is that in your loan?) Did you choose that or was that just what the lender provided? Why did you choose this?

12. Looking back on your experiences in getting a mortgage, what, if anything, would you have liked lenders and brokers to do differently?

- What information, if any, would you have liked to have had but didn't? Why?
- Was there information you feel you received too late to help you make decisions? What information was that?

- Did you understand all the various terminology, or words, used when you were getting a mortgage? How comfortable were you with your ability to understand mortgage terms?
- Do you feel you were ever misled by anyone while getting your loan? What happened?

V. Loan Disclosure Review (38 Minutes)

13. Where did you get specific information about the details of the loan you got?

[PROBE: From the Good Faith Estimate? Truth-in-Lending Form? HUD-1 Form? Discussions by phone or in-person with lenders/brokers? Review of rate sheets? Newspaper listings of rates? Web sites of lenders/brokers?]

Good Faith Estimate:

14.Now, I'd like to talk about some specific documents in more detail. PULL OUT GOOD FAITH ESTIMATE FROM RESPONDENT DOCUMENTS. I'd like you to take a minute and look it over carefully thinking about the clarity and usefulness of it. IF THEY DON'T HAVE DOCUMENTS, USE SAME SAMPLE FROM FOCUS GROUP (vmp version) AND PROCEED FROM THERE.

15. Do you remember receiving this document [or "a document like this" if SAMPLE is used]? [IF YES: When in the process did you receive this document?] [IF NO: GO TO Q17]

16. Is that a reasonable time to make it useful to you? [IF APPROPRIATE: When would be better?]

17. On a scale of 1 to 10, where 1 is "extremely difficult to understand" and 10 is "extremely easy to understand", how understandable is this form to you? Why do you say that? (PROBE FOR SPECIFICS)

18. Let's talk about some of the important terms on the form. Let's start with...

- Loan Origination Fee
- Loan Discount Fee
- Total Estimated Settlement Charges

Ask for each of the above:

- What does this term mean?
- Is this useful to know? Why or why not?
- Is it clear to you? What would make it clearer?

19. Would you say this form is "very useful," "somewhat useful," or "not at all useful" in helping you understand and make decisions about your loan? Why do you say that?

20. What other information, if any, would you like to see included on this form to help you make a decision on the loan?

Truth-in-Lending:

21.PULL OUT TRUTH-IN-LENDING FROM RESPONDENT DOCUMENTS. Again, I'd like you to take a minute and look it over carefully thinking about the clarity and usefulness of it. IF RESPONDENT DOESN'T HAVE DOCUMENT, USE TILA SAMPLE FROM FOCUS GROUP AND PROCEED FROM THERE

22. Do you remember receiving this document [or "a document like this" if sample is used]? [IF YES: When in the process did you receive this document?] [IF NO: GO TO Q24]

23. Is that a reasonable time to make it useful to you? [IF APPROPRIATE: When would be better?]

24. On a scale of 1 to 10, where 1 is "extremely difficult to understand" and 10 is "extremely easy to understand", how understandable is this form to you? Why do you say that? (PROBE FOR SPECIFICS)

25. Let's talk about some of the important terms on the form. Let's start with...

- Annual Percentage Rate
- Finance Charge
- Amount Financed
- Total of Payments
- Pre-payment penalty

Ask for each of the above:

- What does this term mean?
- Is this useful to know? Why or why not?
- Is it clear to you? What would make it clearer?

26. What other information, if any, would you like to see included on this form to help you make a decision on the loan?

27. Would you say this form is "very useful," "somewhat useful," or "not at all useful" in helping you understand and make decisions about your loan? Why do you say that?

Alternative Form:

28. PULL OUT ALTERNATIVE FORM. I'd like to show you a possible alternative document for providing information about mortgage costs that might be used instead of the ones we just looked at. Take a minute and look it over carefully thinking about the clarity and usefulness of it.

29. What do you think of this document? How do you think it compares to the other two documents we just looked at?

PROBE:

- Is this form better or worse than the others?
- Is it easier or more difficult to understand?

30.On a scale of 1 to 10, where 1 is "extremely difficult to understand" and 10 is "extremely easy to understand", how understandable is this form to you? Why do you say that? (PROBE FOR SPECIFICS)?

31.Let's talk about some of the important terms on the form. Let's start with...

- Charge for Discounted Interest Rate [ON PAGE 3]
- Loan Amount [ON PAGE 1]
- Loan Amount Details [ON PAGE 2]

ASK FOR EACH OF THE ABOVE:

- What does this term mean?
- Is this useful to know? Why or why not?
- Is it clear to you? What would make it clearer?

32. Would you say this form is "very useful," "somewhat useful," or "not at all useful" in helping you understand and make decisions about your loan? Why do you say that?

PROBE:

- What do you find useful in this document?
- What do you find not useful or confusing?

33. What other information, if any, would you like to see included on this document to help you make a decision on the loan?

Wrap-Up:

Those are all of the questions I have. Do you have any further comments you would like to make?

Thank You!

APPENDIX C
CONSUMER INTERVIEWS CURRENT DISCLOSURE FORMS

Current Disclosure Forms Used in the Consumer Interviews

The current mortgage cost disclosure forms shown to respondents in the consumer interviews are presented in this appendix. The size of the forms has been reduced to fit the paper and margin sizes of this chapter. The forms used in the testing were on legal-size paper, rather than the letter-size presented here.

Proprietary form used in the consumer interviews

FEDERAL TRUTH-IN LENDING DISCLOSURE STATEMENT

For use with Fixed-Rate, GPM, Balloon Mortgage,
Adjustable or Variable Rate Loans

Date: **11/12/03**
Loan No.: **47231**
Borrowers: **James and Clara Borrower**

Property
Location: **123 Main Street**
Hometown, VA 22030

ANNUAL PERCENTAGE RATE The cost of your credit as a yearly rate	**FINANCE CHARGE** The dollar amount the credit will cost you	Amount Financed The amount of credit provided to you or on your behalf	Total of Payments The amount you will have paid after you have made all payments as scheduled
6.043 %	$ **202,244.34**	$ **172,551.78**	$ **374,796.12**

You have the right to receive at this time an itemization of the Amount Financed.
☐ I want an itemization ☒ I do not want an itemization

Your payment schedule will be:

Number of Payments	Amount of Payments	When Payments Are Due
359	$ **1,041.11**	**monthly starting on 02/01/04**
1	$ **1,037.63**	**ending on 01/01/34**
	$	
	$	
	$	
	$	
	$	

Variable Rate: ☐ This loan has a Variable Rate Feature. Variable Rate Disclosures have been provided to you earlier.

☐ This obligation has a demand Feature.

Insurance: Credit life insurance and credit disability insurance are not required to obtain credit, and will not be provided unless you sign and agree to pay the additional cost. No such insurance will be in force until you have completed an application, the insurance company has issued the policy, the effective date of that policy has arrived and the required premium has been paid.

Type	Premium	Term	Signature
Credit Life	$		I want to apply for credit life insurance. ________ SIGNATURE
Credit Disability	$		I want to apply for credit disability insurance. ________ SIGNATURE
Credit Life and Credit Disability	$		I want to apply for credit life and disability insurance. ________ SIGNATURE

You may obtain property insurance from anyone you want that is acceptable to this institution. If you get the insurance from ____________ you will pay $ ______ for a term of ________

Security: You are giving a security interest in:
☒ the property being purchased
☐ ____________

Late Charge: If payment is late, you will be charged $ ________ / ____ **5.00** % of the payment.

Prepayment: If you pay off early, you
☒ may ☐ will not have to pay a penalty.
☐ may ☐ will not be entitled to a refund of part of the finance charge.

Assumption: Someone buying your home
☒ cannot assume the remainder of the mortgage on the original terms.
☐ may, subject to conditions, be allowed to assume the remainder of the mortgage on the original terms.

A deposit balance ☒ is ☐ is not required. The Annual Percentage Rate does not take into account your required deposit.

See your contract documents for any additional information about nonpayment, default, any required repayment in full before the scheduled date, and prepayment refunds and penalties.

e means an estimate

I/We hereby acknowledge receipt of this disclosure.

________________ / ________ DATE

________________ / ________ DATE

Prepared by: ________________ ________ TITLE

Proprietary form used in the consumer interviews

GOOD FAITH ESTIMATE

Lender:	JL Mortgage Funding
Address:	123 Your Street Mortgagetown, VA 22205
Applicant(s):	James and Clara Borrower
Property Address:	123 Main Street Hometown, VA 22030

Sales Price:	220,000
Base Loan Amount:	176,000
Total Loan Amount:	176,000
Type of Loan:	30 Year Fixed
Date Prepared:	11/12/2003
Rate: 5.87%	Term: 360/360

The information provided below reflects estimates of the charges which you are likely to incur at the settlement of your loan. The fees listed are estimates - the actual charges may be more or less. Your transaction may not involve a fee for every item listed.

The numbers listed beside the estimates generally correspond to the numbered lines contained in the HUD-1 or HUD-1A settlement statement that you will be receiving at settlement. The HUD-1 or HUD-1A settlement statement will show you the actual cost for items paid at settlement.

800 ITEMS PAYABLE IN CONNECTION WITH LOAN:		
801 Loan Origination Fee (1.00 %)	$	1,760.00
802 Loan Discount Fee (%)	$	
803 Appraisal Fee	$	300.00
804 Credit Report	$	
805 Lender's Inspection Fee	$	
806 Mortgage Insurance Application Fee	$	
807 Assumption Fee	$	
808 Mortgage Broker Fee	$	
809 CLO Access Fee	$	
810 Tax Related Service Fee	$	72.00
Administrative Fee	$	650.00
Doc Prep Fee	$	100.00
Courier	$	70.00
	$	
	$	

900 ITEMS REQUIRED BY LENDER TO BE PAID IN ADVANCE:		
901 Interest for 10 day @$ 28.7222 per day	$	287.22
902 Mortgage Insurance Premium	$	
903 Hazard Insurance Premium	$	540.00
	$	
	$	
	$	

1000 RESERVES DEPOSITED WITH LENDER:		
1001 Haz Ins Prem 2 months @$ 45.00	$	90.00
1004 Tax & Assmt Res 9 months @$ 200.00	$	1800.00
	$	
	$	
	$	

"L" designates those costs to be paid by Lender.

1100 TITLE CHARGES:		
1101 Closing or Escrow Fee	$	250.00
1102 Abstract or Title Search	$	125.00
1103 Title Examination	$	
1104 Title Insurance Binder	$	
1105 Document Preparation Fee	$	100.00
1106 Notary Fee	$	10.00
1107 Attorney Fees	$	
1108 Title Insurance	$	774.00
Title Binder	$	50.00
	$	
	$	
	$	

1200 GOVERNMENT RECORDING & TRANSFER CHARGES:		
1201 Recording Fees:	$	75.00
1202 City/County Tax/Stamps:	$	110.00
1203 State Tax/Stamps:	$	330.00
VA Purchase County Transfer 2 of 2	$	110.00
VA Purchase Transfer Tax 2 of 2	$	264.00
	$	
	$	

1300 ADDITIONAL SETTLEMENT CHARGES:		
1301 Survey	$	160.00
1302 Pest Inspection	$	
Flood Certification	$	29.00
	$	
	$	
	$	
TOTAL ESTIMATED SETTLEMENT CHARGES	$	8,056.22

TOTAL ESTIMATED FUNDS NEEDED TO CLOSE:		
Downpayment	$	44,000.00
Est. Closing Costs	$	5,339.00
Est. Prepaid Items/Reserves	$	2,717.22
OTHER: **Earnest Money Deposit**	$	(2,000.00)
TOTAL EST. FUNDS NEEDED TO CLOSE	$	50,056.22

TOTAL ESTIMATED MONTHLY PAYMENT:		
Principal & Interest	$	1,041.11
Real Estate Taxes	$	200.00
Flood & Hazard Insurance	$	45.00
Mortgage Insurance	$	
	$	
TOTAL MONTHLY PAYMENT	$	1,286.11

THIS SECTION TO BE COMPLETED BY LENDER ONLY IF A PARTICULAR PROVIDER OF SERVICE IS REQUIRED. Use of the particular provider is required and the estimate is based on charges of the provider.

ITEM NO.	NAME & ADDRESS OF PROVIDER	TELEPHONE NO.	NATURE OF RELATIONSHIP

These estimates are provided pursuant to the Real Estate Settlement Procedures Act of 1974, as amended (RESPA). Additional information can be found in the HUD Special Information Booklet, which is to be provided to you by your mortgage broker or lender, if your application is to purchase residential real property and the Lender will take a first lien on the property. The undersigned acknowledges receipt of the booklet "Settlement Costs," and the Consumer Handbook on ARM Mortgages, if applicable.

Applicant	Date	Applicant	Date
Applicant	Date	Applicant	Date

☐ This Good Faith Estimate is being provided by , a mortgage broker, and no lender has yet been obtained.

"S" designates those costs to be paid by Seller.

APPENDIX D
CONSUMER INTERVIEWS EXAMPLES OF RESPONDENT COMMENTS ON SELECTED ISSUES

Examples of Respondent Comments on Selected Issues

This appendix presents examples of respondent comments on selected issues from the consumer interviews. Respondent comments are presented on the following topics:

Table D.1	Understanding of GFE discount fee disclosure
Table D.2	Understanding of TILA APR disclosure
Table D.3	Understanding of TILA amount financed disclosure
Table D.4	Understanding of TILA finance charge
Table D.5	Reaction to the prototype disclosures

Table D.1 Examples of Respondent Understanding of the GFE Discount Fee Disclosure

Examples of Respondents Who Misunderstood the Disclosure to Indicate a Discount Received Rather than a Fee Paid:

I asked them. I said where is my discount? It says I'm getting a $2,600 discount where is it? They said no that is what you have to pay. So, it's a trick. It's misleading is what it is. (Interview 51)

I think it's a good thing . . . . Giving me the discount . . . (Interview 39)

It means they will give you, it's like negative points. They have to try and entice you to buy their loan by giving you a discount on the thing. (Interview 31)

That means for some reason if I'm a good girl and I have a coupon, or a code, or something, I would have gotten a discount fee, and why didn't I . . . (Interview 21)

Loan Discount Fee of one and a half percent to me means that they are giving me a discount of one and a half-percent off the value of the loan. And I'm guessing it is because I do have other accounts with them. (Interview 55)

I have no idea. If there is a discount, qualify for some sort of a discount. (Interview 28)

I'm not sure. It's not here . . . . Perhaps the lending institution . . . might have some special program where they discount the Loan Origination Fee by a certain percentage. (Interview 13)

It's zero . . . . Whatever it is we didn't qualify for it. I don't know what it means. (Interview 9)

. . . assume that either the buyer is paying me . . . or somehow I'm getting money off of my fee at settlement. (Interview 32)

They said there is a discount . . . it's from the company. (Interview 5)

Why would there be a discount? They have to give a reason if they are giving you a discount, and if there is a discount I'm not sure. (Interview 18)

Table D.1 (continued)

I'm not sure what they mean by that. I don't remember getting anything like that.

It could have been on my form . . . . Well, if they are going to give you a loan discount, I think you'd like to know why they are giving it to you. (Interview 15)

Examples of Respondents with No Understanding of the Disclosure:

That one I don't know. (Interview 12)

I have no idea what that is. Maybe I better give it [the form] a seven or a six [out of ten]. (Interview 14)

That means nothing to me to be honest with you. (Interview 25) Beats me. (Interview 42)

I'm not sure. (Interview 10)

It doesn't make any sense to me. (Interview 52)

I have no idea what that is. (Interview 22)

I have no idea. (Interview 53)

Again, I have no idea. (Interview 3)

That one I have no idea. (Interview 19)

I don't know what that means . . . when it's a discount and it's your paperwork, you would think you are the one benefitting from it, not them. (Interview 11)

Not sure. (Interview 35)

Examples of Respondents Who Understood Correctly that the Disclosure Indicated a Fee Paid for a Lower Interest Rate or Other Loan Benefit:

Loan Discount Fee well, I'm not sure but I think that is the same as points, meaning you get a lower rate if you pay that upfront. (Interview 36)

Well, I would say that is the Loan Origination Fee dressed up and put in a different name . . . . The two of them are both as I understand it points that are used to bring down the rate that you are paying. (Interview 48)

I'd think loan discount would be them cutting you a break, but they are charging you money to cut you a break. (Interview 34)

Well, I think that gets into the points arena, if I'm not mistaken. And it's a way to adjust—make up for other favorable terms that they may give you, that might be of more interest to you, I'll have to think about that a second. I think that's more in the realm of the points, which is very variable, depending on what you—what the nature was. (Interview 6)

Actually I'm not sure that I know what that means. I would guess that means an additional percentage that you pay in order to bring the rate down. (Interview 23)

I think that is the points, what people commonly refer to as points is the fee you pay upfront to lower the points, or a certain percentage of the loan . . . then you would know how much you are paying upfront. That it lowers your percentage rate. (Interview 8)

Examples of Respondents Who Understood Generally that the Disclosure Indicated a Fee Paid by Them:

Gosh, I've heard that before. That is somehow related to points too . . . . I'm very confused on this now. (Interview 26)

That also is points, a payment. (Interview 49)

I think, I could be wrong about this, when we got refinancing because we went with a broker, part of that went to the broker and part actually went to the lender I believe. That's what I think. I could be wrong. (Interview 29)

I would ask what is a discount point? At the time, I said what's that? . . . I would think it was a fee. (Interview 46)

I can't recall what that is off the top of my head. I think it has something to do with the interest rate. (Interview 20)

Table D.2 Examples of Respondent Understanding of the TILA APR Disclosure

Examples of Respondents Who Misunderstood the APR as the Interest Rate

The interest rate, how much you pay every year on the loan. (Interview 22)

. . . the rate that is legally quoted-- the rate you would calculate mathematically to get the payment. (Interview 6)

Your interest rate, yearly. (Interview 5)

I pay a percentage of what I still owe back to the bank. . . . the interest rate that I'm paying for the year. (Interview 51)

. . . rate of the percentage that they paid on the loan . . . rate at which . . . lending the money. (Interview 39)

That is the APR which can go up every November first. (Interview 14)

. . . it's not the number that I expected to see there, which means maybe I don't know what it is. The Annual Percentage Rate is, yearly interest rate. . . . Well, I'd be surprised if I was the only one that didn't know. (Interview 21)

The Annual Percentage Rate is the rate at which you'll be charged the interest. (Interview 46)

Boy that's a good one. This is the amount of the interest that I'm being charged that is to the principal. . . . Instead of paying 18,000 or something a year, in addition to that I'm paying this amount . . . . (Interview 18)

Moderator: Is it the same as the interest rate that you were quoted that is on the note? Respondent: Oh sure. (Interview 10)

That's the percent of my principal balance that I'm going to be paying over the course of a year. (Interview 12)

That is the actual amount of interest you pay per year. I guess there is some kind of compounding effect in here. (Interview 15)

How much interest is going to be added to the loan. (Interview 3)

. . . we had gone back and forth with the mortgage broker, is that the interest rate is here, but the annual percentage rate is this. We understand now why this figure is never the same as this. . . . they have to take into account if your account is fixed or an adjustable rate. Any time you have an adjustable rate you have to kind of take into account the adjusted amount of your payments into the whole loan and recalculate the percentage.

Table D.2 (continued)

They are looking at it the life of your loan. So, this is a 30-year loan, 6.75 is only on the first five years and then after that, it would basically arbitrarily increase by this much. (Interview 8)

On this one, it's a percentage rate, well it's rounded off, six and a half-percent. It shows the interest rate. (Interview 19)

That is the amount of interest you pay yearly on the loan, the percent of the total loan that you've taken. (Interview 28)

It says here the cost of your credit as a yearly rate. It's a statistic that results from taking the interest rate on the loan and just kind of applying that, compound

interest over the course of a year and then how much interest do you end up paying in a year, and then what is that as percentage of what you borrowed, I think. I know that the Annual Percentage Rate is always a little bit different from the Simple Interest Rate. (Interview 36)

Interest equals principal times rate times time that is the rate. (Interview 48) It's the interest rate on this particular loan. (Interview 49)

This is the 7.13%, and actually it's lower because we get a discount since we are doing a direct debit . . . . how much they are charging each year on the amount that we have left that we owe on the principal. (Interview 55)

Examples of Respondents with No Understanding of the Disclosure

I don't understand this here. . . . that is what I am confused about, the Annual Percentage Rate. (Interview 9)

That is the rate, it's the cost of your credit at the yearly rate . . . there is your Annual Percentage Rate then there is another percentage rate that is like your actual percentage rate. . . . But this is the real rate you're paying. But this is the rate they are charging you. But there is some mystical thing in between there that gives you that . . . I did have it explained to me at one point. Then I said okay I'm paying 5.25 bottom line that is the thing that is important to me. (Interview 20)

. . . I don't know . . . I just always know on anything I've had that the Annual Percentage Rate is always higher. . . . That 's a way for the government to sneak out a little bit more of your money. (Interview 26)

. . . the cost of your credit as a yearly rate is 5.435, even though our interest rate is 5.25. . . . that doesn't really make sense. . . . I don't know. I have no idea. (Interview 29)

This is confusing to me because—and I still don't know if I truly understand it. The APR that threw me off because it wasn't the interest rate. It's not the same thing. (Interview 32)

Well, that's what it's going to cost me. You . . . are actually paying . . . more money. . . . You know the compounding is what throws you off. (Interview 11)

. . . how much it really, really costs . . . . No, I don't understand the discrepancy but I just know that is the way things work. (Interview 33)

I'm not too sure about the APR. I forget how it differs in the actual rate, that I'm not too sure. (Interview 35)

There is this rate, and then there is . . . real rate that you are going to pay which is based on, I'm not sure what. (Interview 42)

Examples of Respondents with a Non-Specific Understanding of the Disclosure

This is the percentage rate of my loan. . . . I'm going to pay that on my loan. (Interview 13)

What you are paying for your money. (Interview 25)

It is a percentage that I will pay per year on the loan. (Interview 52)

That is the rate that I'm going to be paying for that total amount. (Interview 53)

Table D.3 Examples of Respondent Misunderstandings of the TILA Amount Financed Disclosure

Examples of Respondents Who Misunderstood the Amount Financed to be the Loan Amount

That's how much I'm financing, the loan, the principal. (Interview 12) That was actually the loan. . . . that one is clear. (Interview 18)

It's how much I borrowed. (Interview 42)

That is my loan amount. (Interview 21)

That means principal. (Interview 52)

What they are actually going to pay. (Interview 53)

That is the amount borrowed. (Interview 55)

My original loan. How much I originally, how much I borrowed. The total amount borrowed which includes the fees in my case. (Interview 51)

That's how much I borrowed. . . . Well, they have the amount of credit provided to you, or on your behalf. I think that wording is a little strange. . . . I would rather see the amount you borrowed. (Interview 26)

The actual amount of the loan I'm taking out. (Interview 3)

That's basically what you are going to see here, on the settlement sheet, the amount you are going to be in hock for. (Interview 11)

. . . I have assumed, I would have assumed it to be the exact number of the loan . . . it was a different number. (Interview 20)

That is the amount of money that I am buying. (Interview 23)

Table D.4 Examples of Respondent Understanding of the TILA Finance Charge Disclosure

Examples of Respondents Who Misunderstood the Finance Charge to Include Only Interest Payments

That is the actual charge above the principal that has to be paid off. So, that is the actual amount, if you make the payments steadily for the next 30 years that is the actual interest. (Interview 15)

It means what I'm paying in interest. (Interview 31)

It's the interest rate plus the money that they are lending you. (Interview 39)

That is probably the total amount of the interest that you accrue over the life of your loan. So, if you kept this loan for the life of the loan, that's how much you would actually be paying for the loan, to the lender. (Interview 8)

The interest that is going to accrue over the term of the mortgage, if I pay it for all 30 years. (Interview 3)

Well, I think that's—over the full term of the loan, if you've made all the payments, this how much of it would be interest. That's another eye-opener. It would cost me more over the term of the loan, than what I borrowed to borrow it. (Interview 6)

Interest over the life of the loan. (Interview 12)

It means the interest I'm going to pay over the course of the loan. (Interview 14)

That is the total amount I will pay in finance charges in terms of interest to the lender. (Interview 52)

Finance charge is the total amount of interest I'm paying on this loan. (Interview 55)

That's if you were to take the loan, the $225,000 roughly at 8.137 percent this is what I would be paying over 30 years with finance charges. (Interview 13)

You are going to pay the interest with that. (Interview 5)

Examples of Respondents Who Generally Understood the Finance Charge as the "Cost of Credit"

That's the amount beyond, above the principal, that I paid off my loan and the money that I have that is going to them free for nothing. (Interview 48)

That means the amount that the credit is going to cost you if you were to carry it out for the entire amount. (Interview 19)

That's how much I'm paying in order to borrow this much money. (Interview 21)

It means the cost of the money over time. At the end of the road, and by the way with this being a variable rate, that really is an estimate, because they don't know what is going to happen in the last 20 years of the loan, but I believe that is assuming that it stays the same. (Interview 23)

That's what they are charging me to borrow that sum of money. (Interview 26)

Well, it's pretty clear, the dollar amount the credit will cost you. It's going to cost me this much to have this loan, basically double what we borrowed. (Interview 29)

. . . but when all is said and done this is what you are going to be paying if you pay the number of payments throughout the life of the loan. If I was to pay, like say it was 30

years but I paid it off in 15 years then the rate would change. All of that would change wouldn't it? (Interview 46)

The dollar amount the credit will cost you. (Interview 53) What your loan is going to cost you. (Interview 10)

This is exactly how much you actually pay just to get the loan. So, instead of paying a $341,000 loan, you are paying the 641,000 plus. It's just like when you buy a car. You think you buy a $20,000 car and you actually bought a $35,000 car. It's rough. It's just like credit cards. You bought a dress and you thought it was $100. You actually pay $500 for that dress. (Interview 18)

Finance charges that is what you are paying on top of your loan. (Interview 20)

How much it's going to cost you for the loan. That's pretty clear too. It's like, that's more than the house is worth. (Interview 22)

It means what you are paying in total for the money that you are buying. (Interview 25)

That means that is how much the financing of this entire loan amount over the year, over the term of loan is going to cost, which is amazing. (Interview 28)

The amount the credit will cost you . . . . Yeah, that is just basically what the bank is making off of me. (Interview 32)

All the extra money you are going to pay on top of your original loan amount. (Interview 34)

Okay, by the time you are at the end of the loan, you've paid back the money you borrowed and you've paid an awful lot more. An awful lot more is the Total Finance Charge, I think, according to what I see here. (Interview 36)

That is the amount that it cost me to borrow the money. They are making almost double. (Interview 42)

I guess over the term of this loan that is how much you are going to pay on top of the equity value, on top of the value of the loan, which you'll pay over time. (Interview 49)

But what helps me translate [the APR] is the finance charge column which gives you the exact dollar amount. Because that to me makes sense. On a $345,000 loan I'm going to pay $57,000, now that makes sense to me. (Interview 11)

That is the amount you will have paid once the house is paid off. (Interview 9)

Table D.5 Examples of Respondent Reactions to the Prototype Disclosure Form

Examples of Favorable Respondent Reaction to the Prototype Form

Yeah, I think this is a much smarter way to go . . . . That's an improvement, if out of this research you get smarter forms that's good. (Interview 31)

I see a possible replacement . . . . See this is what I've been asking for sitting here. Much clearer, much-much better organized . . . . Better organized and including information that I didn't have before on settlement services, and the services included in the charge. . . . This is terrific. I like this more and more. . . . I'm taking this with me and you're not getting it back (Interview 36)

This would be a miracle if we had this. Oh how wonderful . . . . You know this will never go through the federal government, this is too simple. They like things that are complicated . . . . This is exciting . . . . It's clear to read. It doesn't have all of these lines. All of those lines are very confusing . . . You've got lots of spacing and I think the information is so useful . . . . This is a great form, absolutely. . . . The lender or broker providing this loan is not necessarily shopping on your behalf and providing you with a lower cost loan.

Wow that should be on the front probably. . . . Yes, and the oral promises too, and certainly that is a very good statement. Yeah, oh that would be wonderful. (Interview 11)

This is much better. When you look at this one, the other one is totally insufficient. (Interview 10)

I like it. I like it a lot better than the HUD-1 which is very similar. (Interview 12) It is much clearer. (Interview 14)

You know actually this might be a little clearer, yeah. (Interview 18) I think this is a good document. (Interview 21)

I like it. It's a nice consolidation of the other forms. It's a little easier to read. (Interview 25)

This is much better. (Interview 28)

This is pretty good. I think it's better. (Interview 35)

Actually I like this. I like the Settlement Services Package much better, because I'm sure it contains all of that, it's just not nearly as annoying. . . . It's very clean. It's very straightforward. (Interview 42)

This looks much clearer. (Interview 52)

That's a nice form. . . . Well having said I like the others, I like this one better. I think it's maybe easier to read. It's not good that it takes three pages, but maybe it's necessary. . . . If it didn't have a staple, I'd spread it out. It would be easier . . . (Interview 6)

It's actually very nice, nicely laid out. . . . I think in a way it's better. It's detailed yet it's written probably more for the average person who is not involved in real estate. (Interview 8)

I like it. I like it much better than the other one. . . . Yeah, I can understand where the money is going. . . . I would have liked to have had it to make a decision on ours. It probably would have been a lot easier . . . (Interview 9)

It's real clear. I just think that this one is an easy read. . . . If I could have gotten something like this from three different lenders, it would have made my choice real easy. (Interview 13)

It's very clear. In fact I think this is better than these two. The loan it shows as a 30-year fixed rate, and loan amount, and loan term. It's clear. Then you go down to Our Loan Charges and it shows what they are charging for the interest rate

and the settlement charges, plus the homeowner's insurance. (Interview 19)

It's pretty simple and straightforward. And it would kind of be nice to have these things ahead of time. Then you go in, you talk to your buddies or your friends or someone else. (Interview 22)

This is certainly easier. Looking at this brings back some of the explanations that he had given me. (Interview 39)

This is much easier. This actually looks better. This reads easier . . . That one you had to hunt around. This one you could just go bam, bam, bam. This is much better. (Interview 46)

Someone thought about the customer when they put this together. I think it's much more clear. (Interview 49)

It's a nice little form. (Interview 55)

Examples of Respondents that Suggested that an Itemization of Settlement Costs be Added to the Prototype Form:

This is the forest and that has trees and pieces of grass and stuff which are confusing. This is much better I think . . . . I'm trying to think would it hurt to have the dollar amount in parentheses after each one if there is a cost to each one? I don't know. I think I'd feel better and having said this is the forest and those are the trees there are a couple of redwoods in here that I think you should probably leave. I think it would be better to have a little more detail than that. (Interview 48)

I like it. I would want [a] breakout though of the items in the Settlement Services Package . . . . But I like very much—I'll tell you one other thing that I really like is that it is not on legal paper. (Interview 23)

This so far seems a lot more organized than those other two forms. At least it's a real good attempt at organizing. . . . But perhaps they should itemize that out. (Interview 26)

I like this. This is very organized. I like it because it's sectioned off. It's grouped together by similar—yeah I like it. I think it's a whole lot easier to read than that other one that I had . . . . On the forms that I have, I have to kind of go through and pull out what is important . . . . So, the only part that I don't like is that it didn't break down the settlement service, which is the opposite of mine they broke it down, but they didn't give you a total. (Interview 51)

. . . It says this is what we're doing. This is the cost for it. I would like, I would personally kind of like to see what those are broken down into . . . . I think it's a better one-stop shop and easier to read. Basically it's easier to, you know if it's stapled together nice like this, to come and say here is all of the information I

need on my loan . . . . I think the format that it is in. It looks a little bit more simplistic. Although I'd never see the government going to a document that looks

like this. It does look more simplistic to read. It's broken down more into categories rather than just the litany of charges. It's broken down in small chunks of information . . . . a lot of information presented in one-page . . . . I think it gives you all of the information you need. I think if you could get this type of information from several companies to compare loans now that would be more useful. If they're willing to send you something like that, which I don't think most companies are. (Interview 20)

APPENDIX E CONSUMER TESTING RECRUITMENT SCRIPT AND SCREENER

Mortgage Disclosure Study / Quantitative Consumer Testing
Recruitment Script and Screener

Respondent ID number ____________

Identification of interview location, prime/subprime sample, and other necessary information

____

Respondent name, address, and telephone number

____

1. Hello, may I speak to __________ [USE NAME FROM SAMPLE LIST]

1	Available	—> Continue
2	Not available	—> Ask to speak with person in household who makes or shares decisions on mortgages – if not available, schedule callback
3	No longer at this number	—> Tally and terminate

2. I'm ____________ from Cunningham Research Service, a nationwide market research company. We are not selling anything, we are just doing some consumer research and would like to talk to consumers like you. Could you spare a few minutes to answer some brief questions? Thank you.

   [IF ASKED: We are conducting the research for a government agency that is studying how well consumers understand and use information about mortgage costs, and whether there are ways to make the information more understandable and easier to use when consumers are shopping for a mortgage.][If name of agency is asked: Federal Trade Commission.]

3. In the last two years, that is, since the summer of 2003, have you taken out a mortgage of any kind – to either purchase a home, refinance an existing mortgage, or get a home equity loan or second mortgage?

1	Yes	—> Continue
2	No	—> Terminate and Tally
98	Don't know	—> Terminate and Tally
99	Refused	—> Terminate and Tally

4. When shopping for and making decisions about that mortgage, would you say that you were (a) the main decision-maker for your household, (b) that you shared in the decision-

making, or (c) that someone else in your household was responsible for shopping and making the decisions about the mortgage?

1	a. Main decision-maker	—> Continue
2	b. Shared in decision-making	—> Continue
3	c. Others were responsible	—> Ask to speak with the person responsible. If not available, get name and schedule a callback.
98	Don't know	—> Tally and terminate
99	Refused	—> Tally and terminate

5. Have you or anyone in your household ever worked in . . .
(Read each of the following:)

1 Market research?
2 Advertising or public relations?
3 A bank, mortgage broker, or finance company?
4 Real estate?

IF "YES" TO ANY OF THE ABOVE	—> Terminate and tally
IF "DON'T KNOW" TO ANY OF THE ABOVE	—> Terminate and tally
IF "REFUSED" TO ANY OF THE ABOVE	—> Terminate and tally
IF "NO" TO ALL OF THE ABOVE	—> Continue

6. Have you participated in a market research interview, survey, or focus group in the last 3 months?

1	Yes	—> Terminate and tally
2	No	—> Continue
3	DK	—> Terminate and tally
4	Refused	—> Terminate and tally

7. We would like to invite you to participate in a 20–30 minute research interview on ____ (dates) ______ at ______ (location) ______. At the end of the interview, you will be paid $30 for your participation. I want to stress that the purpose of the interview is strictly for research purposes. We are not selling anything. And your participation will be kept strictly confidential. Are you willing to participate?

IF ASKED —> Provide more information about the address and location of the interview facility.

[IF ASKED: We are conducting the research for a government agency that is studying how well consumers understand and use information about mortgage costs, and whether there are ways to make the information easier to understand and use when consumers are shopping for a mortgage.][If name of agency is asked: Federal Trade Commission.]

1 Yes —> GO TO Q.12
2 No —> GO TO Q.8
3 DK —> GO TO Q.8
4 Refused —> GO TO Q.8

8. I'm sorry to hear that. Why is it you won't be able to come? PROBE FOR REASON. MAKE SURE RESPONDENT UNDERSTANDS WE ARE NOT SELLING ANYTHING.

1 Agree to participate —> Go to Q.12
2 Refuse to participate —> Continue

9. [If answer to Q.4 was "1" ("main decision-maker") —> Terminate and tally]
[If answer to Q.4 was "2" ("shared decision-making") —> Continue]

10. Would the other person in your household who shared in the decision-making about the mortgage be willing to participate in the research interview?

1 Yes —> Continue
2 No —> Terminate and tally
3 Maybe —> Continue
3 DK —> Continue

11. Is he/she available to speak with me at this time?

1 Yes —> Start back at Q.1 with new respondent.
2 No —> Get name and schedule callback

12. FOR ALL SUCCESSFUL RECRUITS: Do you usually wear eyeglasses or contact lenses when you read?

1 Yes —> INSTRUCT RESPONDENT TO: Please bring your eyeglasses or contact lenses with you when you come to the interview. As part of the interview, we will be asking you to look at some information about mortgage costs. We would like you to have your glasses or contacts with you if you usually use them to read. —> Continue
2 No —> Continue

13. Thank you for agreeing to participate in this important research study. Your participation will be very valuable.

APPENDIX F
CONSUMER TESTING QUESTIONNAIRE

Mortgage Disclosure Study / Consumer Testing
Questionnaire

[Note: Questions 17-45 refer to "Loan M" and "Loan V." These loans correspond to the "simple loan" scenario. The loan names in these questions were changed to "Loan K" and "Loan T" for the "complex loan" scenario.]

Cunningham Research respondent ID number ______________

FTC respondent ID number ______________

Sample (prime versus subprime) ______________

Disclosure forms (current versus prototype) ______________

Loan scenario (MV versus KT) ______________

Interview location ______________

Introduction

Hello. I am ______________. Thank you for agreeing to participate in this research interview. As we assured you on the telephone, the interview is for research purposes only. We are not selling anything. Your participation in the research will be kept strictly confidential.

You have been invited to participate in this research interview because you have obtained a mortgage in the last two years or so. We are conducting the research for a government agency that is studying whether there are ways to make mortgage cost information easier to understand for consumers when they are shopping for a mortgage. [*If name of agency is asked: Federal Trade Commission.*] We will ask you some questions about your background and your experience getting mortgages, and then we will show you some information about mortgage costs and ask you some questions about it.

1. Do you usually wear eyeglasses or contact lenses when you read?

 1 Yes —> Continue
 2 No —> Skip to Q.4

2. Do you have your eyeglasses or contact lenses with you today?

 1 Yes —> Skip to Q.4
 2 No —> Continue

3. We will be asking you to read some information about mortgage costs and answer some questions, so if you have difficulty reading without your glasses or contacts, we will have to reschedule you for another time. Could you come back at [time] on [day]? What would be a convenient time for you?

—>Reschedule if possible, then terminate and tally

Demographic Questions

4. (Record sex - do not ask)

1 Male —> Continue
2 Female —> Continue

5. I want to begin by asking you a few questions about yourself. (Show age category card to respondent.) Please look at this card and tell me which of the categories, "A" through "F", describes your age.

1 a. 18 - 24 years old
2 b. 25 - 34 years old
3 c. 35 - 44 years old
4 d. 45 - 54 years old
5 e. 55 - 64 years old
6 f. 65 or more years old
98 g. Don't know (NOT ON CARD)
99 h. Refused (NOT ON CARD)

6. What is the last grade of school you completed?
(DO NOT READ LIST)

1 a. Less than high school graduate
2 b. High school graduate
3 c. Technical/trade school
4 d. Some college / Junior college / Associates degree
5 e. Graduated college
6 f. Graduate/professional school (Masters / PhD / Doctorate / Law school / Medical school) or more
98 g. Don't know
99 h. Refused

7. Are you of Hispanic or Latino origin?
(DO NOT READ LIST)

1 Yes
2 No
98 Don't know
99 Refused

8. (Show race category card to respondent.) Please look at this card and tell me which of the categories "H" through "L" best describes your race. You may select more than one category if more than one describes your race.

1 h. White
2 i. Black or African American
3 j. American Indian or Alaska Native
4 k. Asian
5 l. Native Hawaiian or Other Pacific Islander
97 Hispanic/Latino (VOLUNTEERED, NOT ON CARD)
98 Don't know (NOT ON CARD)
99 Refused (NOT ON CARD)

9. (Show income category card to respondent.) Please look at this card and tell me which of the categories, "H" through "N", best describes your total annual household income.

1 h. Less than $24,999
2 j. $25,000 to $49,999
4 k. $50,000 to $74,999
5 m. $75,000 to $99,999
6 n. $100,000 or more
7 o. Don't know (NOT ON CARD)
8 p. Refused (NOT ON CARD)

Mortgage Experience Questions

(ADD THE FOLLOWING NOTE TO INTERVIEWERS FOR QUESTIONS 10-14 (on the screen for each question): If respondent asks whether to include RENTAL, INVESTMENT, or VACATION properties, say "YES, include all mortgages.")

10. Now I want to ask a few questions about your experience obtaining mortgages. (Show "most recent mortgage date" category card to respondent.) Thinking about the last time you took out a mortgage, please look at this card and tell me which of the categories, "A" through "D", best describes how long ago you took out this mortgage. Count all types of mortgage transactions - either for purchasing a home, refinancing an existing mortgage, obtaining a home equity loan, or

obtaining a second mortgage.

1 a. Less than 6 months ago.
2 b. 6 months ago but less than 1 year ago.
3 c. 1 year ago but less than 2 years ago.
4 d. 2 or more years ago.
98 Don't know (NOT ON CARD)
99 Refused (NOT ON CARD)

11. (Show mortgage purpose category card to respondent.) Please look at this card and tell me which of the following categories, "A" through "D", describes the purpose of your most recent mortgage. You may select more than one category if more than one applies.

1 a. Purchase a home
2 b. Refinance an existing mortgage
3 c. Take cash out / consolidate debts
4 d. Home equity line of credit
5 e. Other (specify) ________________ (NOT ON CARD)
98 Don't know
99 Refused

12. How many different lenders or mortgage brokers did you contact while shopping for that mortgage?

(Record number) ________________
98 Don't know
99 Refused

13. Thinking about the company that you got that mortgage from, had you done business with them before you got that mortgage?

1 Yes
2 No
98 Don't know
99 Refused

14. Now I want to ask you about the total number of mortgages you have ever taken out, no matter how long ago. Again, count all types of mortgage transactions - for purchasing a home, refinancing an existing mortgage, obtaining a home equity loan, or obtaining a second mortgage. And please count all mortgages, no matter how long ago you took them out. Approximately how many times have you taken out a mortgage?

(Record number) ____________________

98 Don't know

99 Refused

Overall loan cost comparison and loan choice questions

(ROTATE THE ORDER IN WHICH THE LOAN FORMS ARE PLACED ON THE TABLE AND THE ORDER IN WHICH THE TWO LOANS ARE REFERRED TO IN QUESTIONS 15 AND 16. THE ROTATIONS SHOULD MATCH ACROSS THE TWO QUESTIONS.)

15. Now I'm going to show you some information about the cost of two different mortgage loans. *(Place the first set of loan forms on the table in front of the respondent.)* Please note that there is more than one page of information for each loan. Please look at this information like you would if you were shopping for a mortgage, and when you are ready, tell me which loan would cost you less. Would Loan __G__ cost you less, would Loan __R__ cost you less, or would both loans cost you the same? (DO NOT READ LIST).

1 Loan __G__

2 Loan __R__

3 Both the same

97 Cannot tell from this information / not enough information (DO NOT READ)

98 Don't know (DO NOT READ)

99 Refused

16. If you were shopping for a mortgage loan and had to choose between one of these two loans, which loan would you choose, Loan __G__ or Loan __R__? (DO NOT READ LIST).

01 Loan __G__

02 Loan __R__

95 Either, both the same

96 Neither

97 Cannot tell from this information / not enough information

98 Don't know

99 Refused

(REMOVE LOANS G AND R FROM TABLE.)

<u>Comparison and identification of individual loan cost items</u>

(PROGRAMMING NOTE: 4 OF THE 8 TEST CELLS WILL USE LOANS LABELED "M" AND "V" FOR THE REMAINDER OF THE QUESTIONNAIRE. THE OTHER 4 CELLS WILL USE LOANS LABELED "K" AND "T". THIS WILL REQUIRE TWO ADJUSTMENTS IN THE PROGRAMMING:
(1) FOR 4 OF THE CELLS, IN ALL QUESTIONS AND RESPONSE CATEGORIES BELOW, THE WORDING "LOAN M" SHOULD BE REPLACED WITH "LOAN K", AND WORDING "LOAN V" SHOULD BE REPLACED WITH "LOAN T".
(2) THE PRE-CODED NUMERICAL RESPONSES WILL DIFFER BETWEEN LOANS M/V AND LOANS K/T. BOTH SETS OF PRE-CODED RESPONSES ARE GIVEN BELOW. NOTES INDICATE WHICH SET IS RELEVANT TO EACH LOAN SCENARIO. ONLY ONE SET OF PRE-CODED RESPONSES SHOULD APPEAR ON THE SCREEN FOR THE INTERVIEWER – THE ONE RELEVANT FOR THE CELL BEING USED.)

(ROTATE THE ORDER IN WHICH THE LOAN FORMS ARE PLACED ON THE TABLE AND THE ORDER IN WHICH THE TWO LOANS ARE REFERRED TO IN QUESTIONS 17, 20, 25, 27, 29, 32, and 34. THE ROTATIONS SHOULD MATCH ACROSS THESE QUESTIONS)

LOAN AMOUNT:

17. Now I'm going to show you the same type of information about two other mortgage loans. *(Place the second set of loan forms on the table in front of the respondent.)* Please look at this information like you would if you were shopping for a mortgage, and when you are ready, I will ask you some questions about it. Again, please note that there is more than one page of information for each loan. *(Allow the respondent a few minutes to look at the information. If the respondent does not volunteer that they are ready, ask:* Are you ready, or would you like a little more time to look at these? *Proceed when ready.)*

Based on the figures shown in these loan documents, in which loan would you be borrowing LESS money? That is, which loan has a lower loan amount? Would you be borrowing less money in Loan <u>M</u>, would you be borrowing less money in Loan <u>V</u>, or would you be borrowing the same amount in both loans?

1 Loan <u>M</u>
2 Loan <u>V</u>
3 Both are the same
97 Cannot tell / not enough information (DO NOT READ)

98 Don't know (DO NOT READ)
99 Refused

18. If you were to take out Loan V, how much money would you be borrowing, that is what is the loan amount in Loan V?
(DO NOT READ LIST)

(FOR LOAN M/V SCENARIO:)

1 $167,066
2 $164,960
3 $160,000

(FOR LOAN K/T SCENARIO:)

4 $189,313
5 $186,147
6 $175,425

(FOR BOTH LOAN SCENARIOS:)

9 Other (specify) ____________________
97 Cannot tell / not enough information
98 Don't know
99 Refused

19. Does Loan V include money borrowed to pay for settlement costs or other up-front charges?

1 Yes
2 No
97 Cannot tell / not enough information (DO NOT READ)
98 Don't know (DO NOT READ)
99 Refused

SETTLEMENT COSTS:

20. Which of these two loans has LOWER settlement charges? Does Loan __M__ have lower settlement charges, does Loan __V__ have lower settlement charges, or do both loans have the same settlement charges?

1 Loan __M__
2 Loan __V__

3 Both the same
97 Cannot tell / not enough information
98 Don't know (DO NOT READ)
99 Refused

21. How much are the settlement charges in Loan M?
(DO NOT READ LIST)

(FOR LOAN M/V SCENARIO:)

1 $6,606
2 $44,606

(FOR LOAN K/T SCENARIO:)

4 $5,303
5 $5,065

(FOR BOTH LOAN SCENARIOS:)

9 Other (specify) ____________________
97 Cannot tell / not enough information
98 Don't know
99 Refused

OPTIONAL COSTS:

22. In Loan V, are there any charges for optional products or services that are NOT required for the loan, that is, for products or services that you would NOT have to buy if you were getting this loan?
(DO NOT READ)

1 Yes —> continue
2 No —> skip to Q.25
97 Cannot tell / not enough information (DO NOT READ) —> skip to Q.25
98 Don't know (DO NOT READ) —> skip to Q.25
99 Refused —> skip to Q.25

23. What products or services are the optional charges for?
(DO NOT READ LIST)

IF RESPONDENT SAYS "INSURANCE" WITHOUT FURTHER SPECIFICATION, ASK "WHAT KIND OF INSURANCE?"

1 Insurance (non-specific)
2 Credit / life / disability insurance
3 Hazard / homeowner's insurance
4 Taxes
9 Other (specify) ____________________
97 Cannot tell / not enough information
98 Don't know
99 Refused

24. How much do the optional products and services cost?
(DO NOT READ LIST)

(FOR LOAN M/V SCENARIO:)

(NO PRE-CODED RESPONSES – USE ONLY COMMON RESPONSES)

(FOR LOAN K/T SCENARIO:)

4 $6,230
5 $3,900 and/plus $2330

(FOR BOTH LOAN SCENARIOS:)

9 Other (specify) ____________________
97 Cannot tell / not enough information
98 Don't know
99 Refused

TOTAL UP-FRONT CHARGES:

25. Which of these two loans has HIGHER total up-front charges? Does Loan __M__ have higher total up-front charges, does Loan __V__ have higher total up-front charges, or do both loans have the same amount of total up-front charges?

1 Loan __M__
2 Loan __V__
3 Both the same
97 Cannot tell / not enough information (DO NOT READ)
98 Don't know (DO NOT READ)
99 Refused

26. How much are the total up-front charges in Loan V?

(DO NOT READ LIST)

(FOR LOAN M/V SCENARIO:)

1 $7,066
2 $38,000

(FOR LOAN K/T SCENARIO:)

4 $13,888
5 $0.00
6 $7,658

(FOR BOTH LOAN SCENARIOS:)

9 Other (specify) ____________________
97 Cannot tell / not enough information
98 Don't know
99 Refused

INTEREST RATE:

27. Which of these two loans has the LOWER interest rate? Does Loan __M__ have the lower interest rate, does Loan __V__ have the lower interest rate, or do both loans have the same interest rate?

1 Loan __M__
2 Loan __V__
3 Both the same
97 Cannot tell / not enough information (DO NOT READ)
98 Don't know (DO NOT READ)
99 Refused

28. What is the interest rate in Loan M?
(DO NOT READ LIST)

(FOR LOAN M/V SCENARIO:)

1 5.75%
2 5.88%

(FOR LOAN K/T SCENARIO:)

4 6.20%
5 6.38%

(FOR BOTH LOAN SCENARIOS:)

9 Other (specify) ______________

97 Cannot tell / not enough information

98 Don't know

99 Refused

APR:

29. Which of these two loans has the LOWER annual percentage rate? The annual percentage rate is sometimes referred to as the "APR." Does Loan __M__ have the lower annual percentage rate, does Loan __V__ have the lower annual percentage rate, or do both loans have the same annual percentage rate?

1 Loan __M__
2 Loan __V__
3 Both the same
97 Cannot tell / not enough information (DO NOT READ)
98 Don't know (DO NOT READ)
99 Refused

30. What is the annual percentage rate, that is, the APR, for Loan M? (DO NOT READ LIST)

(FOR LOAN M/V SCENARIO:)

1 5.88%
2 5.75%

(FOR LOAN K/T SCENARIO:)

4 6.38%
5 6.20%

(FOR BOTH LOAN SCENARIOS:)

9 Other (specify) ______________

97 Cannot tell / not enough information

98 Don't know

99 Refused

31. Sometimes the annual percentage rate for a loan is higher than the interest rate. Why is the APR sometimes higher than the interest rate?

1 APR includes closing costs / settlement costs / up-front costs / additional costs / finance charges / etc.
2 APR is the FINAL interest rate at closing
3 APR is the MAXIMUM that the interest rate can go up to
4 APR includes COMPOUNDING of the interest
9 Other (specify) ____________
97 Cannot tell / not enough information
98 Don't know
99 Refused

CASH AT CLOSING:

32. Which of these two loans would require you to pay LESS cash at the closing table? Would Loan __M__ require less cash at closing, would Loan __V__ require less cash at closing, or would both loans require the same cash at closing?

1 Loan __M__
2 Loan __V__
3 Both the same
97 Cannot tell / not enough information (DO NOT READ)
98 Don't know (DO NOT READ)
99 Refused

33. How much would you have to pay in cash at closing in Loan V? (DO NOT READ LIST)

(FOR LOAN M/V SCENARIO:)

1 $38,000
2 $7,066
3 $47,066

(FOR LOAN K/T SCENARIO:)

4 $0.00
5 $7,658
6 $13,888

(FOR BOTH LOAN SCENARIOS:)

9 Other (specify) ____________________
97 Cannot tell / not enough information
98 Don't know
99 Refused

MONTHLY PAYMENT:

34. Which of these two loans has a LOWER monthly payment, that is, in which loan would your monthly costs be lower? Does Loan __M__ have a lower monthly payment, does Loan __V__ have lower monthly payment, or do both loans have the same monthly payment?

1 Loan __M__
2 Loan __V__
3 Both the same
97 Cannot tell / not enough information (DO NOT READ)
98 Don't know (DO NOT READ)
99 Refused

35. How much would your monthly payment be in Loan M?
(DO NOT READ LIST)

(FOR LOAN M/V SCENARIO:)

1 $1,160
2 $933

(FOR LOAN K/T SCENARIO:)

4 $1,280
5 $1,074

(FOR BOTH LOAN SCENARIOS:)

9 Other (specify) ____________________
97 Cannot tell / not enough information
98 Don't know
99 Refused

ESCROW PAYMENT:

36. Would the monthly payment in Loan M include payments for your property taxes and homeowner's insurance, or would you have to pay for those separately by

yourself?

1 Includes payments for taxes and insurance —> Skip to Q.38
2 Have to pay for those separately by yourself —> Continue
97 Cannot tell / not enough information (DO NOT READ) —> Skip to Q.38
98 Don't know (DO NOT READ) —> Skip to Q.38
99 Refused —> skip to Q.38

37. How much would you have to pay each month for property taxes and homeowner's insurance in Loan M?
(DO NOT READ LIST)

(FOR LOAN M/V SCENARIO:)

1 $166 (for property taxes) and $60 (for homeowner's insurance)
2 $226 (combined)

(FOR LOAN K/T SCENARIO:)

4 $145 (for property taxes) and $60 (for homeowner's insurance)
5 $205 (combined)

(FOR BOTH LOAN SCENARIOS:)

9 Other (specify) ____________
97 Cannot tell / not enough information
98 Don't know
99 Refused

BALLOON PAYMENT:

38. If you took out Loan V and made all of the monthly payments until the end of the loan term, would the last payment amount be the same as the other monthly payments on that loan, more than the other monthly payments on that loan, or less than the other monthly payments on that loan?
(DO NOT READ LIST)

(ROTATE THE ORDER IN WHICH THE THREE RESPONSES ARE LISTED IN THE QUESTION.)

1 Same as the other monthly payments —> Skip to Q.40
2 Less than the other monthly payments —> Continue
3 More than the other monthly payments —> Continue

97 Cannot tell / not enough information (DO NOT READ) —> Skip to Q.40
98 Don't know (DO NOT READ) —> Skip to Q.40
99 Refused —> Skip to Q.40

39. How much would your last monthly payment be in Loan V?
(DO NOT READ LIST)

(FOR LOAN M/V SCENARIO:)

1 $1,237

(FOR LOAN K/T SCENARIO:)

4 $190,568
5 $190,362
6 $1,254
7 $1,049
8 $1,254 plus $189,313
9 $1,049 plus $189,313

(FOR BOTH LOAN SCENARIOS:)

10 Other (specify) ____________________
97 Cannot tell / not enough information
98 Don't know
99 Refused

40. After making the last monthly payment in Loan V, would you still owe any money on the loan?

1 Yes —> Continue
2 No —> Skip to Q.42
97 Cannot tell / not enough information —> Skip to Q.42
98 Don't know —> Skip to Q.42
99 Refused —> Skip to Q.42

41. How much would you still owe on the loan?
(DO NOT READ LIST)

(FOR LOAN M/V SCENARIO:)

(NO PRE-CODED RESPONSES – USE ONLY COMMON RESPONSES)

(FOR LOAN K/T SCENARIO:)

4 $189,313
5 $190,568
6 $190,362

(FOR BOTH LOAN SCENARIOS:)

9 Other (specify) ____________
97 Cannot tell / not enough information
98 Don't know
99 Refused

PREPAY PENALTY:

42. Suppose that you took out Loan M and then TWO years later you wanted to refinance the mortgage with a different lender to get a better interest rate. To get out of Loan M would you have to (a) pay off the remaining balance that you still owed on the loan, (b) pay off the remaining balance plus pay some additional fees, or (c) pay less than the remaining balance?

(ROTATE ORDER OF FIRST THREE RESPONSES)

1 Pay remaining balance only —> Skip to Q.45
2 Pay remaining balance plus additional fees —> Skip to Q.44
3 Pay less than the remaining balance —> Continue to Q.43
4 MAY pay additional fees/penalty (DO NOT READ) —> Skip to Q.44
97 Cannot tell / not enough information (DO NOT READ) —> Skip to Q.45
98 Don't know (DO NOT READ) —> skip to Q.45
99 Refused —> skip to Q.45

43. How much less would you have to pay?
(DO NOT READ LIST)

(FOR LOAN M/V SCENARIO:)

(NO PRE-CODED RESPONSES – USE ONLY COMMON RESPONSES)

(FOR LOAN K/T SCENARIO:)

4 4%
5 $7,017

(FOR BOTH LOAN SCENARIOS:)

9 Other (specify) ______________
97 Cannot tell / not enough information
98 Don't know
99 Refused

All —> skip to Q.45

44. How much more would you have to pay in additional fees?

IF RESPONSE TO Q.42 IS "MAY HAVE TO PAY ADDITIONAL FEES" (I.E., RESPONSE CATEGORY 4), USE THIS ALTERNATIVE WORDING:

How much more MIGHT you have to pay in additional fees?

(DO NOT READ LIST)

(FOR LOAN M/V SCENARIO:)

(NO PRE-CODED RESPONSES – USE ONLY COMMON RESPONSES)

(FOR LOAN K/T SCENARIO:)

4 4%
5 $7,017

(FOR BOTH LOAN SCENARIOS:)

9 Other (specify) ______________
97 Cannot tell / not enough information
98 Don't know
99 Refused

45. Suppose that you took out Loan M and then SIX years later you wanted to refinance the mortgage with a different lender to get a better interest rate. To get out of Loan M, would you have to (a) pay off the remaining balance that you still owed on the loan, (b) pay off the remaining balance plus pay some additional fees, or (c) pay less than the remaining balance?

(ROTATE ORDER OF FIRST THREE RESPONSES)

1 Pay remaining balance only
2 Pay remaining balance plus additional fees
3 Pay less than remaining balance
4 MAY pay additional fees/penalty (DO NOT READ)
97 Cannot tell / not enough information (DO NOT READ)
98 Don't know (DO NOT READ)
99 Refused

46. That is the end of our questions. I want to thank you for taking the time to participate in the study. The government agency that is sponsoring the study is exploring ways to make mortgage costs more understandable for consumers. We are showing different types of forms to different consumers like you to see how easy or difficult the forms are to understand and use. We will then see which way of presenting the information works best. Your participation in the study will be very helpful. Thank you very much.

APPENDIX G
CONSUMER TESTING CURRENT DISCLOSURE FORMS

Current Disclosure Forms Used in the Consumer Testing

The current mortgage cost disclosure forms shown to respondents in the consumer testing are presented in this appendix. The size of the forms has been reduced to fit the paper and margin sizes of this chapter. The forms used in the testing were on legal-size paper, rather than the letter-size presented here, and the text of the forms extended almost to the edge of the paper.

All six versions of the current forms that were used in the testing are presented in this appendix. The format of the forms is the same for all versions, but the specified loan costs vary. The six versions consist of the following loans:

Loans G and R	Used for the overall loan cost and loan choice questions (Questions 15-16) in both the simple-loan and complex-loan scenario groups.
Loans M and V	Used for the individual loan cost questions (Questions 17-45) in the simple-loan scenario group.
Loans K and T	Used for the individual loan cost questions (Questions 17-45) in the complex-loan scenario group.

The test questions, loan-cost scenarios, and loan cost specifications are discussed in detail in the Consumer Testing Methodology section of this chapter.

FEDERAL TRUTH-IN LENDING DISCLOSURE STATEMENT
For use with Fixed-Rate, GPM, Balloon Mortgage,
Adjustable or Variable Rate Loans

Date: 10/14/05
Loan No.: 47231
Borrowers: James and Clara Borrower

LOAN "G"

Property
Location: 123 Your Street
Hometown, VA 22189

ANNUAL PERCENTAGE RATE The cost of your credit as a yearly rate	**FINANCE CHARGE** The dollar amount the credit will cost you	Amount Financed The amount of credit provided to you or on your behalf	Total of Payments The amount you will have paid after you have made all payments as scheduled
6.03 %	$ 201,679.93	$ 172,915.95	$ 374,595.88

You have the right to receive at this time an itemization of the Amount Financed.
☐ I want an itemization ☒ I do not want an itemization

Your payment schedule will be:

Number of Payments	Amount of Payments	When Payments Are Due
360	$ 1,040.52	Monthly beginning 12/01/05
	$	
	$	
	$	
	$	
	$	
	$	

Variable Rate: ☐ This loan has a Variable Rate Feature. Variable Rate Disclosures have been provided to you earlier.

☐ This obligation has a demand Feature.
Insurance: Credit life insurance and credit disability insurance are not required to obtain credit, and will not be provided unless you sign and agree to pay the additional cost. No such insurance will be in force until you have completed an application, the insurance company has issued the policy, the effective date of that policy has arrived and the required premium has been paid.

Type	Premium	Term	Signature
Credit Life	$		I want to apply for credit life insurance. ______ SIGNATURE
Credit Disability	$		I want to apply for credit disability insurance. ______ SIGNATURE
Credit Life and Credit Disability	$		I want to apply for credit life and disability insurance. ______ SIGNATURE

You may obtain property insurance from anyone you want that is acceptable to this institution. If you get the insurance from ______ you will pay $ ______ for a term of ______

Security: You are giving a security interest in:
☒ the property being purchased
☐ ______

Late Charge: If payment is late, you will be charged $ ______ / 5.00 % of the payment.

Prepayment: If you pay off early, you
☐ may ☒ will not have to pay a penalty.
☐ may ☒ will not be entitled to a refund of part of the finance charge.

Assumption: Someone buying your home
☒ cannot assume the remainder of the mortgage on the original terms.
☐ may, subject to conditions, be allowed to assume the remainder of the mortgage on the original terms.

A deposit balance ☐ is ☒ is not required. The Annual Percentage Rate does not take into account your required deposit.
See your contract documents for any additional information about nonpayment, default, any required repayment in full before the scheduled date, and prepayment refunds and penalties.

e means an estimate

I/We hereby acknowledge receipt of this disclosure.

______ / ______ DATE

______ / ______ DATE

Prepared by: ______ ______ TITLE

GOOD FAITH ESTIMATE

LOAN "G"

Lender:	JL Mortgage Company
Address:	123 Main Street Mortgagetown, VA 22189
Applicant(s):	James and Clara Borrower
Property Address:	123 Your Street Hometown, VA 22189

Sales Price:	$220,000.00
Base Loan Amount:	$176,000.00
Total Loan Amount:	$176,000.00
Type of Loan:	Fixed Rate
Date Prepared:	10/14/05
Rate: 5.87%	Term: 30 Year

The information provided below reflects estimates of the charges which you are likely to incur at the settlement of your loan. The fees listed are estimates - the actual charges may be more or less. Your transaction may not involve a fee for every item listed.
The numbers listed beside the estimates generally correspond to the numbered lines contained in the HUD-1 or HUD-1A settlement statement that you will be receiving at settlement. The HUD-1 or HUD-1A settlement statement will show you the actual cost for items paid at settlement.

800 ITEMS PAYABLE IN CONNECTION WITH LOAN:	
801 Loan Origination Fee (1.00 %)	$ 1,760.00
802 Loan Discount Fee (%)	$
803 Appraisal Fee	$ 300.00
804 Credit Report	$
805 Lender's Inspection Fee	$
806 Mortgage Insurance Application Fee	$
807 Assumption Fee	$
808 Mortgage Broker Fee	$
809 CLO Access Fee	$
810 Tax Related Service Fee	$ 82.00
Administrative Fee	$ 650.00
Doc Prep Fee	$ 65.00
Courier	$ 85.00
	$
	$

900 ITEMS REQUIRED BY LENDER TO BE PAID IN ADVANCE:	
901 Interest for 10 day @$ 28.3047 per day	$ 283.05
902 Mortgage Insurance Premium	$
903 Hazard Insurance Premium	$ 540.00
	$
	$
	$

1000 RESERVES DEPOSITED WITH LENDER:	
1001 Haz Ins Prem 2 months @$ 45.00	$ 90.00
1004 Tax & Assmt Res 9 months @$ 183.33	$ 1,650.00
	$
	$
	$

"L" designates those costs to be paid by Lender.

1100 TITLE CHARGES:	
1101 Closing or Escrow Fee	$ 275.00
1102 Abstract or Title Search	$ 150.00
1103 Title Examination	$
1104 Title Insurance Binder	$
1105 Document Preparation Fee	$ 150.00
1106 Notary Fee	$ 20.00
1107 Attorney Fees	$
1108 Title Insurance	$ 774.00
Title Binder	$ 75.00
	$
	$
	$

1200 GOVERNMENT RECORDING & TRANSFER CHARGES:	
1201 Recording Fees:	$ 75.00
1202 City/County Tax/Stamps:	$ 110.00
1203 State Tax/Stamps:	$ 330.00
County Tax	$ 374.00
	$
	$
	$

1300 ADDITIONAL SETTLEMENT CHARGES:	
1301 Survey	$ 180.0
1302 Pest Inspection	$
Flood Certification	$ 34.00
	$
	$
	$
TOTAL ESTIMATED SETTLEMENT CHARGES	$ 8,052.05

TOTAL ESTIMATED FUNDS NEEDED TO CLOSE:	
Downpayment	$ 44,000.00
Est. Closing Costs	$ 5,489.00
Est. Prepaid Items/Reserves	$ 2,563.05
OTHER: Earnest Money	$ (2,000.00)
TOTAL EST. FUNDS NEEDED TO CLOSE	$ 50,052.05

TOTAL ESTIMATED MONTHLY PAYMENT:	
Principal & Interest	$ 1,040.54
Real Estate Taxes	$ 183.33
Flood & Hazard Insurance	$ 45.00
Mortgage Insurance	$
	$
TOTAL MONTHLY PAYMENT	$ 1,268.88

THIS SECTION TO BE COMPLETED BY LENDER ONLY IF A PARTICULAR PROVIDER OF SERVICE IS REQUIRED. Use of the particular provider is required and the estimate is based on charges of the provider.

ITEM NO.	NAME & ADDRESS OF PROVIDER	TELEPHONE NO.	NATURE OF RELATIONSHIP

These estimates are provided pursuant to the Real Estate Settlement Procedures Act of 1974, as amended (RESPA). Additional information can be found in the HUD Special Information Booklet, which is to be provided to you by your mortgage broker or lender, if your application is to purchase residential real property and the Lender will take a first lien on the property. The undersigned acknowledges receipt of the booklet "Settlement Costs," and the Consumer Handbook on ARM Mortgages, if applicable.

Applicant Date Applicant Date

Applicant Date Applicant Date

☐ This Good Faith Estimate is being provided by , a mortgage broker, and no lender has yet been obtained.

"S" designates those costs to be paid by Seller.

FEDERAL TRUTH-IN LENDING DISCLOSURE STATEMENT
For use with Fixed-Rate, GPM, Balloon Mortgage,
Adjustable or Variable Rate Loans

LOAN "R"

Date: 10/14/05
Loan No.: 37912
Borrowers: James and Clara Borrower

Property
Location: 123 Your Street
Hometown, VA 22189

ANNUAL PERCENTAGE RATE The cost of your credit as a yearly rate	**FINANCE CHARGE** The dollar amount the credit will cost you	Amount Financed The amount of credit provided to you or on your behalf	Total of Payments The amount you will have paid after you have made all payments as scheduled
6.03 %	$ 201,679.93	$ 172,915.95	$ 374,595.88

You have the right to receive at this time an itemization of the Amount Financed.
☐ I want an itemization ☒ I do not want an itemization

Your payment schedule will be:

Number of Payments	Amount of Payments	When Payments Are Due
360	$ 1,040.54	Monthly beginning 12/01/05
	$	
	$	
	$	
	$	
	$	
	$	

Variable Rate: ☐ This loan has a Variable Rate Feature. Variable Rate Disclosures have been provided to you earlier.

☐ This obligation has a demand Feature.

Insurance: Credit life insurance and credit disability insurance are not required to obtain credit, and will not be provided unless you sign and agree to pay the additional cost. No such insurance will be in force until you have completed an application, the insurance company has issued the policy, the effective date of that policy has arrived and the required premium has been paid.

Type	Premium	Term	Signature
Credit Life	$		I want to apply for credit life insurance. ________ SIGNATURE
Credit Disability	$		I want to apply for credit disability insurance. ________ SIGNATURE
Credit Life and Credit Disability	$		I want to apply for credit life and disability insurance. ________ SIGNATURE

You may obtain property insurance from anyone you want that is acceptable to this institution. If you get the insurance from ________________ you will pay $ ________ for a term of ________________

Security: You are giving a security interest in:
☒ the property being purchased
☐ ________________

Late Charge: If payment is late, you will be charged $ ________ / 5.00 % of the payment.

Prepayment: If you pay off early, you
☐ may ☒ will not have to pay a penalty.
☐ may ☒ will not be entitled to a refund of part of the finance charge.

Assumption: Someone buying your home
☒ cannot assume the remainder of the mortgage on the original terms.
☐ may, subject to conditions, be allowed to assume the remainder of the mortgage on the original terms.

A deposit balance ☐ is ☒ is not required. The Annual Percentage Rate does not take into account your required deposit.

See your contract documents for any additional information about nonpayment, default, any required repayment in full before the scheduled date, and prepayment refunds and penalties.

e means an estimate

I/We hereby acknowledge receipt of this disclosure.

________________ / ________ DATE

________________ / ________ DATE

Prepared by: ________________ ________ TITLE

GOOD FAITH ESTIMATE

LOAN "R"

Lender:	FS Mortgage Company
Address:	456 Main Street Mortgagetown, VA 22189
Applicant(s):	James and Clara Borrower
Property Address:	123 Your Street Hometown, VA 22189

Sales Price:	$220,000.00
Base Loan Amount:	$176,000.00
Total Loan Amount:	$176,000.00
Type of Loan:	Fixed Rate
Date Prepared:	10/14/05
Rate: 5.87% Term:	30 Year

The information provided below reflects estimates of the charges which you are likely to incur at the settlement of your loan. The fees listed are estimates - the actual charges may be more or less. Your transaction may not involve a fee for every item listed.

The numbers listed beside the estimates generally correspond to the numbered lines contained in the HUD-1 or HUD-1A settlement statement that you will be receiving at settlement. The HUD-1 or HUD-1A settlement statement will show you the actual cost for items paid at settlement.

800 ITEMS PAYABLE IN CONNECTION WITH LOAN:		
801 Loan Origination Fee (%)	$	2,590.00
802 Loan Discount Fee (%)	$	
803 Appraisal Fee	$	300.00
804 Credit Report	$	
805 Lender's Inspection Fee	$	
806 Mortgage Insurance Application Fee	$	
807 Assumption Fee	$	
808 Mortgage Broker Fee	$	
809 CLO Access Fee	$	
810 Tax Related Service Fee	$	25.00
Administrative Fee	$	52.00
Doc Prep Fee	$	60.00
Courier	$	15.00
	$	
	$	

900 ITEMS REQUIRED BY LENDER TO BE PAID IN ADVANCE:		
901 Interest for 10 day @$ 28.30 per day	$	47 283.05
902 Mortgage Insurance Premium	$	
903 Hazard Insurance Premium	$	540.00
	$	
	$	
	$	

1000 RESERVES DEPOSITED WITH LENDER:		
1001 Haz Ins Prem 2 months @$ 45.00	$	90.00
1004 Tax & Assmt Res 9 months @$ 183.33	$	1,650.00
	$	
	$	
	$	

"L" designates those costs to be paid by Lender.

1100 TITLE CHARGES:		
1101 Closing or Escrow Fee	$	110.00
1102 Abstract or Title Search	$	30.00
1103 Title Examination	$	
1104 Title Insurance Binder	$	
1105 Document Preparation Fee	$	30.00
1106 Notary Fee	$	10.00
1107 Attorney Fees	$	
1108 Title Insurance	$	248.00
Title Binder	$	15.00
	$	
	$	
	$	

1200 GOVERNMENT RECORDING & TRANSFER CHARGES:		
1201 Recording Fees:	$	75.00
1202 City/County Tax/Stamps:	$	110.00
1203 State Tax/Stamps:	$	330.00
County Tax	$	374.00
	$	
	$	
	$	

1300 ADDITIONAL SETTLEMENT CHARGES:		
1301 Survey	$	70.00
1302 Pest Inspection	$	
Flood Certification	$	24.00
	$	
	$	
	$	
TOTAL ESTIMATED SETTLEMENT CHARGES	$	7,026.05

TOTAL ESTIMATED FUNDS NEEDED TO CLOSE:		
Downpayment	$	44,000.00
Est. Closing Costs	$	4,463.00
Est. Prepaid Items/Reserves	$	2,563.05
OTHER: Earnest Money	$	(2,000.00)
TOTAL EST. FUNDS NEEDED TO CLOSE	$	49,026.05

TOTAL ESTIMATED MONTHLY PAYMENT:		
Principal & Interest	$	1,040.54
Real Estate Taxes	$	183.33
Flood & Hazard Insurance	$	45.00
Mortgage Insurance	$	
	$	
TOTAL MONTHLY PAYMENT	$	1,268.88

THIS SECTION TO BE COMPLETED BY LENDER ONLY IF A PARTICULAR PROVIDER OF SERVICE IS REQUIRED. Use of the particular provider is required and the estimate is based on charges of the provider.

ITEM NO.	NAME & ADDRESS OF PROVIDER	TELEPHONE NO.	NATURE OF RELATIONSHIP

These estimates are provided pursuant to the Real Estate Settlement Procedures Act of 1974, as amended (RESPA). Additional information can be found in the HUD Special Information Booklet, which is to be provided to you by your mortgage broker or lender, if your application is to purchase residential real property and the Lender will take a first lien on the property. The undersigned acknowledges receipt of the booklet "Settlement Costs," and the Consumer Handbook on ARM Mortgages, if applicable.

Applicant	Date	Applicant	Date
Applicant	Date	Applicant	Date

☐ This Good Faith Estimate is being provided by , a mortgage broker, and no lender has yet been obtained.

"S" designates those costs to be paid by Seller.

FEDERAL TRUTH-IN LENDING DISCLOSURE STATEMENT
For use with Fixed-Rate, GPM, Balloon Mortgage,
Adjustable or Variable Rate Loans

LOAN "M"

Date: 10/14/05
Loan No.: 53926
Borrowers: James and Clara Borrower

Property Location: 123 Your Street
Hometown, VA 22189

ANNUAL PERCENTAGE RATE The cost of your credit as a yearly rate	**FINANCE CHARGE** The dollar amount the credit will cost you	Amount Financed The amount of credit provided to you or on your behalf	Total of Payments The amount you will have paid after you have made all payments as scheduled
5.88 %	$ 178,459.61	$ 157,678.36	$ 336,137.97

You have the right to receive at this time an itemization of the Amount Financed.
☐ I want an itemization ☒ I do not want an itemization

Your payment schedule will be:

Number of Payments	Amount of Payments	When Payments Are Due
360	$ 933.72	Monthly beginning 12/01/05
	$	
	$	
	$	
	$	
	$	
	$	

Variable Rate: ☐ This loan has a Variable Rate Feature. Variable Rate Disclosures have been provided to you earlier.

☐ This obligation has a demand Feature.

Insurance: Credit life insurance and credit disability insurance are not required to obtain credit, and will not be provided unless you sign and agree to pay the additional cost. No such insurance will be in force until you have completed an application, the insurance company has issued the policy, the effective date of that policy has arrived and the required premium has been paid.

Type	Premium	Term	Signature	
Credit Life	$		I want to apply for credit life insurance.	SIGNATURE
Credit Disability	$		I want to apply for credit disability insurance.	SIGNATURE
Credit Life and Credit Disability	$		I want to apply for credit life and disability insurance.	SIGNATURE

You may obtain property insurance from anyone you want that is acceptable to this institution. If you get the insurance from ____________ you will pay $ ________ for a term of ____________

Security: You are giving a security interest in:
☒ the property being purchased
☐ ____________

Late Charge: If payment is late, you will be charged $ ____________ / 5.00 % of the payment.

Prepayment: If you pay off early, you
☐ may ☒ will not have to pay a penalty.
☐ may ☒ will not be entitled to a refund of part of the finance charge.

Assumption: Someone buying your home
☒ cannot assume the remainder of the mortgage on the original terms.
☐ may, subject to conditions, be allowed to assume the remainder of the mortgage on the original terms.

A deposit balance ☐ is ☒ is not required. The Annual Percentage Rate does not take into account your required deposit.

See your contract documents for any additional information about nonpayment, default, any required repayment in full before the scheduled date, and prepayment refunds and penalties.

e means an estimate

I/We hereby acknowledge receipt of this disclosure.

____________ / ____________ DATE

____________ / ____________ DATE

Prepared by: ____________ ____________ TITLE

Lender:	JL Mortgage Company
Address:	123 Main Street Mortgagetown, VA 22189
Applicant(s):	James and Clara Borrower
Property Address:	123 Your Street Hometown, VA 22189

LOAN "M"

GOOD FAITH ESTIMATE

Sales Price:	$200,000.00
Base Loan Amount:	$160,000.00
Total Loan Amount:	$160,000.00
Type of Loan:	Fixed Rate
Date Prepared:	10/14/05
Rate: 5.75%	Term: 30 Year

The information provided below reflects estimates of the charges which you are likely to incur at the settlement of your loan. The fees listed are estimates - the actual charges may be more or less. Your transaction may not involve a fee for every item listed.
The numbers listed beside the estimates generally correspond to the numbered lines contained in the HUD-1 or HUD-1A settlement statement that you will be receiving at settlement. The HUD-1 or HUD-1A settlement statement will show you the actual cost for items paid at settlement.

800 ITEMS PAYABLE IN CONNECTION WITH LOAN:		
801 Loan Origination Fee (%)	$	1,400.00
802 Loan Discount Fee (%)	$	
803 Appraisal Fee	$	200.00
804 Credit Report	$	
805 Lender's Inspection Fee	$	
806 Mortgage Insurance Application Fee	$	
807 Assumption Fee	$	
808 Mortgage Broker Fee	$	
809 CLO Access Fee	$	
810 Tax Related Service Fee	$	50.00
Administrative Fee	$	450.00
Doc Prep Fee	$	100.00
Courier	$	50.00
	$	
	$	

900 ITEMS REQUIRED BY LENDER TO BE PAID IN ADVANCE:		
901 Interest for 8 day @$ 25.2055 per day	$	201.64
902 Mortgage Insurance Premium	$	
903 Hazard Insurance Premium	$	720.00
	$	
	$	
	$	

1000 RESERVES DEPOSITED WITH LENDER:		
1001 Haz Ins Prem 2 months @$ 60.00	$	120.00
1004 Tax & Assmt Res 9 months@$ 166.67	$	1,500.00
	$	
	$	
	$	

"L" designates those costs to be paid by Lender.

1100 TITLE CHARGES:		
1101 Closing or Escrow Fee	$	200.00
1102 Abstract or Title Search	$	125.00
1103 Title Examination	$	
1104 Title Insurance Binder	$	
1105 Document Preparation Fee	$	75.00
1106 Notary Fee	$	10.00
1107 Attorney Fees	$	
1108 Title Insurance	$	540.00
Title Binder	$	50.00
	$	
	$	
	$	

1200 GOVERNMENT RECORDING & TRANSFER CHARGES:		
1201 Recording Fees:	$	50.00
1202 City/County Tax/Stamps:	$	100.00
1203 State Tax/Stamps:	$	250.00
County Tax	$	275.00
	$	
	$	
	$	

1300 ADDITIONAL SETTLEMENT CHARGES:		
1301 Survey	$	120.00
1302 Pest Inspection	$	
Flood Certification	$	20.00
	$	
	$	
	$	
TOTAL ESTIMATED SETTLEMENT CHARGES	$	6,606.64

TOTAL ESTIMATED FUNDS NEEDED TO CLOSE:		
Downpayment	$	40,000.00
Est. Closing Costs	$	4,065.00
Est. Prepaid Items/Reserves	$	2,541.64
OTHER: Earnest Money	$	(2,000.00)
TOTAL EST. FUNDS NEEDED TO CLOSE	$	44,606.64

TOTAL ESTIMATED MONTHLY PAYMENT:		
Principal & Interest	$	933.72
Real Estate Taxes	$	166.67
Flood & Hazard Insurance	$	60.00
Mortgage Insurance	$	
	$	
TOTAL MONTHLY PAYMENT	$	1,160.38

THIS SECTION TO BE COMPLETED BY LENDER ONLY IF A PARTICULAR PROVIDER OF SERVICE IS REQUIRED. Use of the particular provider is required and the estimate is based on charges of the provider.

ITEM NO.	NAME & ADDRESS OF PROVIDER	TELEPHONE NO.	NATURE OF RELATIONSHIP

These estimates are provided pursuant to the Real Estate Settlement Procedures Act of 1974, as amended (RESPA). Additional information can be found in the HUD Special Information Booklet, which is to be provided to you by your mortgage broker or lender, if your application is to purchase residential real property and the Lender will take a first lien on the property. The undersigned acknowledges receipt of the booklet "Settlement Costs," and the Consumer Handbook on ARM Mortgages, if applicable.

Applicant	Date	Applicant	Date
Applicant	Date	Applicant	Date

☐ This Good Faith Estimate is being provided by , a mortgage broker, and no lender has yet been obtained.

"S" designates those costs to be paid by Seller.

FEDERAL TRUTH-IN LENDING DISCLOSURE STATEMENT
For use with Fixed-Rate, GPM, Balloon Mortgage,
Adjustable or Variable Rate Loans

Date: 10/14/05
Loan No.: 72315
Borrowers: James and Clara Borrower

LOAN "V"

Property
Location: 123 Your Street
Hometown, VA 22189

ANNUAL PERCENTAGE RATE The cost of your credit as a yearly rate	**FINANCE CHARGE** The dollar amount the credit will cost you	Amount Financed The amount of credit provided to you or on your behalf	Total of Payments The amount you will have paid after you have made all payments as scheduled
6.02 %	$ 191,774.69	$ 164,960.00	$ 356,734.69

You have the right to receive at this time an itemization of the Amount Financed.
☐ I want an itemization ☒ I do not want an itemization

Your payment schedule will be:

Number of Payments	Amount of Payments	When Payments Are Due
360	$ 990.93	Monthly beginning 12/01/05
	$	
	$	
	$	
	$	
	$	
	$	

Variable Rate: ☐ This loan has a Variable Rate Feature. Variable Rate Disclosures have been provided to you earlier.

☐ This obligation has a demand Feature.

Insurance: Credit life insurance and credit disability insurance are not required to obtain credit, and will not be provided unless you sign and agree to pay the additional cost. No such insurance will be in force until you have completed an application, the insurance company has issued the policy, the effective date of that policy has arrived and the required premium has been paid.

Type	Premium	Term	Signature
Credit Life	$		I want to apply for credit life insurance. ______ SIGNATURE
Credit Disability	$		I want to apply for credit disability insurance. ______ SIGNATURE
Credit Life and Credit Disability	$		I want to apply for credit life and disability insurance. ______ SIGNATURE

You may obtain property insurance from anyone you want that is acceptable to this institution. If you get the insurance from ______ you will pay $ ______ for a term of ______

Security: You are giving a security interest in:
☒ the property being purchased
☐ ______

Late Charge: If payment is late, you will be charged $ ______ / 5.00 % of the payment.

Prepayment: If you pay off early, you
☐ may ☒ will not have to pay a penalty.
☐ may ☒ will not be entitled to a refund of part of the finance charge.

Assumption: Someone buying your home
☒ cannot assume the remainder of the mortgage on the original terms.
☐ may, subject to conditions, be allowed to assume the remainder of the mortgage on the original terms.

A deposit balance ☐ is ☒ is not required. The Annual Percentage Rate does not take into account your required deposit.

See your contract documents for any additional information about nonpayment, default, any required repayment in full before the scheduled date, and prepayment refunds and penalties.

e means an estimate

I/We hereby acknowledge receipt of this disclosure.

______ / ______ DATE

______ / ______ DATE

Prepared by: ______ ______ TITLE

Lender:	FS Mortgage Company	**GOOD FAITH ESTIMATE**	
Address:	456 Main Street Mortgagetown, VA 22189	Sales Price:	$200,000.00
		Base Loan Amount:	$160,000.00
	LOAN "V"	Total Loan Amount:	$167,066.04
Applicant(s):	James and Clara Borrower	Type of Loan:	Fixed Rate
Property Address:	123 Your Street Hometown, VA 22189	Date Prepared:	10/14/05
		Rate: 5.90% Term:	30 Year

The information provided below reflects estimates of the charges which you are likely to incur at the settlement of your loan. The fees listed are estimates - the actual charges may be more or less. Your transaction may not involve a fee for every item listed.
The numbers listed beside the estimates generally correspond to the numbered lines contained in the HUD-1 or HUD-1A settlement statement that you will be receiving at settlement. The HUD-1 or HUD-1A settlement statement will show you the actual cost for items paid at settlement.

800 ITEMS PAYABLE IN CONNECTION WITH LOAN:		1100 TITLE CHARGES:	
801 Loan Origination Fee (%)	$ 900.00	1101 Closing or Escrow Fee	$ 275.00
802 Loan Discount Fee (%)	$	1102 Abstract or Title Search	$ 250.00
803 Appraisal Fee	$ 150.00	1103 Title Examination	$
804 Credit Report	$	1104 Title Insurance Binder	$
805 Lender's Inspection Fee	$	1105 Document Preparation Fee	$ 125.00
806 Mortgage Insurance Application Fee	$	1106 Notary Fee	$ 40.00
807 Assumption Fee	$	1107 Attorney Fees	$
808 Mortgage Broker Fee	$	1108 Title Insurance	$ 675.00
809 CLO Access Fee	$	Title Binder	$ 50.00
810 Tax Related Service Fee	$ 50.00		$
Administrative Fee	$ 625.00		$
Doc Prep Fee	$ 150.00		$
Courier	$ 75.00		
	$	1200 GOVERNMENT RECORDING & TRANSFER CHARGES:	
	$	1201 Recording Fees:	$ 50.00
900 ITEMS REQUIRED BY LENDER TO BE PAID IN ADVANCE:		1202 City/County Tax/Stamps:	$ 100.00
		1203 State Tax/Stamps:	$ 250.00
901 Interest for 8 day @$ 27.0052 per day	$ 216.04	County Tax	$ 275.00
902 Mortgage Insurance Premium	$		$
903 Hazard Insurance Premium	$ 960.00		$
	$		$
	$	1300 ADDITIONAL SETTLEMENT CHARGES:	
	$	1301 Survey	$ 175.00
1000 RESERVES DEPOSITED WITH LENDER:		1302 Pest Inspection	$
1001 Haz Ins Prem 2 months@$ 80.00	$ 160.00	Flood Certification	$ 40.00
1004 Tax & Assmt Res 9 months@$ 166.67	$ 1,500.00		$
	$		$
	$		$
	$	TOTAL ESTIMATED SETTLEMENT CHARGES	$ 7,066.04

"L" designates those costs to be paid by Lender.

TOTAL ESTIMATED FUNDS NEEDED TO CLOSE:		TOTAL ESTIMATED MONTHLY PAYMENT:	
Downpayment	$ 40,000.00	Principal & Interest	$ 990.93
Est. Closing Costs	$	Real Estate Taxes	$ 166.67
Est. Prepaid Items/Reserves	$	Flood & Hazard Insurance	$ 80.00
OTHER: Earnest Money	$ (2,000.00)	Mortgage Insurance	$
TOTAL EST. FUNDS NEEDED TO CLOSE	$ 38,000.00		$
		TOTAL MONTHLY PAYMENT	$ 1,237.60

THIS SECTION TO BE COMPLETED BY LENDER ONLY IF A PARTICULAR PROVIDER OF SERVICE IS REQUIRED. Use of the particular provider is required and the estimate is based on charges of the provider.

ITEM NO.	NAME & ADDRESS OF PROVIDER	TELEPHONE NO.	NATURE OF RELATIONSHIP

These estimates are provided pursuant to the Real Estate Settlement Procedures Act of 1974, as amended (RESPA). Additional information can be found in the HUD Special Information Booklet, which is to be provided to you by your mortgage broker or lender, if your application is to purchase residential real property and the Lender will take a first lien on the property. The undersigned acknowledges receipt of the booklet "Settlement Costs," and the Consumer Handbook on ARM Mortgages, if applicable.

Applicant	Date	Applicant	Date
Applicant	Date	Applicant	Date

☐ This Good Faith Estimate is being provided by , a mortgage broker, and no lender has yet been obtained.

"S" designates those costs to be paid by Seller.

FEDERAL TRUTH-IN LENDING DISCLOSURE STATEMENT

For use with Fixed-Rate, GPM, Balloon Mortgage, Adjustable or Variable Rate Loans

LOAN "K"

Date: 10/14/05

Loan No.: 21782

Borrowers: James and Clara Borrower

Property Location: 123 Your Street
Hometown, VA 22189

ANNUAL PERCENTAGE RATE The cost of your credit as a yearly rate	**FINANCE CHARGE** The dollar amount the credit will cost you	Amount Financed The amount of credit provided to you or on your behalf	Total of Payments The amount you will have paid after you have made all payments as scheduled
6.38 %	$ 214,725.92	$ 172,066.61	$ 386,792.53

You have the right to receive at this time an itemization of the Amount Financed.

☐ I want an itemization ☒ I do not want an itemization

Your payment schedule will be:

Number of Payments	Amount of Payments	When Payments Are Due
360	$ 1,074.42	Monthly beginning 12/01/05
	$	
	$	
	$	
	$	
	$	
	$	

Variable Rate: ☐ This loan has a Variable Rate Feature. Variable Rate Disclosures have been provided to you earlier.

☐ This obligation has a demand Feature.

Insurance: Credit life insurance and credit disability insurance are not required to obtain credit, and will not be provided unless you sign and agree to pay the additional cost. No such insurance will be in force until you have completed an application, the insurance company has issued the policy, the effective date of that policy has arrived and the required premium has been paid.

Type	Premium	Term	Signature	
Credit Life	$		I want to apply for credit life insurance.	SIGNATURE
Credit Disability	$		I want to apply for credit disability insurance.	SIGNATURE
Credit Life and Credit Disability	$		I want to apply for credit life and disability insurance.	SIGNATURE

You may obtain property insurance from anyone you want that is acceptable to this institution. If you get the insurance from __________ you will pay $ ______ for a term of ________

Security: You are giving a security interest in:

☐ the property being purchased

☒ __________

Late Charge: If payment is late, you will be charged $ ______ / 5.00 % of the payment.

Prepayment: If you pay off early, you

☒ may ☐ will not have to pay a penalty.

☐ may ☒ will not be entitled to a refund of part of the finance charge.

Assumption: Someone buying your home

☒ cannot assume the remainder of the mortgage on the original terms.

☐ may, subject to conditions, be allowed to assume the remainder of the mortgage on the original terms.

A deposit balance ☐ is ☒ is not required. The Annual Percentage Rate does not take into account your required deposit.

See your contract documents for any additional information about nonpayment, default, any required repayment in full before the scheduled date, and prepayment refunds and penalties.

e means an estimate

I/We hereby acknowledge receipt of this disclosure.

__________ / ______ DATE

__________ / ______ DATE

Prepared by: __________ ______ TITLE

Proprietary form used in the consumer testing

GOOD FAITH ESTIMATE

LOAN "K"

Lender:	**JL Mortgage Company**
Address:	**123 Main Street** **Mortgagetown, VA 22189**
Applicant(s):	**James and Clara Borrower**
Property Address:	**123 Your Street** **Hometown, VA 22183**

Sales Price:	
Base Loan Amount:	$175,425.00
Total Loan Amount:	$175,425.00
Type of Loan:	Fixed Rate
Date Prepared:	10/14/05
Rate: 6.20% Term:	30 Year

The information provided below reflects estimates of the charges which you are likely to incur at the settlement of your loan. The fees listed are estimates - the actual charges may be more or less. Your transaction may not involve a fee for every item listed.

The numbers listed beside the estimates generally correspond to the numbered lines contained in the HUD-1 or HUD-1A settlement statement that you will be receiving at settlement. The HUD-1 or HUD-1A settlement statement will show you the actual cost for items paid at settlement.

800 ITEMS PAYABLE IN CONNECTION WITH LOAN:		
801 Loan Origination Fee (%)	$	2,400.00
802 Loan Discount Fee (%)	$	
803 Appraisal Fee	$	200.00
804 Credit Report	$	
805 Lender's Inspection Fee	$	
806 Mortgage Insurance Application Fee	$	
807 Assumption Fee	$	
808 Mortgage Broker Fee	$	
809 CLO Access Fee	$	
810 Tax Related Service Fee	$	50.00
Administrative Fee	$	450.00
Doc Prep Fee	$	100.00
Courier	$	50.00
	$	
	$	

900 ITEMS REQUIRED BY LENDER TO BE PAID IN ADVANCE:		
901 Interest for 8 day @$ 29.7982 per day	$	238.38
902 Mortgage Insurance Premium	$	
903 Hazard Insurance Premium	$	
	$	
	$	
	$	

1000 RESERVES DEPOSITED WITH LENDER:		
1001 Haz Ins Prem @$	$	
1004 Tax & Assmt Res @$	$	
	$	
	$	
	$	

"L" designates those costs to be paid by Lender.

1100 TITLE CHARGES:		
1101 Closing or Escrow Fee	$	200.00
1102 Abstract or Title Search	$	125.00
1103 Title Examination	$	
1104 Title Insurance Binder	$	
1105 Document Preparation Fee	$	75.00
1106 Notary Fee	$	10.00
1107 Attorney Fees	$	
1108 Title Insurance	$	540.00
Title Binder	$	50.00
	$	
	$	
	$	

1200 GOVERNMENT RECORDING & TRANSFER CHARGES:		
1201 Recording Fees:	$	50.00
1202 City/County Tax/Stamps:	$	100.00
1203 State Tax/Stamps:	$	250.00
County Tax	$	275.00
	$	
	$	
	$	

1300 ADDITIONAL SETTLEMENT CHARGES:		
1301 Survey	$	120.00
1302 Pest Inspection	$	
Flood Certification	$	20.00
	$	
	$	
	$	
TOTAL ESTIMATED SETTLEMENT CHARGES	$	5,303.38

TOTAL ESTIMATED FUNDS NEEDED TO CLOSE:		
Downpayment	$	
Est. Closing Costs	$	5,065.00
Est. Prepaid Items/Reserves	$	238.38
OTHER:	$	
TOTAL EST. FUNDS NEEDED TO CLOSE	$	5,303.38

TOTAL ESTIMATED MONTHLY PAYMENT:		
Principal & Interest	$	1,074.42
Real Estate Taxes	$	
Flood & Hazard Insurance	$	
Mortgage Insurance	$	
	$	
TOTAL MONTHLY PAYMENT	$	1,074.42

THIS SECTION TO BE COMPLETED BY LENDER ONLY IF A PARTICULAR PROVIDER OF SERVICE IS REQUIRED. Use of the particular provider is required and the estimate is based on charges of the provider.

ITEM NO.	NAME & ADDRESS OF PROVIDER	TELEPHONE NO.	NATURE OF RELATIONSHIP

These estimates are provided pursuant to the Real Estate Settlement Procedures Act of 1974, as amended (RESPA). Additional information can be found in the HUD Special Information Booklet, which is to be provided to you by your mortgage broker or lender, if your application is to purchase residential real property and the Lender will take a first lien on the property. The undersigned acknowledges receipt of the booklet "Settlement Costs," and the Consumer Handbook on ARM Mortgages, if applicable.

Applicant	Date	Applicant	Date
Applicant	Date	Applicant	Date

☐ This Good Faith Estimate is being provided by , a mortgage broker, and no lender has yet been obtained.

"S" designates those costs to be paid by Seller.

FEDERAL TRUTH-IN LENDING DISCLOSURE STATEMENT
For use with Fixed-Rate, GPM, Balloon Mortgage,
Adjustable or Variable Rate Loans

LOAN "T"

Date: 10/14/05
Loan No.: 26457
Borrowers: James and Clara Borrower

Property
Location: 123 Your Street
Hometown, VA 22189

ANNUAL PERCENTAGE RATE The cost of your credit as a yearly rate	**FINANCE CHARGE** The dollar amount the credit will cost you	Amount Financed The amount of credit provided to you or on your behalf	Total of Payments The amount you will have paid after you have made all payments as scheduled
6.88 %	$ 129,059.36	$ 186,147.50	$ 315,206.86

You have the right to receive at this time an itemization of the Amount Financed.
☐ I want an itemization ☒ I do not want an itemization

Your payment schedule will be:

Number of Payments	Amount of Payments	When Payments Are Due
119	$ 1,049.11	Monthly beginning 12/01/05 and ending 10/01/15
1	$ 190,362.54	11/01/15
	$	
	$	
	$	
	$	
	$	

Variable Rate: ☐ This loan has a Variable Rate Feature. Variable Rate Disclosures have been provided to you earlier.

☐ This obligation has a demand Feature.

Insurance: Credit life insurance and credit disability insurance are not required to obtain credit, and will not be provided unless you sign and agree to pay the additional cost. No such insurance will be in force until you have completed an application, the insurance company has issued the policy, the effective date of that policy has arrived and the required premium has been paid.

Type	Premium	Term	Signature
Credit Life	$ 3,900.00	10 years	I want to apply for credit life insurance. SIGNATURE
Credit Disability	$ 2,330.00	10 years	I want to apply for credit disability insurance. SIGNATURE
Credit Life and Credit Disability	$		I want to apply for credit life and disability insurance. SIGNATURE

You may obtain property insurance from anyone you want that is acceptable to this institution. If you get the insurance from ______ you will pay $ ______ for a term of ______

Security: You are giving a security interest in:
☐ the property being purchased
☒ the property located at 123 Your St., Hometown, VA 22189

Late Charge: If payment is late, you will be charged $ ______ / 5.00 % of the payment.

Prepayment: If you pay off early, you
☐ may ☒ will not have to pay a penalty.
☐ may ☒ will not be entitled to a refund of part of the finance charge.

Assumption: Someone buying your home
☒ cannot assume the remainder of the mortgage on the original terms.
☐ may, subject to conditions, be allowed to assume the remainder of the mortgage on the original terms.

A deposit balance ☐ is ☒ is not required. The Annual Percentage Rate does not take into account your required deposit.
See your contract documents for any additional information about nonpayment, default, any required repayment in full before the scheduled date, and prepayment refunds and penalties.
e means an estimate
I/We hereby acknowledge receipt of this disclosure.

______ / ______ DATE

______ / ______ DATE

Prepared by: ______ ______ TITLE

GOOD FAITH ESTIMATE

LOAN "K"

Lender: FS Mortgage Company
Address: 456 Main Street
Mortgagetown, VA 22189
Applicant(s): James and Clara Borrower
Property Address: 123 Your Street
Hometown, VA 22189

Sales Price:
Base Loan Amount: $175,425.00
Total Loan Amount: $175,425.00
Type of Loan: Fixed Rate
Date Prepared: 10/14/05
Rate: 6.20% Term: 30 Year

The information provided below reflects estimates of the charges which you are likely to incur at the settlement of your loan. The fees listed are estimates - the actual charges may be more or less. Your transaction may not involve a fee for every item listed.
The numbers listed beside the estimates generally correspond to the numbered lines contained in the HUD-1 or HUD-1A settlement statement that you will be receiving at settlement. The HUD-1 or HUD-1A settlement statement will show you the actual cost for items paid at settlement.

800 ITEMS PAYABLE IN CONNECTION WITH LOAN:	
801 Loan Origination Fee (%)	$ 2,400.00
802 Loan Discount Fee (%)	$
803 Appraisal Fee	$ 200.00
804 Credit Report	$
805 Lender's Inspection Fee	$
806 Mortgage Insurance Application Fee	$
807 Assumption Fee	$
808 Mortgage Broker Fee	$
809 CLO Access Fee	$
810 Tax Related Service Fee	$ 50.00
Administrative Fee	$ 450.00
Doc Prep Fee	$ 100.00
Courier	$ 50.00
	$
	$

900 ITEMS REQUIRED BY LENDER TO BE PAID IN ADVANCE:	
901 Interest for 8 day @$29.7982 per day	$ 238.39
902 Mortgage Insurance Premium	$
903 Hazard Insurance Premium	$
	$
	$
	$

1000 RESERVES DEPOSITED WITH LENDER:	
1001 Haz Ins Prem @$	$
1004 Tax & Assmt Res @$	$
	$
	$
	$

"L" designates those costs to be paid by Lender.

1100 TITLE CHARGES:	
1101 Closing or Escrow Fee	$ 200.00
1102 Abstract or Title Search	$ 125.00
1103 Title Examination	$
1104 Title Insurance Binder	$
1105 Document Preparation Fee	$ 75.00
1106 Notary Fee	$ 10.00
1107 Attorney Fees	$
1108 Title Insurance	$ 540.00
Title Binder	$ 50.00
	$
	$
	$

1200 GOVERNMENT RECORDING & TRANSFER CHARGES:	
1201 Recording Fees:	$ 50.00
1202 City/County Tax/Stamps:	$ 100.00
1203 State Tax/Stamps:	$ 250.00
County Tax	$ 275.00
	$
	$
	$

1300 ADDITIONAL SETTLEMENT CHARGES:	
1301 Survey	$ 120.00
1302 Pest Inspection	$
Flood Certification	$ 20.00
	$
	$
	$
TOTAL ESTIMATED SETTLEMENT CHARGES	$ 5,303.39

TOTAL ESTIMATED FUNDS NEEDED TO CLOSE:	
Downpayment	$ 5,065.00
Est. Closing Costs	$ 238.39
Est. Prepaid Items/Reserves	$
OTHER:	$
TOTAL EST. FUNDS NEEDED TO CLOSE	$ 5,303.39

TOTAL ESTIMATED MONTHLY PAYMENT:	
Principal & Interest	$ 1,074.42
Real Estate Taxes	$
Flood & Hazard Insurance	$
Mortgage Insurance	$
	$
TOTAL MONTHLY PAYMENT	$ 1,074.42

THIS SECTION TO BE COMPLETED BY LENDER ONLY IF A PARTICULAR PROVIDER OF SERVICE IS REQUIRED. Use of the particular provider is required and the estimate is based on charges of the provider.

ITEM NO.	NAME & ADDRESS OF PROVIDER	TELEPHONE NO.	NATURE OF RELATIONSHIP

These estimates are provided pursuant to the Real Estate Settlement Procedures Act of 1974, as amended (RESPA). Additional information can be found in the HUD Special Information Booklet, which is to be provided to you by your mortgage broker or lender, if your application is to purchase residential real property and the Lender will take a first lien on the property. The undersigned acknowledges receipt of the booklet "Settlement Costs," and the Consumer Handbook on ARM Mortgages, if applicable.

Applicant Date Applicant Date

Applicant Date Applicant Date

☐ This Good Faith Estimate is being provided by , a mortgage broker, and no lender has yet been obtained.

"S" designates those costs to be paid by Seller.

Appendix H
Consumer Testing Prototype Disclosure Forms

Prototype Disclosure Forms Used in the Consumer Testing

The prototype mortgage cost disclosure forms shown to respondents in the consumer testing are presented in this appendix. The prototype forms used in the testing were presented on legal-size paper, the same as presented here.

All six versions of the prototype forms that were used in the testing are presented in this appendix. The format of the forms is the same for all versions, but the specified loan costs vary. The six versions consist of the following loans:

Loans G and R	Used for the overall loan cost and loan choice questions (Questions 15-16) in both the simple-loan and complex-loan scenario groups.
Loans M and V	Used for the individual loan cost questions (Questions 17-45) in the simple-loan scenario group.
Loans K and T	Used for the individual loan cost questions (Questions 17-45) in the complex-loan scenario group.

The test questions, loan-cost scenarios, and loan cost specifications are discussed in detail in the Consumer Testing Methodology section of this chapter.

Mortgage Loan Offer
JL Mortgage Company
123 Main Street
Mortgagetown, Virginia 22189
(703) 555-2767

LOAN "G"

Page 1 of 3

Borrower: James and Clara Borrower
Property Location: 123 Your Street, Hometown, VA 22189
Offer Date: October 14, 2005

This page provides a summary of your loan, our charges for the loan, and your loan payments. See pages 2 and 3 for important details on each of these items.

YOUR LOAN

Loan Type Summary	30 year fixed-rate
Loan Amount	$ 176,000.00
Loan Term	30 years (360 monthly payments)

OUR LOAN CHARGES

Interest Rate	5.87%	Fixed rate
Up-Front Charges	$ 8,052.05	Total settlement charges
	$ 0.00	Charges for optional products and services
	$ 8,052.05	Total up-front charges
Monthly-Billed Charges	None	
Annual Percentage Rate (APR)	6.03%	The cost of credit, including both interest payments and other finance charges, expressed as an annual rate.

YOUR LOAN PAYMENTS

Cash Due at Closing	$ 50,052.05	
Monthly Payments	$ 1,268.88	Payments number 1–360 (Includes required payments for property taxes and hazard insurance)
Balloon Payment	None	

PENALTIES AND LATE FEES

Prepayment Penalty	None
Late Fee	A 5% late fee will be charged on payments more than 7 days late.

JL Mortgage Company	LOAN "G"	Page 2 of 3

This page and the next provide explanations and important details about your loan amount, our charges for the loan, and your loan payments. See page 1 for a summary of these items.

HOME PURCHASE DETAILS

Home Purchase	$ 220,000.00	Home price
	$ 44,000.00	Down payment
	$ 176,000.00	Amount of home price financed

LOAN AMOUNT DETAILS

Loan Amount	$ 176,000.00	Financed home purchase
	$ 0.00	Financed settlement charges
	$ 0.00	Financed charges for optional products and services
	$ 176,000.00	Total Loan Amount

OPTIONAL CHARGES DETAILS

Optional Products and Services Charges	None

CASH DUE AT CLOSING DETAILS

Cash Due at Closing	$ 44,000.00	Down payment
	$ 8,052.05	Settlement charges
	$ (2,000.00)	Earnest money deposit credited to borrower
	$ 50,052.05	Total cash due at closing

MONTHLY PAYMENT DETAILS

Monthly Payment	Itemization of initial monthly payment	
	$ 1,040.54	Principal and interest
	$ 183.33	Property tax escrow
	$ 45.00	Hazard (homeowners) insurance
	$ 0.00	Private mortgage insurance (PMI)
	$ 0.00	Monthly-billed optional products or services
	$ 1,268.88	Total initial monthly payment

Taxes and Insurance	Property taxes and hazard insurance ARE included in your monthly loan payment.

JL Mortgage Company LOAN "G" Page 3 of 3

SETTLEMENT CHARGES DETAILS

This page lists the settlement services included in the settlement charges shown on page 1. ALL of the settlement services you need to close the loan are included.

Settlement Services Package	$5,489.00	This package includes the following services:

Origination and lender services	Title services
Loan origination	Settlement agent
Appraisal	Title search and examination
Credit report	Title document preparation
Lender's property survey	Lender's title insurance
Lender's property inspection	Attorney services
Pest inspection	Notary fee
Government taxes and fees	
County recording fee	State and local tax stamps

Interest Charge for Partial Month	$ 283.05	This charge is for the daily interest charges from the day of your settlement until the end of the month. For this loan this amount is $ 28.3047 per day for 10 days (if your closing date is 10/22/05).
Prepaid Items	$ 0.00 $ 540.00	Property taxes (0 months at $____ per month) Hazard insurance (12 months at $ 45.00 per month)
Reserves Deposited with the Lender	$1,650.00 $ 90.00	Property taxes (9 months at $ 183.33 per month) Hazard insurance (2 months at $ 45.00 per month)
Total Settlement Charges	**$8,052.05**	**Total Settlement Charges**

HOW TO PROTECT YOURSELF

COMPARISON SHOP TO FIND THE BEST DEAL — The lender or broker providing this loan is not necessarily shopping on your behalf or providing you with the lowest cost loan.

DO NOT RELY ON ORAL PROMISES TO CHANGE THESE TERMS — Obtain all changes in writing.

SAVE THIS OFFER SHEET AND COMPARE TO DOCUMENTS AT CLOSING — Before you sign any papers at your loan closing (loan settlement), make sure that the costs have not been increased.

Federal law requires that this offer sheet be provided to the borrower within three (3) business days after the borrower has applied for a loan. If the loan terms change prior to acceptance by the borrower, a new offer sheet must be provided. Notify the Federal Trade Commission (FTC) if the lender does not abide by the terms set forth in this offer or does not provide this offer sheet within three days of application: Federal Trade Commission (FTC), 600 Pennsylvania Avenue, N.W., Washington D.C., 20580, telephone (877) FTC-HELP (382-4357), web site www.ftc.gov.

Mortgage Loan Offer

FS Mortgage Company

456 Main Street

Mortgagetown, Virginia 22189

(703) 555-2767

LOAN "R"

Page 1 of 3

Borrower: James and Clara Borrower

Property Location: 123 Your Street, Hometown, VA 22189

Offer Date: October 14, 2005

This page provides a summary of your loan, our charges for the loan, and your loan payments. See pages 2 and 3 for important details on each of these items.

YOUR LOAN

Loan Type Summary	30 year fixed-rate
Loan Amount	$ 176,000.00
Loan Term	30 years (360 monthly payments)

OUR LOAN CHARGES

Interest Rate	5.87%	Fixed rate
Up-Front Charges	$ 7,026.05	Total settlement charges
	$ 0.00	Charges for optional products and services
	$ 7,026.05	Total up-front charges
Monthly-Billed Charges	None	
Annual Percentage Rate (APR)	6.03%	The cost of credit, including both interest payments and other finance charges, expressed as an annual rate.

YOUR LOAN PAYMENTS

Cash Due at Closing	$ 49,026.05	
Monthly Payments	$ 1,268.88	Payments number 1–360 (includes required payments for property taxes and hazard insurance)
Balloon Payment	None	

PENALTIES AND LATE FEES

Prepayment Penalty	None
Late Fee	A 5% late fee will be charged on payments more than 7 days late.

FS Mortgage Company	LOAN "R"	Page 2 of 3

This page and the next provide explanations and important details about your loan amount, our charges for the loan, and your loan payments. See page 1 for a summary of these items.

HOME PURCHASE DETAILS

Home Purchase	$ 220,000.00	Home price
	$ 44,000.00	Down payment
	$ 176,000.00	Amount of home price financed

LOAN AMOUNT DETAILS

Loan Amount	$ 176,000.00	Financed home purchase
	$ 0.00	Financed settlement charges
	$ 0.00	Financed charges for optional products and services
	$ 176,000.00	Total Loan Amount

OPTIONAL CHARGES DETAILS

Optional Products and Services Charges	None

CASH DUE AT CLOSING DETAILS

Cash Due at Closing	$ 44,000.00	Down payment
	$ 7,026.05	Settlement charges
	$ (2,000.00)	Earnest money deposit credited to borrower
	$ 49,026.05	Total cash due at closing

MONTHLY PAYMENT DETAILS

Monthly Payment	Itemization of initial monthly payment	
	$ 1,040.54	Principal and interest
	$ 183.33	Property tax escrow
	$ 45.00	Hazard (homeowners) insurance
	$ 0.00	Private mortgage insurance (PMI)
	$ 0.00	Monthly-billed optional products or services
	$ 1,268.88	Total initial monthly payment

Taxes and Insurance	Property taxes and hazard insurance ARE included in your monthly loan payment.

FS Mortgage Company	LOAN "R"	Page 3 of 3

SETTLEMENT CHARGES DETAILS

This page lists the settlement services included in the settlement charges shown on page 1. ALL of the settlement services you need to close the loan are included.

Settlement Services Package	$4,463.00	This package includes the following services: __Origination and lender services__: Loan origination; Appraisal; Credit report; Lender's property survey; Lender's property inspection; Pest inspection __Title services__: Settlement agent; Title search and examination; Title document preparation; Lender's title insurance; Attorney services; Notary fee __Government taxes and fees__: County recording fee; State and local tax stamps
Interest Charge for Partial Month	$ 283.05	This charge is for the daily interest charges from the day of your settlement until the end of the month. For this loan this amount is $ 28.3047 per day for 10 days (if your closing date is 10/22/05).
Prepaid Items	$ 0.00 $ 540.00	Property taxes (0 months at $_____ per month) Hazard insurance (12 months at $ 45.00 per month)
Reserves Deposited with the Lender	$1,650.00 $ 90.00	Property taxes (9 months at $ 183.33 per month) Hazard insurance (2 months at $ 45.00 per month)
Total Settlement Charges	**$7,026.05**	**Total Settlement Charges**

HOW TO PROTECT YOURSELF

COMPARISON SHOP TO FIND THE BEST DEAL — The lender or broker providing this loan is not necessarily shopping on your behalf or providing you with the lowest cost loan.

DO NOT RELY ON ORAL PROMISES TO CHANGE THESE TERMS — Obtain all changes in writing.

SAVE THIS OFFER SHEET AND COMPARE TO DOCUMENTS AT CLOSING — Before you sign any papers at your loan closing (loan settlement), make sure that the costs have not been increased.

Federal law requires that this offer sheet be provided to the borrower within three (3) business days after the borrower has applied for a loan. If the loan terms change prior to acceptance by the borrower, a new offer sheet must be provided. Notify the Federal Trade Commission (FTC) if the lender does not abide by the terms set forth in this offer or does not provide this offer sheet within three days of application: Federal Trade Commission (FTC), 600 Pennsylvania Avenue, N.W., Washington D.C., 20580, telephone (877) FTC-HELP (382-4357), web site www.ftc.gov.

Mortgage Loan Offer
JL Mortgage Company
123 Main Street
Mortgagetown, Virginia 22189
(703) 555-2767

LOAN "M"

Page 1 of 3

Borrower: James and Clara Borrower — Offer Date: October 14, 2005
Property Location: 123 Your Street, Hometown, VA 22189

This page provides a summary of your loan, our charges for the loan, and your loan payments. See pages 2 and 3 for important details on each of these items.

YOUR LOAN

Loan Type Summary	30 year fixed-rate	
Loan Amount	$ 160,000.00	
Loan Term	30 years (360 monthly payments)	

OUR LOAN CHARGES

Interest Rate	5.75%	Fixed rate
Up-Front Charges	$ 6,606.64	Total settlement charges
	$ 0.00	Charges for optional products and services
	$ 6,606.64	Total up-front charges
Monthly-Billed Charges	None	
Annual Percentage Rate (APR)	5.88%	The cost of credit, including both interest payments and other finance charges, expressed as an annual rate.

YOUR LOAN PAYMENTS

Cash Due at Closing	$ 44,606.64	
Monthly Payments	$ 1,160.38	Payments number 1–360 (Includes required payments for property taxes and hazard insurance)
Balloon Payment	None	

PENALTIES AND LATE FEES

Prepayment Penalty	None
Late Fee	A 5% late fee will be charged on payments more than 7 days late.

JL Mortgage Company	LOAN "M"	Page 2 of 3

This page and the next provide explanations and important details about your loan amount, our charges for the loan, and your loan payments. See page 1 for a summary of these items.

HOME PURCHASE DETAILS

Home Purchase	$ 200,000.00	Home price
	$ 40,000.00	Down payment
	$ 160,000.00	Amount of home price financed

LOAN AMOUNT DETAILS

Loan Amount	$ 160,000.00	Financed home purchase
	$ 0.00	Financed settlement charges
	$ 0.00	Financed charges for optional products and services
	$ 160,000.00	Total Loan Amount

OPTIONAL CHARGES DETAILS

Optional Products and Services Charges	None

CASH DUE AT CLOSING DETAILS

Cash Due at Closing	$ 40,000.00	Down payment
	$ 6,606.64	Settlement charges
	$ (2,000.00)	Earnest money deposit credited to borrower
	$ 44,606.64	Total cash due at closing

MONTHLY PAYMENT DETAILS

Monthly Payment	Itemization of initial monthly payment	
	$ 933.72	Principal and interest
	$ 166.67	Property tax escrow
	$ 60.00	Hazard (homeowners) insurance
	$ 0.00	Private mortgage insurance (PMI)
	$ 0.00	Monthly-billed optional products or services
	$ 1,160.38	Total initial monthly payment
Taxes and Insurance	Property taxes and hazard insurance ARE included in your monthly loan payment.	

JL Mortgage Company | LOAN "M" | Page 3 of 3

SETTLEMENT CHARGES DETAILS

This page lists the settlement services included in the settlement charges shown on page 1. ALL of the settlement services you need to close the loan are included.

Settlement Services Package	$4,065.00	This package includes the following services: Origination and lender services: Loan origination; Appraisal; Credit report; Lender's property survey; Lender's property inspection; Pest inspection Title services: Settlement agent; Title search and examination; Title document preparation; Lender's title insurance; Attorney services; Notary fee Government taxes and fees: County recording fee; State and local tax stamps
Interest Charge for Partial Month	$ 201.64	This charge is for the daily interest charges from the day of your settlement until the end of the month. For this loan this amount is $ 25.2055 per day for 8 days (if your closing date is 10/24/05).
Prepaid Items	$ 0.00 $ 720.00	Property taxes (0 months at $____ per month) Hazard insurance (12 months at $ 60.00 per month)
Reserves Deposited with the Lender	$1,500.00 $ 120.00	Property taxes (9 months at $ 166.67 per month) Hazard insurance (2 months at $ 60.00 per month)
Total Settlement Charges	$6,606.64	Total Settlement Charges

HOW TO PROTECT YOURSELF

COMPARISON SHOP TO FIND THE BEST DEAL — The lender or broker providing this loan is not necessarily shopping on your behalf or providing you with the lowest cost loan.

DO NOT RELY ON ORAL PROMISES TO CHANGE THESE TERMS — Obtain all changes in writing.

SAVE THIS OFFER SHEET AND COMPARE TO DOCUMENTS AT CLOSING — Before you sign any papers at your loan closing (loan settlement), make sure that the costs have not been increased.

Federal law requires that this offer sheet be provided to the borrower within three (3) business days after the borrower has applied for a loan. If the loan terms change prior to acceptance by the borrower, a new offer sheet must be provided. Notify the Federal Trade Commission (FTC) if the lender does not abide by the terms set forth in this offer or does not provide this offer sheet within three days of application: Federal Trade Commission (FTC), 600 Pennsylvania Avenue, N.W., Washington D.C., 20580, telephone (877) FTC-HELP (382-4357), web site www.ftc.gov.

Mortgage Loan Offer

FS Mortgage Company

456 Main Street
Mortgagetown, Virginia 22189
(703) 555-2767

LOAN "V"

Page 1 of 3

Borrower: James and Clara Borrower
Property Location: 123 Your Street, Hometown, VA 22189

Offer Date: October 14, 2005

This page provides a summary of your loan, our charges for the loan, and your loan payments. See pages 2 and 3 for important details on each of these items.

YOUR LOAN

Loan Type Summary	30 year fixed-rate
Loan Amount	$ 167,066.04
Loan Term	30 years (360 monthly payments)

OUR LOAN CHARGES

Interest Rate	5.90%	Fixed rate
Up-Front Charges	$ 7,066.04	Total settlement charges
	$ 0.00	Charges for optional products and services
	$ 7,066.04	Total up-front charges
Monthly-Billed Charges	None	
Annual Percentage Rate (APR)	6.02%	The cost of credit, including both interest payments and other finance charges, expressed as an annual rate.

YOUR LOAN PAYMENTS

Cash Due at Closing	$ 38,000.00	
Monthly Payments	$ 1,237.60	Payments number 1–360 (Includes required payments for property taxes and hazard insurance)
Balloon Payment	None	

PENALTIES AND LATE FEES

Prepayment Penalty	None
Late Fee	A 5% late fee will be charged on payments more than 7 days late.

FS Mortgage Company	LOAN "V"	Page 2 of 3

This page and the next provide explanations and important details about your loan amount, our charges for the loan, and your loan payments. See page 1 for a summary of these items.

HOME PURCHASE DETAILS

Home Purchase	$ 200,000.00	Home price
	$ 40,000.00	Down payment
	$ 160,000.00	Amount of home price financed

LOAN AMOUNT DETAILS

Loan Amount	$ 160,000.00	Financed home purchase
	$ 7,066.04	Financed settlement charges
	$ 0.00	Financed charges for optional products and services
	$ 167,066.04	Total Loan Amount

OPTIONAL CHARGES DETAILS

Optional Products and Services Charges	None

CASH DUE AT CLOSING DETAILS

Cash Due at Closing	$ 40,000.00	Down payment
	$ 0.00	Settlement charges
	$ (2,000.00)	Earnest money deposit credited to borrower
	$ 38,000.00	Total cash due at closing

MONTHLY PAYMENT DETAILS

Monthly Payment	Itemization of initial monthly payment	
	$ 990.93	Principal and interest
	$ 166.67	Property tax escrow
	$ 80.00	Hazard (homeowners) insurance
	$ 0.00	Private mortgage insurance (PMI)
	$ 0.00	Monthly-billed optional products or services
	$ 1,237.60	Total initial monthly payment
Taxes and Insurance	Property taxes and hazard insurance ARE included in your monthly loan payment.	

FS Mortgage Company | **LOAN "V"** | Page 3 of 3

SETTLEMENT CHARGES DETAILS

This page lists the settlement services included in the settlement charges shown on page 1. ALL of the settlement services you need to close the loan are included.

Settlement Services Package	$4,230.00	This package includes the following services: <u>Origination and lender services</u>: Loan origination; Appraisal; Credit report; Lender's property survey; Lender's property inspection; Pest inspection <u>Title services</u>: Settlement agent; Title search and examination; Title document preparation; Lender's title insurance; Attorney services; Notary fee <u>Government taxes and fees</u>: County recording fee; State and local tax stamps
Interest Charge for Partial Month	$ 216.04	This charge is for the daily interest charges from the day of your settlement until the end of the month. For this loan this amount is $ 27.0052 per day for 8 days (if your closing date is 10/24/05).
Prepaid Items	$ 0.00 $ 960.00	Property taxes (0 months at $_____ per month) Hazard insurance (12 months at $ 80.00 per month)
Reserves Deposited with the Lender	$1,500.00 $ 160.00	Property taxes (9 months at $ 166.67 per month) Hazard insurance (2 months at $ 80.00 per month)
Total Settlement Charges	**$7,066.04**	**Total Settlement Charges**

HOW TO PROTECT YOURSELF

COMPARISON SHOP TO FIND THE BEST DEAL — The lender or broker providing this loan is not necessarily shopping on your behalf or providing you with the lowest cost loan.

DO NOT RELY ON ORAL PROMISES TO CHANGE THESE TERMS — Obtain all changes in writing.

SAVE THIS OFFER SHEET AND COMPARE TO DOCUMENTS AT CLOSING — Before you sign any papers at your loan closing (loan settlement), make sure that the costs have not been increased.

Federal law requires that this offer sheet be provided to the borrower within three (3) business days after the borrower has applied for a loan. If the loan terms change prior to acceptance by the borrower, a new offer sheet must be provided. Notify the Federal Trade Commission (FTC) if the lender does not abide by the terms set forth in this offer or does not provide this offer sheet within three days of application: Federal Trade Commission (FTC), 600 Pennsylvania Avenue, N.W., Washington D.C., 20580, telephone (877) FTC-HELP (382-4357), web site www.ftc.gov.

Mortgage Loan Offer

JL Mortgage Company
123 Main Street
Mortgagetown, Virginia 22189
(703) 555-2767

LOAN "K"

Page 1 of 3

Borrower: James and Clara Borrower
Property Location: 123 Your Street, Hometown, VA 22189

Offer Date: October 14, 2005

This page provides a summary of your loan, our charges for the loan, and your loan payments. See pages 2 and 3 for important details on each of these items.

YOUR LOAN

Loan Type Summary	30 year fixed-rate
Loan Amount	$ 175,425.00
Loan Term	30 years (360 monthly payments)

OUR LOAN CHARGES

Interest Rate	6.20%	Fixed rate
Up-Front Charges	$ 5,303.39	Total settlement charges
	$ 0.00	Charges for optional products and services
	$ 5,303.39	Total up-front charges
Monthly-Billed Charges	None	
Annual Percentage Rate (APR)	6.38%	The cost of credit, including both interest payments and other finance charges, expressed as an annual rate.

YOUR LOAN PAYMENTS

Cash Due at Closing	$ 5,303.39	
Monthly Payments	$ 1,074.42	Payments number 1–360 (Does NOT include required payments for property taxes and hazard insurance.)
Balloon Payment	None	

PENALTIES AND LATE FEES

Prepayment Penalty	A penalty of four percent (4%) of the prepaid loan balance will be charged if the loan is paid off during the first five years. An immediate refinancing of the loan would result in a penalty of $7,017.00.
Late Fee	A 5% late fee will be charged on payments more than 7 days late.

JL Mortgage Company	LOAN "K"	Page 2 of 3

This page and the next provide explanations and important details about your loan amount, our charges for the loan, and your loan payments. See page 1 for a summary of these items.

LOAN AMOUNT DETAILS

Loan Amount	$ 150,000.00	Refinance current mortgage loan
	$ 20,000.00	Cash paid to borrower
	$ 5,425.00	Consolidation of borrower's other debts
	$ 0.00	Financed settlement charges
	$ 0.00	Financed charges for optional products and services
	$ 175,425.00	Total Loan Amount

OPTIONAL CHARGES DETAILS

Optional Products and Services Charges	None

CASH DUE AT CLOSING DETAILS

Cash Due at Closing	$ 5,303.39	Settlement charges
	$ 5,303.39	Total cash due at closing

MONTHLY PAYMENT DETAILS

Monthly Payment	Itemization of initial monthly payment	
	$ 1,074.42	Principal and interest
	$ 0.00	Property tax escrow
	$ 0.00	Hazard (homeowners) insurance
	$ 0.00	Private mortgage insurance (PMI)
	$ 0.00	Monthly-billed optional products or services
	$ 1,074.42	Total initial monthly payment

Taxes and Insurance

Property taxes and hazard insurance are NOT included in your monthly loan payment. You will be responsible for paying these additional required costs yourself. Your additional monthly costs will be:

$	145.83	Property taxes
$	60.00	Hazard insurance
$	205.83	Total additional monthly costs

JL Mortgage Company	LOAN "K"	Page 3 of 3

SETTLEMENT CHARGES DETAILS

This page lists the settlement services included in the settlement charges shown on page 1. ALL of the settlement services you need to close the loan are included.

Settlement Services Package	$5,065.00	This package includes the following services: Origination and lender services: Loan origination; Appraisal; Credit report; Lender's property survey; Lender's property inspection; Pest inspection Title services: Settlement agent; Title search and examination; Title document preparation; Lender's title insurance; Attorney services; Notary fee Government taxes and fees: County recording fee; State and local tax stamps
Interest Charge for Partial Month	$ 238.39	This charge is for the daily interest charges from the day of your settlement until the end of the month. For this loan this amount is $ 29.7982 per day for 8 days (if your closing date is 10/24/05).
Prepaid Items	$ 0.00 $ 0.00	Property taxes (__ months at $_____ per month) Hazard insurance (__ months at $____ per month)
Reserves Deposited with the Lender	$ 0.00 $ 0.00	Property taxes (__ months at $____ per month) Hazard insurance (__ months at $____ per month)
Total Settlement Charges	$5,303.39	Total Settlement Charges

HOW TO PROTECT YOURSELF

COMPARISON SHOP TO FIND THE BEST DEAL — The lender or broker providing this loan is not necessarily shopping on your behalf or providing you with the lowest cost loan.

DO NOT RELY ON ORAL PROMISES TO CHANGE THESE TERMS — Obtain all changes in writing.

SAVE THIS OFFER SHEET AND COMPARE TO DOCUMENTS AT CLOSING — Before you sign any papers at your loan closing (loan settlement), make sure that the costs have not been increased.

Federal law requires that this offer sheet be provided to the borrower within three (3) business days after the borrower has applied for a loan. If the loan terms change prior to acceptance by the borrower, a new offer sheet must be provided. Notify the Federal Trade Commission (FTC) if the lender does not abide by the terms set forth in this offer or does not provide this offer sheet within three days of application: Federal Trade Commission (FTC), 600 Pennsylvania Avenue, N.W., Washington D.C., 20580, telephone (877) FTC-HELP (382-4357), web site www.ftc.gov.

Mortgage Loan Offer

FS Mortgage Company

456 Main Street

Mortgagetown, Virginia 22189

(703) 555-2767

LOAN "T"

Page 1 of 3

Borrower: James and Clara Borrower

Offer Date: October 14, 2005

Property Location: 123 Your Street, Hometown, VA 22189

This page provides a summary of your loan, our charges for the loan, and your loan payments. See pages 2 and 3 for important details on each of these items.

YOUR LOAN

Loan Type Summary	10 year interest-only balloon	
Loan Amount	$ 189,313.43	
Loan Term	10 years (120 monthly payments)	

OUR LOAN CHARGES

Interest Rate	6.65%	Fixed rate
Up-Front Charges	$ 7,658.43	Total settlement charges
	$ 6,230.00	Charges for optional products and services
	$ 13,888.43	Total up-front charges
Monthly-Billed Charges	None	
Annual Percentage Rate (APR)	6.88%	The cost of credit, including both interest payments and other finance charges, expressed as an annual rate.

YOUR LOAN PAYMENTS

Cash Due at Closing	$ 0.00	
Monthly Payments	$ 1,254.95	Payments number 1–119 (includes required payments for property taxes and hazard insurance.)
Balloon Payment	$ 190,568.38	Payment number 120 – You will have to pay this amount at the end of the 10 year loan term.

PENALTIES AND LATE FEES

Prepayment Penalty	None
Late Fee	A 5% late fee will be charged on payments more than 7 days late.

FS Mortgage Company	LOAN "T"	Page 2 of 3

This page and the next provide explanations and important details about your loan amount, our charges for the loan, and your loan payments. See page 1 for a summary of these items.

LOAN AMOUNT DETAILS

Loan Amount	$ 150,000.00	Refinance current mortgage loan
	$ 20,000.00	Cash paid to borrower
	$ 5,425.00	Consolidation of borrower's other debts
	$ 7,658.43	Financed settlement charges
	$ 6,230.00	Financed charges for optional products and services
	$ 189,313.43	Total Loan Amount

OPTIONAL CHARGES DETAILS

Optional Products and Services Charges	$ 3,900.00	Credit life insurance
	$ 2,330.00	Credit disability insurance
	$ 6,230.00	Total Optional Product and Services Charges

These products and services are NOT required for the loan. Tell your loan provider if you do not wish to purchase them and make sure that you obtain a revised offer sheet with these charges removed.

CASH DUE AT CLOSING DETAILS

Cash Due at Closing	$ 0.00

MONTHLY PAYMENT DETAILS

Monthly Payment — Itemization of initial monthly payment

	$ 1,049.11	Principal and interest
	$ 145.83	Property tax escrow
	$ 60.00	Hazard (homeowners) insurance
	$ 0.00	Private mortgage insurance (PMI)
	$ 0.00	Monthly-billed optional products or services
	$ 1,254.95	Total initial monthly payment

Taxes and Insurance	Property taxes and hazard insurance ARE included in your monthly loan payment.

FS Mortgage Company	LOAN "T"	Page 3 of 3

SETTLEMENT CHARGES DETAILS

This page lists the settlement services included in the settlement charges shown on page 1. ALL of the settlement services you need to close the loan are included.

Settlement Services Package	$5,230.00	This package includes the following services: *Origination and lender services*: Loan origination; Appraisal; Credit report; Lender's property survey; Lender's property inspection; Pest inspection *Title services*: Settlement agent; Title search and examination; Title document preparation; Lender's title insurance; Attorney services; Notary fee *Government taxes and fees*: County recording fee; State and local tax stamps
Interest Charge for Partial Month	$ 275.93	This charge is for the daily interest charges from the day of your settlement until the end of the month. For this loan this amount is $ 34.4914 per day for 8 days (if your closing date is 10/24/05).
Prepaid Items	$ 0.00 $ 720.00	Property taxes (0 months at $_____ per month) Hazard insurance (12 months at $ 60.00 per month)
Reserves Deposited with the Lender	$1,312.50 $ 120.00	Property taxes (9 months at $ 145.83 per month) Hazard insurance (2 months at $ 60.00 per month)
Total Settlement Charges	**$7,658.43**	**Total Settlement Charges**

HOW TO PROTECT YOURSELF

COMPARISON SHOP TO FIND THE BEST DEAL — The lender or broker providing this loan is not necessarily shopping on your behalf or providing you with the lowest cost loan.

DO NOT RELY ON ORAL PROMISES TO CHANGE THESE TERMS — Obtain all changes in writing.

SAVE THIS OFFER SHEET AND COMPARE TO DOCUMENTS AT CLOSING — Before you sign any papers at your loan closing (loan settlement), make sure that the costs have not been increased.

Federal law requires that this offer sheet be provided to the borrower within three (3) business days after the borrower has applied for a loan. If the loan terms change prior to acceptance by the borrower, a new offer sheet must be provided. Notify the Federal Trade Commission (FTC) if the lender does not abide by the terms set forth in this offer or does not provide this offer sheet within three days of application: Federal Trade Commission (FTC), 600 Pennsylvania Avenue, N.W., Washington D.C., 20580, telephone (877) FTC-HELP (382-4357), web site www.ftc.gov.

References

[1] Outstanding mortgage debt and annual originations figures were obtained, respectively, from "Mortgage Loans Outstanding, Quarterly – 1952-2006," and "1-4 Family Mortgage Originations 1990-2005," both from the Mortgage Bankers Association of America ("MBAA").

[2] The TILA statement discloses the "annual percentage rate" ("APR"), "finance charge," "amount financed," "total of payments," payment schedule, charges for optional credit insurance, any late payment fee, and an indication of whether a prepayment penalty

may apply to the loan. For purchase-money loans, creditors must provide the disclosures within three days of receiving a consumer's written application, but many also provide the disclosures again at closing, even though it is not required unless certain costs have changed beyond specified tolerances. For refinance loans, creditors must provide the disclosures prior to consummation of the loan, which most do at closing. See Ralph J. Rohner and Fred H. Miller, Truth in Lending, Robert A. Cook, Alvin C. Harrell, and Elizabeth Huber, editors, Chicago: American Bar Association, Section of Business Law, 2000; and National Consumer Law Center, *Truth in Lending*, 5th edition, 2003. The GFE provides an itemized disclosure of several dozen individual settlement costs. The disclosures must be provided within three days of receiving a consumer's written application. *See* Department of Housing and Urban Development ("HUD"), *RESPA - Real Estate Settlement Procedures Act*, [online], <http://www.hud.gov/offices/hsg/sfh/res/respa_hm.cfm?>, (March 28, 2007). *See also* Thomas A. Durkin and Gregory E. Elliehausen, "*Financial Economics of Information Disclosure: Applications to Truth-In-Lending (tentative title),*" Oxford University Press, forthcoming, for a review of the purpose, history, content, and difficulties of Truth-inLending disclosures; a discussion of other consumer financial disclosures, including the GFE; and an analysis of the theoretical basis provided for consumer disclosures by the economics of information.

[3] President Lyndon B. Johnson, *Special Message to the Congress on Consumer Interests*, March 21st, 1966, <http://www.presidency.ucsb.edu/ws/index.php?pid=27505> (April 2, 2007)

[4] *See* 15 U.S.C. Section 1601(a).

[5] *See* 12 U.S.C. Section 2601(a)–(b)(1). The findings also stated that consumers needed to be protected from "unnecessarily high settlement charges caused by certain abusive practices that have developed in some areas of the country," and that additional purposes of the statute were to eliminate kickbacks and referral fees, reduce the amounts home buyers are required to place in escrow accounts, and reform local recordkeeping of land title information. *See* 12 U.S.C. Section 2601(a), (b)(2)–(4).

[6] *See,* for example, Durkin and Elliehausen, *supra* note 2, and Thomas A. Durkin and Gregory Elliehausen, "Disclosure as a Consumer Protection," in *The Impact of Public Policy on Consumer Credit*, edited by Thomas A. Durkin and Michael E. Staten, Kluwer Academic Publishers: Boston, 2002.

[7] National Consumer Law Center, *supra* note 2.

[8] Economic Growth and Regulatory Paperwork Reduction Act of 1996 (Pub. L. 104-208, 110 Stat. 3009), Section 2101.

[9] FRB and HUD, *Joint Report to the Congress Concerning Reform to the Truth in Lending Act and the Real Estate Settlement Procedures Act*, July 1998. The two agencies had earlier concluded that regulatory changes would not significantly improve the disclosures, and that legislative changes were needed to accomplish the goals of Congress. *See* FRB, "Truth in Lending; request for comments" press release, March 31, 1997 (also published in 62 *Fed. Reg.* 15624-26 (April 2, 1997); and Laurence H. Meyer, Governor, FRB, *Disclosure requirements for home mortgage loans,* testimony before the Subcommittee on Financial Institutions and Regulatory Relief, of the Committee on Banking, Housing, and Urban Affairs, U.S. Senate, July 15, 1997.

[10] The recommended changes to the TILA disclosures included adding the interest rate, revising the explanation of the APR, eliminating the "amount financed" figure, and expanding the definition of "finance charge" to include virtually all costs required to close the loan. The agencies also recommended that lenders offering the proposed guaranteed settlement packages not be required to itemize the costs of each settlement service, as required in the current GFE. The agencies also recommended a number of substantive prohibitions and requirements aimed at reducing abusive lending practices. *See* FRB and HUD, *supra* note 9.

[11] HUD and the U.S. Department of Treasury ("HUD and Treasury"), *Curbing Predatory Home Mortgage Lending*, joint report, June 20, 2000.

[12] HUD, "Real Estate Settlement Procedures Act (RESPA); Simplifying and Improving the Process of Obtaining Mortgages To Reduce Settlement Costs to Consumers; Proposed Rule," 67 *Fed. Reg.* 49134–74 (July 29, 2002).

[13] HUD, Office of Policy Development and Research, *Economic Analysis and Initial Regulatory Flexibility Analysis for RESPA Proposed Rule to Simplify and Improve the Process of Obtaining Mortgages to Reduce Settlement Costs to Consumers,* July, 2002.

[14] Federal Trade Commission ("FTC") staff submitted comments that generally supported the HUD proposal, but raised concerns about several issues, including the proposed broker compensation disclosures. *See* FTC, Staff of the Bureau of Economics, Bureau of Consumer Protection, and Office of Policy Planning, *Comment on Proposed Amendments to the Regulations Implementing the Real Estate Settlement Procedures Act,* Docket No. FR-4727-P-01, October 28, 2002. In 2004, the FTC released a study, based on testing with over 500 recent mortgage customers, that showed that the proposed broker compensation disclosures confused consumers, leading many to choose loans that were more expensive, and created a substantial consumer bias against broker loans, even when the broker loans cost the same or less than direct lender loans, because the disclosures would have been required of brokers but not direct lenders. *See* FTC, Bureau of Economics Staff Report, James M. Lacko and Janis K. Pappalardo, *The Effect of Mortgage Broker Compensation Disclosures on Consumers and Competition: A Controlled Experiment,* February 2004.

[15] HUD, Alphonso Jackson, Acting Secretary, "RESPA Final Rule (RIN 2502-AH85)," letter to John Graham, Administrator, Office of Information and Regulatory Affairs, Office of Management and Budget, March 22, 2004.

[16] *See* FRB, "Truth in Lending," Advance Notice of Proposed Rulemaking, December 3, 2004 (published in 69 *Fed. Reg.* 70925-36 (December 8, 2004)). In statements since it announced the review, FRB officials have stated that they intend to use extensive consumer testing "to determine what information is most important to consumers, when that information is useful, what language and formats work best, and how disclosures can be simplified, prioritized, and organized to reduce complexity and information overload." *See* FRB, Sandra F. Braunstein, Director, Division of Consumer and Community Affairs, letter to Orice M. Williams, Director, Financial Markets and Community Investment, Government Accountability Office ("GAO"), Sept. 6, 2006, included as an appendix to GAO, *Alternative Mortgage Products—Impact on Defaults Remains Unclear, but Disclosure of Risks to Borrowers Could Be Improved*, report to the Chairman, Subcommittee on Housing and Transportation, Committee on Banking, Housing, and Urban Affairs, U.S. Senate, September 2006.

[17] *See* GAO, *supra* note 16. In assessing the readability of the disclosures, the GAO used guidelines presented in Securities Exchange Commission ("SEC"), *A Plain English Handbook: How to Create Clear SEC Disclosure Documents* (1998). Although written to help guide the drafting of SEC disclosure documents, the handbook is a valuable resource that can greatly aid the design of any consumer disclosures, particularly those involving complex information.

[18] OCC, FRB, Federal Deposit Insurance Corporation, Office of Thrift Supervision, and National Credit Union Administration, *Interagency Guidance on Nontraditional Mortgage Product Risks,* September 29, 2006 (published in 71 *Fed. Reg.* 58609-18 (October 4, 2006)); and *Illustrations of Consumer Information for Nontraditional Mortgage Products,* May 31, 2007 (published in 72 *Fed. Reg.* 31825-32 (June 8, 2007)).

[19] *See* FRB, 2006, *supra* note 16.

[20] *See* Brian Bucks and Karen Pence, "Do Homeowners Know Their House Values and Mortgage Terms?" Finance and Economics Discussion Series Working Paper 2006-03, FRB Janujary 2006.

[21] *See* Jinkook Lee and Jeanne M. Hogarth, "The Price of Money: Consumers' Understanding of APRs and Contract Interest Rates," *Journal of Public Policy and Marketing*, 18(1), Spring 1999, pages 66-76.

[22] *See* FTC, 2004, *supra* note 14.

[23] These studies examine TILA disclosures in general, and are not usually related specifically to mortgage loans. A detailed review of the consumer surveys that examine these issues, as well as surveys that examine consumer views of which loan terms are important, the availability of information on loan costs, the extent of consumer search for such information, and the extent to which consumers shop for credit, *see* Durkin and Elliehausen, *supra* note 2; and Durkin and Elliehausen, *supra* note 6. A general study of consumer mortgage shopping behavior is presented in Jinkook Lee and Jean M. Hogarth, "Consumer Information Search for Home Mortgages: Who, What, How Much, and What Else?" *Financial Services Review*, 9 (3), Fall 2000, pp. 277–98.

[24] FTC actions against mortgage lenders, brokers, and servicers include *FTC v. Mortgages Para Hispanos.Com Corp.*, No. 4:06-CV-00019 (E.D. Tex. filed Jan. 18, 2006); *FTC v. Ranney*, No. 04-F-1065 (D. Colo. 2005) (judgment against ind. def.), (D. Colo. 2004) (judgment against corp. defs.); *FTC v. Capital City Mortgage Corp.*, No. 1 :98CV-00237 (D.D.C. 2005) (stipulated order with relief defs.), (D.D.C. 2004) (consent decree with ind. def.); *FTC v. Chase Fin. Funding*, No. SACV 04-549 (C.D. Cal. filed May 12, 2004); *United States v. Fairbanks Capital Corp.*, No. 03-122 19 (D. Mass. 2003); *FTC v. Diamond*, No. 02-C-5078, (N.D. Ill. 2003); *United States v. Mercantile Mortgage Co.*, No. 02-C-5079 (N.D. Ill. 2002); *FTC v. Associates First Capital Corp.*, No. 1 :01-CV-00606 (N.D. Ga. 2002); *FTC v. First Alliance Mortgage Co.*, No. SA CV 00-964 (C.D. Cal. 2002); *United States v. Action Loan Co.*, No. 3:00CV-511-H (W.D. Ky. 2000); *FTC v. Nu West, Inc.*, C00-1197 (W.D. Wash. 2000); *United States v. Delta Funding Corp.*, No. CV-00-1872 (E.D.N.Y. 2000); *FTC v. Barry Cooper Prop.*, No. 99-07782 (C.D. Cal. 1999); *FTC v. Capitol Mortgage Corp.*, No. 2:99CV580 (D. Utah 1999); *FTC v. CLS Fin. Serv., Inc.*, No. 99-CV-1215 (W.D. Wash. 1999); *FTC v. Granite Mortgage*, LLC, No. 99-CV-289 (E.D. Ky. 1999); *FTC v. Interstate Res. Corp.*, No. 1:99-CV5988 (S.D.N.Y. 1999); *FTC v. LAP Fin. Serv., Inc.*, No. 3:99-CV-496 (W.D. Ky. 1999); *FTC v. Wasatch Credit Corp.*, No. 99-

CV-579 (D. Utah 1999); *In re First Plus Fin. Group, Inc.*, FTC Docket No. C-3984 (2000); *In re Fleet Fin., Inc.*, 128 F.T.C. 479 (1999).

[25] *See* FTC, Letter to Jennifer L. Johnson, Secretary, FRB, in response to a request for public comments regarding the "Home Equity Lending Market," Docket No. OP-1253, September 14, 2006.

[26] The same method was used for the focus group of subprime borrowers. Respondents for the prime borrower focus group were recruited from a commercially available list of recent mortgage customers in the Washington D.C. area, obtained by the research contractor.

[27] The procedure for subprime mortgages was complicated by the fact that the courthouse records were not organized by lender, but by trustee. But courthouse employees explained that lender names sometimes appear in the trustee field. Such records, when found, were included in the sample. Also, when a trustee name appeared to be consistently paired with a particular subprime lender, searches on the trustee name were used to identify mortgages from the corresponding lender. This procedure proved effective—all of the interview respondents who had been identified as subprime had indeed obtained their recent mortgage from a subprime lender.

[28] Transactions involving both a closed-ended mortgage and a home equity line of credit were common, and were included in the sample

[29] [29] In 2000, 55 percent of the persons aged 25 or older in Montgomery County had a Bachelor's degree or higher, compared to 24 percent in the country as a whole. In 2004, the median household income in Montgomery County was $76,957, compared to $44,334 for the country as a whole. *See* U.S. Census Bureau, State and County QuickFacts. Montgomery County data available at:____http://quickfacts.census.gov/ qfd/states/24/24031.html; U.S. data available at: ttp://quickfacts.census.gov /qfd/states/24000.html.

[30] In 2005, 32 percent of the population of Montgomery County was non-white, compared to 20 percent in the country as a whole. The county had a higher proportion of African Americans than the country as a whole (16.4 versus 12.8 percent, respectively), roughly the same proportion of Hispanics (13.6 versus 14.4 percent), and a substantially higher proportion of Asian Americans (13.2 versus 4.3 percent, respectively).

[31] The script used for the final wave of recruiting is presented in Appendix A. Some relatively minor changes were made to the script during the course of the recruiting.

[32] Compensation was raised to $150 on one of the days on which interviews were conducted, because a snowstorm had developed and the additional compensation encouraged attendance.

[33] Thirty-eight interviews were conducted, but due to technical difficulties, two interviews could not be transcribed with sufficient clarity for further analysis, leaving 36 interviews in the final sample.

[34] With the exception of gender, demographic data for interviews with couples are based on responses from the respondent who answered the screening questionnaire. Also, throughout this chapter, the term "respondent," in the singular, is used to refer to the participant or participants of a particular interview, regardless of whether the interview was conducted with a single individual or a couple.

[35] The final interview guide is presented in Appendix B. Some changes were made to the original guide after both the first interview and the first wave of interviews. For

example, the first interview suggested that it would be feasible to include questions about the draft prototype disclosure, and this was added for subsequent interviews. Additional specific questions about the prototype were added after the initial wave of interviews.

[36] The sample GFE and TILA forms are presented in Appendix C. The sample GFE was an enhanced version that included information not required by the current regulations, including the amount of money borrowed, the interest rate, the total monthly payment amount, an itemization of the monthly payment, the cash due at closing, and the total settlement charges. Many lenders use some variation of an enhanced GFE that goes beyond the regulatory requirements. The form used in the tests followed this practice so that it would more closely reflect the information that many consumers actually receive. The use of an enhanced GFE implies, however, that the test results will understate any problems that consumers may have with a GFE that merely complies with the regulations. For additional discussion of the reasons for using the enhanced version of the form, *see* Section 4.1, below. The TILA statement consisted of the disclosures required for closed-end, fixed-rate residential mortgages (*see* 12 C.F.R. § 226.18).

[37] Although most questions asked in the interviews were of a qualitative nature, the understandability ratings are more quantitative, and are more typical of questions used in a structured survey.

[38] If the borrower was seeking a loan primarily for business purposes, the transaction would have been exempt from TILA and RE SPA requirements, and the lender would not have been required to provide the TILA and GFE disclosures. The borrower, however, did receive the disclosures.

[39] In some cases, respondents seemed to rely on the reputation of the prime-lender affiliate of the subprime lender from whom they had obtained their loans. Several respondents continued to refer to their lenders using the name of the prime-lender affiliates, rather than the name of the subprime affiliates who actually provided the loans.

[40] The TILA statement consisted of the disclosures required for closed-end, fixed-rate residential mortgages. *See* 12 C.F.R. § 226.18.

[41] Examination of a number of GFEs suggests that many include additional loan cost information not required by the regulations, and that the information included, and the presentation format, differs widely across lenders. The regulations governing the GFE merely specify a list of individual settlement costs that must be disclosed and allows lenders to present the disclosures in any format they choose. This results in wide variation in the disclosure formats used by different lenders and the types of additional information provided.

[42] TILA statements may exhibit some differences across lenders, but the forms are far more standardized and the differences largely confined to variations in the presentation of the information.

[43] The questionnaire is presented in Appendix F.

[44] The two loans also had the same APR. These could be the same, even though one loan had higher settlement costs, because not all settlement charges are classified as finance charges under TILA and included in the APR calculation.

[45] The loans used in the first part of the test were similar to the loans in the simple-loan scenario used in the second part of the test (as described below), because they did not include the types of complicating features that appeared in the complex-loan scenario.

[46] The time period varied somewhat across interview locations, depending on the size of the mortgage market. Because smaller markets had fewer mortgage transactions per month, obtaining a similarly sized sample of loans as obtained in the larger markets (particularly for subprime loans) required samples going back farther in time. The customer list for nine of the interview sites included mortgages recorded up to about 2 years prior to the interviews (more precisely, the oldest records ranged between 21 and 28 months at these sites). The oldest records for the other three sites were recorded only 16 to 18 months prior to the interview. At all sites, the most recent mortgage records in the customer list were about four months old at the time of the interviews.

[47] A copy of the screening questionnaire is provided in Appendix E.

[48] Borrowers with more than one mortgage during the sample period were classified as subprime if at least one of the mortgages was obtained from a subprime lender, even though the other mortgages may have been from prime lenders.

[49] Although the prime and subprime classifications are based on the identity of the lender rather than the features of the loan or the credit history of the borrower, throughout this report the more succinct phrase of "prime and subprime borrowers" is often used to refer to the two groups of respondents rather than the longer phrase of "borrowers who obtained their loans from prime and subprime lenders."

[50] *See* HUD, *HUD Subprime and Manufactured Home Lender List,* [online], <http://www.huduser.org/datasets/manu.html >, (April 27, 2007). The list consists of lenders that specialize in subprime lending and who report loan data to the FRB and other federal regulatory agencies under the Home Mortgage Disclosure Act. The list also includes lenders, separately identified, who specialize in lending for manufactured homes.

[51] For a description of the size requirements for reporting under HMDA, *see* Federal Financial Institutions Examination Council, *Who reports HMDA data?* [online], <http://www.ffiec.gov/hmda/reporter.htm>, (April 27, 2007). For the HMDA statute and regulations more generally, *see*, respectively, 12 U.S.C. Section 2801 and 12 C.F.R. Section 203.1–6.

[52] Additional detail on the combined and excluded questions is provided in the monthly payment and balloon payment sections of the results chapter.

[53] The omitted questions asked respondents to identify the types of optional products or services included in the loan, the charges for the optional products or services, the amount of the prepayment penalty, and the charges for property taxes and homeowner's insurance not included in the monthly payment. Questions that merely asked whether such costs were present in the loans were included in the aggregation.

[54] *See* FRB and HUD, *supra* note 9.

[55] One of the simple purchase loans ("Loan V") also contains financed settlement costs.

[56] These figures may be useful for checking the accuracy of the disclosed APR but are of less value to consumer borrowing and shopping decisions. Because few consumers are likely to attempt to check the accuracy of the disclosed APR, the presence of these figures in a consumer shopping document merely adds clutter to the form. Some of the

information, such as the "amount financed" disclosure, may even confuse and mislead consumers.

[57] The focus on total rather than individual settlement costs is similar to the approach proposed by HUD for its proposed guaranteed mortgage packages. In its proposal, HUD argued that focusing on total settlement costs would make shopping for a mortgage easier and result in lower settlement costs for consumers. *See* HUD, 2002, *supra* notes 12 and 13. The focus of the prototype form on the total settlement costs rather than detailed itemization, however, does not require the use of packaged mortgage services. The focus of the prototype is on how information on settlement costs is presented to borrowers, not on how the underlying transaction is structured.

[58] The numerical amount will overstate the penalty that would be incurred if something less than the entire original principal were prepaid. This amount will be close to the actual penalty during the first few years of the loan, however, because most of the loan payments during the first few years go towards interest payments rather than reduction of principal.

[59] TILA also requires a written disclosure of the cost of the insurance and the fact that it is not required for the loan.

[60] Although adding a signature requirement would make it more likely that optional items are included in the loan only if the consumer wishes to purchase them, the purchase may not be truly voluntary and optional, even if the consumer signs a statement that indicates the desire to purchase the optional items, if the lender used deceptive practices to obscure the disclosures or induce the signature. Whether the insurance is truly optional is ultimately a question of fact. *See* note 92, *infra*.

[61] As noted above in footnote 57, although the prototype form uses the phrase "package" when referring to the settlement services charge, it would not necessarily require the types of packages outlined by HUD in its 2002 proposal. All that is necessary is that the cost of the various settlement services be disclosed as a single price rather than itemized as in the current GFE. Whether this is accomplished through a HUD-type package or simply an aggregation of the individual costs is not material to the disclosure or its intended use by consumers.

[62] The FTC does not intervene to resolve the complaints of individual consumers, but may take action when a pattern of complaints indicates the possibility of a more widespread problem. The suggestion that consumers notify the FTC of problems was intended to provide a mechanism by which the agency could become aware of patterns of problems from particular lenders. Banking agencies also could be added to the suggested contact list.

[63] The 19 percentage point improvement represents a 31 percent increase over the result obtained with the current forms

[64] The differences between the simple- and complex-loan scenarios were statistically significant in both disclosure groups, as was the difference across the disclosure groups.

[65] The differences across the two loan scenarios were statistically significant at the one percent level.

[66] The analysis of incorrect and "don't know" responses presented in the text and Table 6.3 are based on the results of 19 questions for the simple-loan scenario and 23 questions for the complex-loan scenario, two questions fewer than included in the analysis earlier in this section. Two questions, which pertained to monthly payments and balloon

payments, were excluded because each consisted of multi-question sequences for which it is not always possible to uniquely classify responses as either "incorrect" or "don't know." Respondents may have provided different types of responses in different parts of the sequence.

[67] Although one of the four differences was not statistically significant.

[68] The difference between prime and subprime borrowers, across both disclosure groups and loan-cost scenarios, shown in the first row of Table 6.4, was statistically significant, but the differences in specific disclosure form or loan-cost scenario groups were not statistically significant. The lack of significance in the specific groups may be due to the smaller sample sizes.

[69] Although in both scenarios the improvement achieved by the prototype form was slightly larger for subprime borrowers than prime borrowers, the differences, which amounted to less than one percentage point, were not statistically significant.

[70] Across both disclosure-form groups, respondents in the simple- and complex-loan scenarios, respectively, answered 74 and 67 percent of the questions correctly, a difference of seven percentage points. The difference increases to 10 percentage points among respondents viewing the current disclosure forms. These differences are statistically significant.

[71] Across both disclosure form groups, prime respondents in the simple-loan scenario answered 75 percent of the questions correctly, compared to 65 percent for subprime respondents in the complex-loan scenario, a difference of 10 percentage points. The difference increases to 13 percentage points among respondents viewing the current disclosure forms. These differences are statistically significant.

[72] The prototype form increased the percentage of questions answered correctly by 15.6 percentage points among prime respondents in the simple loan scenario, but 22.4 percentage points among subprime respondents in the complex-loan scenario, a difference of 6.8 percentage points. This difference is statistically significant.

[73] Thirteen of the differences were statistically significant in the simple-loan scenario and16 were statistically significant in the complex-loan scenario.

[74] *See* Questions 15 and 16 in Appendix F.

[75] The APRs also were identical in the two loans. The APRs could be identical, even though one loan had higher settlement costs, because not all settlement charges are considered to be financed under TILA and included in the APR calculation.

[76] The loans were similar to the loans in the simple-loan scenario used in the second part of the test, because they did not include the types of complicating features that appeared in the complex-loan scenario.

[77] Unless otherwise noted, all differences described in the text are statistically significant at the five percent level or better.

[78] In an earlier FTC study that used this same question and test procedure, 90 percent of the respondents correctly identified the less expensive loan (*see* FTC, 2004, *supra* note 14). The higher level of accuracy is likely due to the simplicity of the disclosure forms tested in the earlier study. In one version tested, the form was only a half a page long, contained only nine cost figures (in contrast to several dozen in the forms tested here), and highlighted the one figure that differed between the two loans. In another version tested, the form spread across two pages but had no more than a half of page of information on each, contained only 12 cost figures across the two pages, and also

highlighted the figure that differed between the loans. When information on the yield spread premium was added to these forms, the proportion of respondents correctly identifying the less expensive loan dropped to 63 to 72 percent.

[79] The earlier FTC study also used this same question (*see* the previous footnote and FTC, 2004, *supra* note 14). In two versions of the disclosure form tested, 85 and 94 percent of the respondents correctly chose the loan that was less expensive. These figures fell to 65 to 70 percent when information on the yield spread premium was added to the forms.

[80] In the loan cost question, 11 and 12 percent of the respondents in the current- and prototype-form groups, respectively, identified the more expensive loan as less expensive. Twenty-four and 12 percent of the respondents said that both loans cost the same. One to two percent of each group said that they either did not know or did not have enough information. In the loan choice question, 18 and 12 percent of the respondents in the current- and prototype-form groups, respectively, either chose the more expensive loan or said "either loan, both cost the same." The remaining respondents said either "neither loan," "don't know," "not enough information," or refused to answer the question.

[81] *See* Questions 17–19 in Appendix F. In these and other questions, text shown in capital letters, such as "LESS," indicates words that interviewers were instructed to emphasize when reading the question. Dual loan names, such as "Loan V(T)" indicate the loan to be used in the question for each of the two loan-cost scenarios, with the loan for the simple-loan scenario provided first and the loan for the complex-loan scenario provided second in parentheses.

[82] In both scenarios, most of the respondents who did not identify the correct loan identified the wrong loan instead—14 and four percent of the current- and prototype-form respondents, respectively, in the simple-loan scenario, and 37 and 15 percent in the complex-loan scenario. Other respondents said that either the loan amount was the same in both loans, they did not know, they did not have enough information, or they refused to answer the question.

[83] Some unscrupulous lenders have taken advantage of this confusion to deceive consumers about the size of the loan. *See*, for example, *FTC v. First Alliance Mortgage Co.*, *supra* note 24.

[84] The "amount financed" disclosed on the TILA statement is equal to the loan amount, including everything financed by the lender, minus the amount of points and other prepaid finance charges (as defined by the TILA regulations) paid on the loan. If a consumer took out a $100,000 mortgage and was charged $10,000 (10 percent) in points and other prepaid finance charges, the total loan amount would be $100,000, but the "amount financed" would be $90,000 ($100,000 minus $10,000). If this same consumer financed the charges by rolling them into the loan principal, the total loan amount would $110,000 but the "amount financed" would be $100,000 ($100,000 plus $10,000 minus $10,000). This may lull some consumers into believing that they are not paying points, because points do not appear to be added to the loan amount and points are not being paid in cash at closing. Although the settlement charges would be detailed in the GFE and HUD-1 forms, the amount-financed disclosure may lead some consumers to conclude that settlement charges need not be carefully scrutinized in these forms.

[85] The figure at the top of the GFE was labeled "total loan amount." A "base loan amount" also was disclosed, with the difference between the two consisting of any financed settlement charges.

[86] This may understate the proportion of respondents who did not recognize that charges were financed because the question required merely a "yes" or "no" answer, making it easy for respondents who did not know the answer to simply guess "yes" or "no." On average, half of those guessing would provide the correct answer, inflating the overall percentage of correct answers.

[87] *See* Questions 20 and 21 in Appendix F.

[88] About 85 percent of the respondents who did not select the correct loan selected the other loan instead. The rest said that both loans had the same charges, they did not know, or they could not tell from the information provided.

[89] Only five percent of the prototype-form group made that same error. The difference between the two groups was statistically significant at the one percent level.

[90] Only nine percent of the other current-forms respondents (that is, those who did not incorrectly provide the amount of cash due at closing in the second question) made this same mistake.

[91] The difference between the two scenarios was significant at the one percent level. In the complex-loan scenario, the current-forms result was five percentage points higher than in the prototype-form group, but the difference was not statistically significant.

[92] For credit insurance to be considered optional under TILA, three conditions must be met: the insurance must not be required by the creditor and this fact must disclosed to the borrower in a written statement; the charges for the insurance must be disclosed to the borrower; and the borrower must sign or initial an affirmative written request that indicates that they wish to purchase the insurance. If the required disclosures are not made, or if the borrower does not sign the agreement, any charges imposed for the insurance are considered mandatory, rather than optional, and must be considered part of the finance charge and included in the APR calculation. The insurance may not be truly optional, however, even if these requirements are met, if, for example, the lender uses deceptive practices to obscure the disclosures or mislead borrowers. Whether the insurance is truly optional is ultimately a question of fact. *See*, for example, *In re Tower Loan*, 115 FTC 140 (1992); *In re Money Tree*, 123 FTC 1187 (1997); *FTC v. Stewart Fin. Co. Holdings, Inc.*, Civ. No. 1:03-CV-2648-JTC (N.D. Ga. 2005); and *FTC v. Associates First Capital Corp.*, *supra* note 24.

[93] *See* Questions 22–24 in Appendix F.

[94] As noted in footnote 92, above, one of the requirements for credit insurance to be considered optional under TILA is that the borrower must sign or initial an affirmative written request that indicates agreement to purchase the insurance (and the cost of the insurance, and the fact that it is not required, must be disclosed). Signatures were not present on the TILA statement used in the tests, but the disclosed insurance charges were financed, added to the loan amount (which was disclosed in the GFE), and used to calculate the monthly and balloon loan payments.

[95] Thirty percent said that optional charges were not included in the loan costs and 13 percent said that they either did not know or did not have enough information.

[96] In the question asking respondents to identify the optional items, 10 current-forms respondents were counted as incorrect even though they said "credit insurance,"

because they also listed other items in their answers that were not optional. In addition to saying "credit insurance," all 10 also said "homeowner's" or "hazard insurance," and three also listed "taxes." If these 10 are counted as correct, the percentage correct in the current-forms group would increase by 5 percentage points, to 31 percent correct, leaving 69 percent who did not recognize that the credit insurance was optional.

[97] Of the prototype-form respondents who correctly answered the first optional-charges question, 87 and 98 percent then correctly identified the optional items and charges, respectively, in the two follow-up questions. Of the current-form respondents who correctly answered the first question, only 45 and 60 percent correctly identified the items and charges.

[98] Similar results also were found in the simple loan scenario, where the loan did not contain credit insurance or any other optional charges. In the initial question, 47 percent of current-form respondents correctly responded that the loan did not contain any charges for optional items, compared to 87 percent of prototype-form respondents, an improvement of 39 percentage points.

[99] Similarly, 40 percent failed to correctly identify the amount of optional charges in the second follow-up question. In contrast, only 13 and two percent the prototype-form respondents who correctly noted that optional charges were included in the loan failed to correctly identify the optional items and charges, respectively.

[100] The items included homeowners' insurance, taxes, flood certification, pest inspection, survey, and various other fees. Respondents providing these incorrect items amounted to 28 percent of the current-forms group; only five percent of the prototype group made the same type of error. Almost identical percentages—28 and eight percent in the current and prototype groups, respectively—made the same type of error in the simple-loan scenario, where none of the items were optional.

[101] Under federal law, lenders can legitimately require that consumers purchase credit insurance to obtain the loan, but then the insurance costs would be considered a finance charge, and would increase the disclosed APR.

[102] *See*, for example, *FTC v. Associates First Capital Corp.*, *supra* note 24. In order to settle the legal complaint, Citigroup Inc. and CitiFinancial Credit Company, the successor corporations to Associates, agreed to pay $215 million in redress to consumers who had been charged for credit insurance.

[103] As noted earlier, for purchase-money loans, creditors must provide the disclosures within three days of receiving a consumer's written application, but many also provide the disclosures again at closing, even though it is not required unless certain costs have changed beyond specified tolerances. For refinance loans, creditors must provide the disclosures prior to consummation of the loan, and most typically do so at closing.

[104] Although, as noted above, adding a signature requirement would make it more likely that optional items are included in the loan only if the consumer wishes to purchase them, the purchase may not be truly voluntary and optional, even if the consumer signs a statement that indicates the desire to purchase the optional items, if the lender used deceptive practices to obscure the disclosures or induce the signature. Whether the insurance is truly optional is ultimately a question of fact. *See* note 92, *supra*.

[105] *See* Questions 25 and 26 in Appendix F.

[106] The APR provides a measure of the overall cost of the loan, including interest, up-front charges, and other credit costs, and can be used to compare loan offers. In some

situations, however, the APR may produce inaccurate comparisons, such as when borrowers do not intend to hold the loan for the full term, because they intend to either move or refinance in the near future. In these circumstances, evaluation of the interest rate and other loan terms becomes more important.

[107] *See* Questions 27 and 28 in Appendix F.

[108] The differences between the two groups were not statistically significant.

[109] The APR is less useful, however, in some borrowing situations, where it can lead to inaccurate comparisons of loan alternatives. The APR is calculated under the assumption that the loan is held for the full term, and will provide an inaccurate measure of the cost of the loan for a borrower who intends to move or refinance before the end of the term.

[110] *See* Questions 29–3 1 in Appendix F.

[111] The differences between the forms were not statistically significant.

[112] The difference between the results is statistically significant at the one percent level in both scenarios.

[113] Combining the results of the interest rate and APR questions shows that 53 percent of current-forms respondents provided the correct rate in both questions, compared to 77 percent of the prototype-form group, an improvement of 24 percentage points.

[114] Respondents were counted as providing a correct answer if they said that the APR also included, for example, "closing costs," "settlement costs," "up-front costs" "additional costs," or "finance charges." Although these answers do not include the precise legal specifications that appear in the regulation that defines the APR (Regulation Z), they indicate that the respondent had a workable, intuitive concept of the difference between the two rates.

[115] 115 Across the two loan scenarios, about one-quarter of the respondents in both groups said they "did not know" why the APR was sometimes higher than the interest rate, and another three-to-four percent said that they "could not tell / did not enough information." The most common incorrect answers were that the APR included compounding of the interest rate (22 and 13 percent of the current- and prototype-form groups, respectively), the APR was the final rate at closing (13 and 10 percent, respectively), and the APR was the maximum to which the interest rate can rise (seven and two percent, respectively).

[116] *See* Questions 32 and 33 in Appendix F.

[117] The differences between the groups were not statistically significant.

[118] The differences between the two loan cost scenarios were statistically significant for both disclosure-form groups. The differences between the two disclosure-form groups in the complex scenario were not statistically significant.

[119] Although settlement costs also were financed in the simple-loan scenario, a down payment on the house purchase was due at closing and disclosed.

[120] About half of the prototype-form respondents who gave such an answer provided only the amount of settlement charges; the other half provided the sum of settlement and optional charges. Virtually all of the current-forms respondents who gave such an answer provided only the amount of settlement charges.

[121] *See*, for example, *FTC v. Associates First Capital Corp.; FTC v. Diamond*; and *United States v. Mercantile Mortgage Co.*, *supra* note 24.

[122] *See* Questions 34–37 in Appendix F.

[123] These figures are as a percentage of all of the respondents in each group. Of the respondents who recognized that taxes and insurance were to be paid separately, 20 and 90 percent of current- and prototype-forms groups, respectively, correctly identified the amount of the costs. In current-forms group, 63 percent said they could not tell from the information and 12 percent said they did not know.

[124] The monthly tax and insurance costs could appear in two places in the current forms used in the tests. One place the costs could appear is in the itemization of the monthly payment, into "principal and interest," "real estate taxes," "flood and hazard insurance," and "mortgage insurance," that appears in the GFE. (This is a feature of the enhanced GFE used in the study but is not required by the regulations governing the form.) For this loan, however, the tax and insurance portions of the itemization were left blank because these items were not included in the payment to the lender. The second place the costs could appear is in the itemization of "reserves deposited with the lender" in the GFE, which provides the monthly tax and insurance costs, the number of months held in reserve and the total dollar amounts. These items were left blank in the test form for this loan because the loan did not include reserves.

[125] Sixty-nine and 95 percent of the current- and prototype-form respondents, respectively, provided the total payment amount, including taxes and insurance, and 88 and 96 percent of these recognized that the payment included taxes and insurance. Twenty-seven percent of the current-forms respondents provided only the principal and interest portion of the payment, and only 46 percent of these recognized that it did not include taxes and insurance.

[126] Some lenders may offer loans with unusually low monthly payments and attempt to deceptively conceal, or affirmatively misrepresent, the presence of a large balloon payment at the end of the loan. *See*, for example, *FTC v. Diamond*; *United States v. Mercantile Mortgage Co.*; and *FTC v. Capital City Mortgage Corp.*; *supra* note 24.

[127] *See* Questions 38–41 in Appendix F.

[128] Responses were counted as correct regardless of whether the amount included the regular monthly payment portion of the final payment, and regardless of whether it included the escrow for taxes and insurance, because the responses indicated that the respondent had knowledge of a large balloon payment at the end of the loan and these details affected the amount by less than one percentage point.

[129] About 83 percent of these respondents provided the balloon amount when asked for the amount of the last payment. About nine percent provided it when asked how much they would still owe after the last payment. Another nine percent provided it in response to both questions.

[130] Similar results also were found in the simple-loan scenario, in which the loan did not contain a balloon payment. Seventy-eight and 73 percent of the respondents in the current- and prototype-form groups, respectively, correctly recognized that their last payment would be the same as their other monthly payments. The difference between the groups was not statistically significant.

[131] The substantial proportion of respondents who were unaware of the balloon payment also raises questions about how well borrowers are aware of the risk that a substantial increase in monthly payments may occur in adjustable-rate and payment option loans.

[132] The FTC has brought legal actions against lenders and mortgage brokers for such practices. *See*, for example, *FTC v. Diamond*; *United States v. Mercantile Mortgage Co.*; and *FTC v. Chase Fin. Funding*; *supra* note 24.

[133] The questions used the term "additional fees" rather than "prepayment penalties" in order to prevent respondents from simply matching the phrase to the form, regardless of whether they understood the implications of the disclosure, thus providing a better gauge of respondent understanding. This seems unlikely to have confused respondents because the questions made a clear distinction between merely paying off the loan balance or having to pay something more, regardless of what the additional amounts were called.

[134] *See* Questions 42–45 in Appendix F.

[135] TILA statements used by some lenders make this even less informative with the two check-boxes indicating that borrowers either "may" or "may not" have to pay a penalty.whether a prepayment penalty would be assessed.

[136] Most of the respondents who failed to recognize the prepayment penalty provided an incorrect answer rather than simply saying that they did not know or could not tell. About 70 percent of these respondents in each disclosure group (amounting to about 25 percent of all of the respondents in each group) said they would have to pay only the remaining balance on the loan, and another five to ten percent said they would have to pay less than the remaining balance.

[137] Respondents were counted as correct if they said that the additional fees would be either "four percent" or "$7,017." The latter figure corresponds to what the penalty would be if the entire original loan balance had been refinanced. The actual penalty after two years would be about $6,856, because the loan balance would be slightly lower (approximately $171,143 rather the original $175,425). The $7,017 figure is counted as correct, even though the actual penalty would be slightly smaller, because the response indicates an understanding that a substantial penalty would be assessed and its approximate size.

[138] The current-forms respondents who provided the correct response may have inappropriately observed the interviewer's computer screen and selected one of pre-coded responses listed there.

[139] The five percentage point difference between the two groups was not statistically significant.

[140] In the current- and prototype groups, respectively, 13 and 14 percent of respondents incorrectly believed that they would have to pay additional fees, one and two percent believed that they "may" have to pay such fees, four and six percent believed that they would have to pay less than the balance, eight percent of each said they did not have enough information, and four and five percent said they did not know.

[141] These are combined results across both loan scenarios and both disclosure forms.

INDEX

A

B

C

D

E

W

Y